HISTORIC HOTELS OF TEXAS

A Traveler's Guide

LIZ CARMACK

Texas A&M University Press   College Station

The paper used in this book
meets the minimum requirements
of the American National Standard for Permanence
of Paper for Printed Library Materials, Z39.48-1984.
Binding materials have been chosen for durability.

PHOTO CREDITS:

front cover—Driskill Hotel, courtesy Driskill Hotel

back cover —The Fairmount, by Doug Jacobson; Renaissance Casa de Palmas, by Jeff
Carmack; Hotel Blessing, by J. Griffis Smith/TxDOT; Antlers Hotel, by Liz Carmack

frontmatter—The Fairmount (p. i), by Doug Jacobson; InterContinental Stephen F. Austin
Hotel (title page), courtesy InterContinental Stephen F. Austin Hotel; and Nutt House
Historic Hotel (p. xv), by Liz Carmack

LIBRARY OF CONGRESS
CATALOGING-IN-PUBLICATION DATA

Carmack, Liz.
  Historic hotels of Texas : a traveler's guide / Liz Carmack. — 1st ed.
     p. cm.
  Includes index.
  ISBN-13: 978-1-58544-608-7 (flexbound : alk. paper)
  ISBN-10: 1-58544-608-4 (flexbound)
  1. Hotels–Texas–Guidebooks.   2. Historic buildings–Texas–Guidebooks.
  I. Title.
  TX907.3.T4C37   2007
  910.4609764–dc22   2007003213

For my mother,

TULULA INEZ HOWELL

✥ CONTENTS

🙖 PREFACE

An Oklahoma native, I moved to Austin in 1988 after living for a while in England. Shortly after returning to the United States, I visited my aunt in San Antonio for the first time in many years. We strolled along the River Walk, bought Mexican folk art at El Mercado, and wandered around the exhibits at the Alamo. Culture shock does not begin to describe what I felt during that brief visit. Everywhere we went I sensed a pervasive state patriotism and was awestruck after my small taste of Texas' history and mingling cultures. By later working at Texas institutions—the state's House of Representatives, the Lady Bird Johnson Wildflower Center, and KLRU-TV—I was immersed in Texas politics and the state's natural beauty, culture, and history. I now realize why Texans are so proud, and I am happy to call myself a nonnative Texan.

The seed for this book was planted by an appreciation for my adopted state and an interest in old Texas travel guides, which I collect and which my husband and I have used, along with newer references, to plan dozens of excursions. Two books were particularly helpful for finding unusual, historic lodging for our trips—*Historic Texas Hotels and Country Inns* by Linda Johnson and Sally Ross, and *A Guide to Historic Texas Inns and Hotels* by Ann Ruff—but neither were updated beyond 1982.

In 2004 Shannon Davies and Texas A&M University Press agreed that a current guide to historic Texas hotels was needed and encouraged my dream to write one. During my nearly two years of research, my original list of thirty-five operating historic hotels grew to sixty-four. I visited each of the operating hotels featured in this book primarily during 2005 and 2006, and I spent at least one night in all but a handful. I started out a fan of historic hotels and, after writing this book, remain so. Although some hotels are decidedly more appealing and comfortable than others, I see value in each one and appreciate their peculiarities and individual charms.

I also made trips to many of the closed and repurposed hotels mentioned in the "Closed but Not Forgotten Hotels" section. One of the high points of that research was taking a three-hour guided tour of the Baker Hotel in Mineral Wells, which included climbing fourteen flights of pitch-dark stairs by flashlight and squeezing through broken windows to clamber onto the hotel's windy, rooftop terrace.

I checked the amenities, rates, and other particulars of the operating hotels as late as possible in 2007 before the book went to print. Some of the hotels included here were for sale or undergoing renovation as I wrote this book. Some may shut their doors, while others that had been closed for years will reopen. This book will be updated periodically to reflect changes, but to do this, I will depend largely upon information provided by the hotels, local residents, and readers like you who share my love for this subject. Please visit www.historictexashotels.com to share information and comments.

❧ ACKNOWLEDGMENTS

This book would not have been possible without the help of dozens of individuals who were generous with their time, knowledge, advice, and support.

I am most grateful to those who read all or part of the draft manuscript and provided feedback on style, organization, and factual content; they include Judith Singer Cohen, Shannon Davies, Dr. Archie P. McDonald, Dr. Charles Schultz, John and Kate Wong Troesser, Ed Van De Vort, Frances B. Vick, Dale Weisman, and Mindy Wilson.

Wayne Bell of the Texas Historical Commission provided important early guidance for my research and helped me develop the initial list of hotels. Charles Sadnick and Greg Smith, of the commission, helped me confirm which hotels are on the National Register of Historic Places and which ones have Texas historical markers. Janie Headrick, also of the commission, provided encouragement and connected me with dozens of county historians and Main Street Program staff. These local residents and dozens of others shared tips about many hotels, both open and closed.

During interviews, more than eighty people around the state provided information on Texas hotels and their communities. I appreciate all of them, but special thanks go to Robert W. Brown, Jayne Catrett, Mary Kate Durham, John Haywood, Jan Johnson, David Mycue, Ona Lea Pierce, Ruth Harrison Pierce, Susan Pritchett, and Travis Roberts.

Dozens of county history museums and public libraries across the state were excellent resources, and their wonderful staff and volunteers were a great help. Several historical archives and their competent archivists were key to my research, including the Archives of the Big Bend at Sul Ross State University, Alpine; the Austin History Center, Austin; the Carnegie Center of Brazos Valley History, Bryan; the Jane Burges Perrenot Research Center, El Paso; the Galveston and Texas History Center at the Rosenberg Library, Galveston; the Hospitality Industry Archives within the Conrad N. Hilton College of Hotel and Restaurant Management at the University of Houston,

Houston; the Museum of South Texas History, Edinburg; the Panhandle Plains Museum, Canyon; the Tarrant County Archives, Fort Worth; the Steen Library at Stephen F. Austin University, Nacogdoches; and the Texas Historical Commission Library, Austin.

Most of the hotels allowed me to stay one night free or granted me a reduced room rate. This book could not have been accomplished otherwise, but no business paid to be included, and no hotel was omitted because its owners didn't offer to assist me with the cost of lodging. The "About This Book and How to Use It" section details the criteria I used to select the hotels included here.

My husband, Jeff, spent hours editing my draft manuscript, took some of the hotel photos, and provided encouragement and unwavering support throughout this long project. To him I owe the greatest thanks of all.

HISTORIC HOTELS OF TEXAS

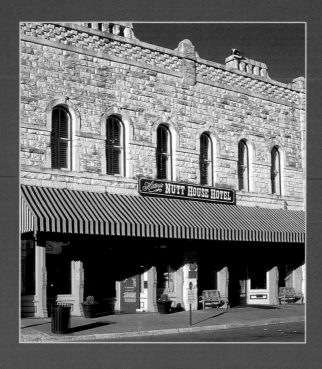

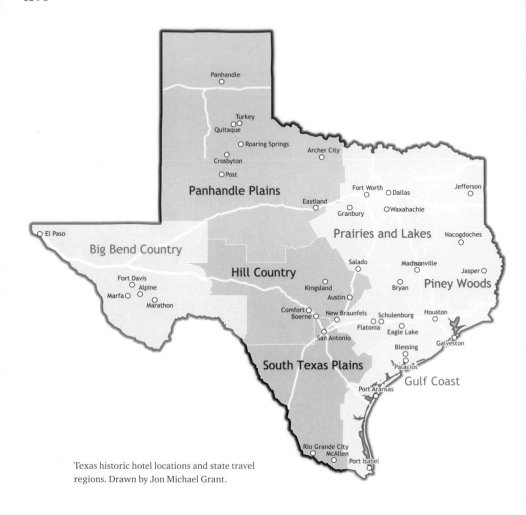

Texas historic hotel locations and state travel
regions. Drawn by Jon Michael Grant.

About This Book and How to Use It

This book is a travel guide to sixty-four operating historic hotels in Texas. Each of the featured hotels met three criteria: it is at least fifty years old; it originally opened as a hotel or, if not, became one and has operated as such for the majority of the time since the building was completed; and it offers lodging today.

A handful of hotels meeting all three criteria were not included because they are now budget accommodations that primarily serve long-term residents and are not frequented by tourists or business travelers. In addition, the Stagecoach Inn and the Comfort Common are in the book despite not strictly meeting the third criterion. I included them because of their age (in both cases their original buildings are more than one hundred years old) and because even though guests can't stay in the original inns, lodging is offered on their properties.

ORGANIZED BY SEVEN REGIONS

The hotels featured are grouped by the seven regions used in the *Texas State Travel Guide.* The regions are Big Bend Country, Gulf Coast, Hill Country, Panhandle Plains, Piney Woods, Prairies and Lakes, and South Texas Plains. The hotel summaries are listed alphabetically by city within each region. A map at the beginning of each region's section shows the cities where hotels are located. A map at the beginning of this section shows the locations of all sixty-four historic hotels.

Order a free copy of the *Texas State Travel Guide* at 800-8888-TEX or through the TravelTex Web site, www.traveltex.com.

YEAR ASSOCIATED WITH EACH HOTEL

The year listed with each hotel is the year the original lodging building was completed. In many instances, these historic buildings took more than one year to construct. If the year of completion is uncertain, the most likely decade or year the building was completed is preceded by "circa." Some hotels have additional historic buildings on their properties that are used for lodging. Some hotels have added to their original buildings.

HOTELS ARE NOT RATED

In talking to lodgers and innkeepers, I found that travelers have a surprising variety of tastes and range of standards. One disappointed guest thought a hotel "too rustic" despite its terry bathrobes, carefully decorated rooms, heated outdoor pool, fine dining restaurant, and spa. And while basic accommodations, minimal amenities, and cobwebs under furniture would send many people packing, others didn't mind "roughing it" at some hotels. They instead considered these conditions a colorful part of their travel adventure. So rather than rate or rank these hotels, I've tried to provide enough information in each summary to help you decide which ones will suit you. See the "Why Choose a Historic Hotel and What to Expect" section for an overview.

CONTACT HOTEL FOR RESERVATIONS AND INFORMATION ABOUT LATEST RATES AND AMENITIES

Specific information about each hotel's facilities, amenities, and rates is provided in each hotel summary. This information was checked as close to publication as possible, but particulars can change. It's best to check the hotel's Web site (most have one) and contact the hotel in advance to double-check rates, make reservations, and inquire about specific amenities or other features that matter to you.

HOTEL GHOSTS

A few hotel summaries mention ghosts, but this book focuses on other details and by no means presents a complete discussion of reported hauntings at every hotel. For more comprehensive coverage of ghosts in Texas lodging, see *Haunted Texas Vacations* by Lisa Farwell, *Texas Guide to Haunted Restaurants, Taverns & Inns* by Robert Wlokarski and Anne Powell Wlokarski, and *Best Tales of Texas Ghosts* by Docia Schultz Williams.

During my hotel visits I heard lots of ghost stories from innkeepers, hotel staff, and guests. My only "close encounter" occurred at 10 P.M. one night in the Jefferson Hotel in Jefferson. My husband decided to photograph the deserted hallway before we walked down to what the hotel calls its haunted room. The digital photo revealed what can only be described as a floating pink blob in the middle of the hall that was otherwise not visible. We wordlessly exchanged a glance and quickly retreated to our room. The next morning we leafed through a notebook filled with guests' handwritten accounts of many more strange encounters.

ADDITIONAL HISTORIC ACCOMMODATION IN TEXAS

Texas has a plethora of historic accommodations in addition to the hotels featured in this book. Other lodging that you might want to explore includes:

—*Inns, cabins, and other accommodations at state and national parks.* These include the Landmark Inn in Castroville, the Indian Lodge in Davis Mountains State Park, and the cabins in the basin of the Chisos Mountains of Big Bend National Park. See the Web sites of the National Park Service, www.nps.gov, or the Texas Parks and Wildlife Department, www.tpwd.state.tx.us.

—*Tourist courts and motels.* These first appeared along the nation's highways during the 1920s (a few appeared earlier) for the new automobile tourists. Many, like the San Jose Motel in Austin and the Rainbow Courts Motel in Rockdale, have either been revamped into trendy boutique destinations or preserved to evoke a nostalgic travel experience.

—*Bed and breakfast inns.* B&Bs generally offer fewer rooms than do hotels and occupy single-family homes or a group of multiple individual properties. Dozens of books and Web sites provide references to historic Texas B&Bs. Hospitality Accommodations of Texas (HAT), which is described further in the "Why Choose a Historic Hotel and What to Expect" section, is also a great resource. A few of the historic hotels in this book call themselves B&Bs because they offer a complimentary breakfast with lodging.

KEY TO "ESSENTIALS" SECTION FOR EACH HOTEL

Contact: This item includes the hotel's physical address (and mailing address, if different), its toll-free and local telephone numbers, and its fax number (if it has one). The hotel's Web site and e-mail address are listed if it has them. Before you arrive, check the Web site or call the hotel for its latest rates, to ask about particular amenities, and to make reservations.

Rooms: This indicates the number of guest rooms, including suites, the hotel offers and provides a description of the type of bathroom facilities (private or shared) and what type of fixtures are available in bathrooms throughout the hotel. Types of fixtures may include claw-foot tubs with or without a shower attachment, traditional bathtub/shower combinations, Jacuzzi tubs, walk-in showers, and bathtubs. Types of beds listed may include king, queen, full, and twin. Most hotels offer some rooms that have more than one bed.

Rates: These rates are for one night per room, double occupancy. The range is from the cheapest room to the most expensive (often a suite). For some hotels it includes accommodation associated with the hotel but not in the hotel building, such as off-site guesthouses. These rates do not include taxes. Every effort was made to provide the most current rates, but they are subject to change. *It is always best to contact the hotel for current rates and for information about special packages or long-term rates.* Hotels often vary their rates based upon demand, day of the week, and time of the year. If you seek a reservation during a special event in the community or during the peak tourist season, be prepared to pay more. The scale I used:

$ = $70 or less
$$ = $71–$180
$$$ = $181–$300
$$$$ = more than $300

Some hotels include a continental or full breakfast with the room price. If so, this is listed next to the rate.

Room amenities: The hotels in this book offer anywhere from dozens of room amenities to none. This item lists up to nine of the most common room amenities guests can expect: phone, TV, coffee maker (with complimentary coffee), hair dryer, iron and ironing board, robe, room service, and Internet connection. "Wi-fi" means high-speed wireless Internet connection. "Wired Internet" means high-speed wired Internet connection. If the connection is free, this is noted. "Room service" means the hotel offers room service of some variety. The larger hotels usually provide twenty-four-hour room service. At smaller hotels, room service may be offered only when the hotel's restaurant is open. Call the hotel or check its Web site for information about other room amenities that are important to you.

Facilities: Hotel restaurant(s) and bar hours of operation are listed. Again, these are subject to change. If the hotel has a business center, a fitness center on-site (no matter how small), a pool, whirlpool, or complimentary car service, these are listed. If the hotel accommodates groups, this listing includes the largest number of people the hotel can host for an event at which attendees are standing, such as a reception. Contact the hotel for specifics regarding meeting and banquet facilities and about available off-site recreation facilities. Here is also where I note other features, such as a guest laundry room. If there is no Internet access in guest rooms, but it's available elsewhere, I note it here.

Smoking: "Designated rooms" means there are guest rooms in which smoking is allowed. If smoking is allowed in the hotel bar or other public areas, this is noted. You can always assume that smoking is allowed outside the hotel. If there are no spaces inside the hotel designated for smokers, the listing reads, "outdoors only."

Credit cards: The cards the hotel accepts are abbreviated as follows: V = Visa; MC = MasterCard; AE = American Express; DC = Diners Club; D = Discover; JCB = Japan Credit Bureau. The few hotels that accept only cash and check are noted.

Parking: Location and description of hotel guest parking, including any charges and whether it is through a valet only, are indicated. Many urban hotels offer valet parking only and charge a fee per night, which includes unlimited "in and out" from the hotel garage. These rates, too, are subject to change. If you're willing to walk, public garages in urban areas can be cheaper but are often a block or more away from the hotel and don't usually offer "in and out" privileges.

Accessibility: This listing indicates "disabled access" if at least one guest room has features installed to aid people with disabilities. Large urban properties are more likely to have rooms that meet strict Americans with Disabilities Act requirements for lodging. I also note when hotels have guest rooms on the ground floor and elevators for those who have trouble climbing stairs. Contact the hotel to inquire about facilities to meet your specific needs.

Pets: If pets are welcome, any fee or deposit is also listed. Special amenities provided for pets are also noted.

Author's tips: Here you'll find my recommendations for area events, businesses, or restaurants. I sometimes also include insider tidbits about the hotel, such as details about special rooms, hotel policies toward children, and whether light sleepers should pack earplugs.

National Register of Historic Places: This item notes whether the building is included in this federal registry.

Texas historical marker: This indicates whether a Texas historical marker is associated with the hotel.

Texas Heritage Trails Program: This specifies the heritage tourism region that the hotel is within as designated by the Texas Historical Commission's Texas Heritage Trails Program. The region's Web site is provided as a travel planning resource.

Visitor information: The local chamber of commerce or convention and visitors bureau contact information and Web site are listed at the end of each entry as a travel planning resource.

Why Choose a Historic Hotel and What to Expect

INDIVIDUALITY AND TANGIBLE LINKS TO TEXAS HISTORY

One of the most attractive features of historic hotels is that they offer refreshing individuality in a world homogenized by big-box retail stores and chain hotels and motels. Although some historic hotels have similarities, each is a unique property with a singular look and atmosphere. Modern chain hotels and motels, on the other hand, bank on their uniformity of architectural style, decor, facilities, and amenities. This predictability may be comforting, but cookie-cutter lodging gives guests no sense of place. A night spent at one chain in Dallas is not unlike staying at the same one in San Antonio or Lubbock.

Some of the larger historic hotels do have corporate owners and are operated by companies such as Wyndham, InterContinental, Hilton, and Marriott. But these companies have usually taken great pains to preserve or restore the architectural details of their historic properties, and they highlight the hotel's individual flavor, unique features, and history. Most historic Texas hotels are owned by real people instead of big corporations.

The stories of historic hotels are intertwined with the histories of their communities. Many were constructed during booming economic times: the cotton market was bullish, or oil wells were thick as tumbleweeds in the Panhandle. Others began as resorts for families traveling by rail for vacations in West Texas, the Hill Country, and the Gulf Coast. Several hoteliers are well known for more than owning businesses; some were Texas pioneers, town founders, cattle barons, civic and business leaders, or hardworking widows doing their best to provide for their children.

Probably the most notable Texas hotelier is Conrad Hilton. His start in the lodging business came in 1919, when he purchased the Mobley Hotel in Cisco during an oil boom. In 1924 he built in Dallas the first high-rise hotel to carry his name (now the Hotel Indigo). By the start of the Depression, his empire had grown to nine Texas properties. Today, the Hilton family of hotels spans the globe with more than two thousand properties. (Read more about Hilton in the "Closed but Not Forgotten Hotels" section.)

The architectural heritage of this state includes a significant number of hotel buildings. From the Gulf Coast to the Big Bend, hotels designed decades ago by famed architectural firms, such as Trost and Trost, and accomplished architects, such as Joseph

Each of the state's historic hotels has its own story. Here are a few of the interesting details:

- Teddy Roosevelt recruited some of his Rough Riders, the nation's first volunteer cavalry, in the Menger Hotel bar in San Antonio.
- Rock Hudson, Elizabeth Taylor, James Dean, and other cast and crew working on the film *Giant* made the Hotel Paisano in Marfa their headquarters in 1955.
- The Chicago White Sox and other national baseball teams stayed at the Rogers Hotel in Waxahachie during spring training from 1916 to 1921.
- The rambling Luther Hotel in Palacios was cut into three pieces, moved by mule one-half mile from its original location, and reassembled shortly after it was constructed in 1903.
- Four hotels still lodging guests today were designed by noted architect of the Southwest Henry C. Trost of the firm Trost and Trost. They are: Camino Real Hotel (originally Hotel Paso del Norte) in El Paso; the Holland Hotel in Alpine; the Gage Hotel in Marathon; and Hotel Paisano in Marfa. In addition, Trost designed the 1930 art deco tower addition to the Driskill Hotel in Austin. Closed Texas hotels designed by Trost include the El Capitan in Van Horn and the Hotel Cortez (originally Orndorff Hotel) and Plaza Hotel (originally Hilton Hotel) in El Paso.
- The Jefferson Hotel in Jefferson was originally a cotton warehouse across from the docks on Big Cypress Bayou in the 1850s. At that time, Jefferson was the state's leading inland port.
- The Driskill Hotel in Austin is the last remaining grand Victorian hotel in Texas and since it opened in 1886 has been the scene of numerous inaugural balls for Texas governors.
- The lobby of the Tarpon Inn in Port Aransas displays thousands of tarpon scales, including one autographed by President Franklin D. Roosevelt, who fished off the Texas coast in 1937.

Finger and Alfred Giles, contribute to the character of their communities. Several are Recorded Texas Historic Landmarks or are on the National Register of Historic Places.

Almost all Texas historic hotels have some original interior fixtures and other remaining architectural details—such as light fixtures, flooring, and woodwork—that help make them distinctive and provide tactile links to the past. A few hotel lobbies are mini museums and display newspaper clippings from the hotel's grand opening and yellowed hotel registers inked with autographs of entertainers, Civil War generals, or presidents. But the many ordinary patrons who signed these registers contributed most to the essence of these establishments. For them, these buildings were the locus for their day-to-day activities, places where they could do business, politick, and socialize. This continues today. Out-of-towners and locals alike create memories and participate in life's important and routine events—whether celebrating a wedding or a birthday, participating in a civic or political meeting, or attending a business conference or family reunion.

HOTELS TO SUIT MANY TASTES

During my hotel visits, I found accommodations that would appeal to different kinds of travelers and fit many of the reasons people travel. *Are you the outdoorsy type who wants to bring a hunting rifle or bicycle into your hotel room?* Some historic hotels frequented by hunters and cyclists allow this. *Do you want to spend the weekend ordering room service, drinking champagne, and tucked into a king-sized bed with handmade duvet and pressed sheets?* Pampering guests is the main goal at many upscale historic hotels. *Does your treasured pet travel with you everywhere, even when you're in San Antonio on business?* Pets and their devoted owners get special treatment at some historic hotels. *Do you love talking with locals about their community's history and enjoy soaking up the area's ambience?* Historic hotels in rural areas offer many opportunities to mix with friendly locals. *Do you need to stay connected to work or home while traveling?* Many historic hotels offer Internet access.

Because people have different travel styles, requirements for comfort, reasons for travel, and travel budgets, I've tried to describe each hotel with plenty of details. You should be able to use the hotel summaries to guide you to the hotel that's right for your particular trip and tastes.

LEVELS OF SERVICE, AMENITIES, AND COSTS

Those who shy away from staying at historic hotels might do so because they assume they'll have to share a bathroom with other guests or because they expect to find limited facilities and amenities. While the level of amenities and services vary greatly across the state, only a handful of hotels offer the most basic accom-

HOTELS TO SUIT VARIED TRAVELERS AND TRIPS

The hotels below are organized according to one or more of the features that I think might appeal to guests based on their particular tastes, interests, and reasons for travel. *This is by no means a complete listing of each of these hotel's significant features. Several hotels could be placed in more than one category, but to keep the list manageable, I have listed some under only one or two.* See the individual hotel summaries for more complete information about each hotel.

Romance and Celebratory Occasions
The Adolphus, Dallas
Comfort Common, Comfort
Driskill Hotel, Austin
The Fairmount, San Antonio
Gage Hotel, Marathon
Hotel Garza, Post
Hotel ZaZa, Houston
Meyer Bed and Breakfast on
    Cypress Creek, Comfort
Nutt House Historic Hotel,
    Granbury
Olle Hotel, Flatonia
Swann Hotel Bed and Breakfast,
    Jasper

Cycling and Motorcycle Tours
Belle-Jim Hotel, Jasper
Gage Hotel, Marathon
Holland Hotel, Alpine
Hotel Limpia, Fort Davis
Hotel Paisano, Marfa
Hotel Turkey, Turkey
Rocksprings Hotel, Rocksprings

Sportsman Lodge, Quitaque
Veranda Historic Inn, Fort Davis
Von Minden Hotel, Schulenburg
Ye Kendall Inn, Boerne

Local Color
Belle-Jim Hotel, Jasper
Casa de Palmas, McAllen
Fredonia Hotel, Nacogdoches
Hotel Blessing, Blessing
Hotel Turkey, Turkey
Hotel Paisano, Marfa
Luther Hotel, Palacios
Tremont House, Galveston

Texas Country or Cowboy Charm
Gage Hotel, Marathon
Hotel Turkey, Turkey
Miss Molly's Hotel, Fort Worth
Sportsman Lodge, Quitaque
Stockyards Hotel, Fort Worth

Hunting or Angling Trips
Farris Hotel, Eagle Lake
Hotel Turkey, Turkey
Luther Hotel, Palacios
Sportsman Lodge, Quitaque
Spur Hotel, Archer City
Tarpon Inn, Port Aransas
Travelers Inn, Roaring Springs
Queen Isabel Inn, Port Isabel
Yacht Club Hotel, Port Isabel

Ghost Hunting
Driskill Hotel, Austin
Excelsior House, Jefferson
Faust Hotel, New Braunfels
Jefferson Hotel, Jefferson
Menger Hotel, San Antonio
Prince Solms Inn, New Braunfels
Sheraton Gunter Hotel, San
    Antonio
Von Minden Hotel, Schulenberg

Business Travelers
Alden Houston, Houston
The Adolphus, Dallas
Driskill Hotel, Austin
The Fairmount, San Antonio
Fort Worth Hilton, Fort Worth
Hotel Indigo, Dallas
InterContinental Stephen F. Austin
    Hotel, Austin
The Lancaster, Houston
LaSalle Hotel, Bryan
St. Anthony Hotel, San Antonio
Sheraton Gunter Hotel, San
    Antonio
Stoneleigh Hotel and Spa, Dallas
Warwick Melrose Hotel, Dallas

Destination Restaurants or Bars
The Adolphus, Dallas
Antlers Hotel, Kingsland
Belle-Jim Hotel, Jasper
Camino Real Hotel, El Paso
Hotel Blessing, Blessing
Driskill Hotel, Austin
Faust Hotel, New Braunfels
Holland Hotel, Alpine
InterContinental Stephen F. Austin
    Hotel, Austin
Jefferson Hotel, Jefferson
Smith House, Crosbyton
Stagecoach Inn, Salado
The Woodbine Hotel, Madisonville
Ye Kendall Inn, Boerne

History Buff Destination
Crockett Hotel, San Antonio
Eastland Hotel, Eastland
Excelsior House, Jefferson
Hotel Galvez, Galveston
La Borde House, Rio Grande City
Menger Hotel, San Antonio
Sheraton Gunter Hotel, San
    Antonio

Smith House, Crosbyton
Rogers Hotel, Waxahachie
Texan Hotel, Panhandle

Pets Pampered
The Fairmount, San Antonio
Holland Hotel, Alpine
Hotel Lawrence, Dallas
Hotel ZaZa, Houston
Sheraton Gunter Hotel, San
    Antonio
Warwick Melrose Hotel, Dallas

Local Live Music
Driskill Hotel, Austin
Hotel Turkey, Turkey
InterContinental Stephen F. Austin
    Hotel, Austin
Miss Molly's Hotel, Fort Worth
Sportsman Lodge, Quitaque
Spur Hotel, Archer City
Stockyards Hotel, Fort Worth
Hotel Texas, Fort Worth

Architectural Standouts
The Adolphus, Dallas
Driskill Hotel, Austin
Camino Real Hotel, McAllen
Courtyard Fort Worth Doubletree/
    Blackstone, Fort Worth
Hotel Galvez, Galveston
Hotel Paisano, Marfa
Menger Hotel, San Antonio
Veranda Historic Inn, Fort Davis
The Woodbine Hotel, Madisonville

Whimsical, Chic, or Unusual Interior Decor
Alden Houston, Houston
Havana Riverwalk Inn, San
    Antonio
Hotel Indigo, Dallas
Hotel ZaZa, Houston

modations. Not surprisingly, these also offer the least expensive nightly rates, from about $25 to about $80 for guest rooms and suites. At these hotels, guests will likely share bath facilities, although some offer a few rooms with private baths. Furnishings and decor can be spare, a bit worn, and utilitarian. Amenities may be minimal—picture a tiny bar of Cashmere Bouquet soap on the bathroom sink, which has separate taps for hot and cold water. Those willing to forgo a few creature comforts may find that, taken on their own terms, these hotels have their special charms.

The majority of Texas' historic hotels have a wider selection of facilities and amenities and offer mid-range prices. Rates can run from around $50 for a standard room to about $600 for a suite. In this group, most have private baths although a couple of these hotels offer guests a choice of private bath or shared facilities. A few of these mid-range hotels are in major cities, but most are in smaller communities. A goodly number don't have room service, but several have a restaurant and bar on premises. Many offer a complimentary continental or full breakfast

The remaining one-third of the state's historic hotels offer what you would expect from any first-class urban hotel, including valet parking (for a fee), doormen, bell captains, room service, at least one restaurant and bar, and fitness, meeting, and banquet facilities. Many of these hotels have a concierge who can skillfully arrange for tickets to a sold-out event or track down a guest's favorite Scotch. Some of these hotels are operated by international hotel companies and have hundreds of guest rooms and suites. Almost all the rooms at these accommodations have private baths, and at the more posh facilities, the marble-clad bathrooms have multiple showerheads and Jacuzzi tubs and are stocked with designer toiletries and terry robes. The nightly room rates at most of these hotels begin at roughly $100 for a standard room and can run as high as $3,000 for the largest, most well-appointed suite.

ATMOSPHERE AND DECOR

Not surprisingly, the mid-sized and smaller hotels generally offer more intimate surroundings. Guests have more personal contact with innkeepers, fellow guests, and locals. Accommodations in smaller towns also offer the most relaxed, informal ambience. At these hotels, locals chat with guests over meals prepared from scratch in the hotel restaurant. Resident innkeepers insist their patrons call them by their first names and volunteer to drive ill lodgers to the doctor. The innkeeper's decorating touch at some of the mid-sized and smaller hotels can make the accommodations feel like large homes. Family antiques or some of the hotel's original furnishings are sometimes scattered throughout these buildings. You might find family photos, personal art collections, or locally made crafts dotting the walls. A few have

TIPS FOR STAYING IN SMALL HISTORIC HOTELS

In general, guests booking accommodations at hotels with fewer than thirty rooms should be aware of a few things, although not all of these items may apply.

- Claw-foot bathtubs. Love them or loathe them, these tubs are offered at many smaller hotels. They can be awkward to climb into and out of, but they are great for a luxuriant soak. Some come with shower attachments. Inquire in advance about bathroom facilities if this concerns (or appeals to) you.
- No TV. If you bring reading material to wile away quiet evening hours at TV-less facilities, it's best to pack a clip-on book light. You might not have a well-positioned bedside lamp.
- Train noise. Many hotels were built alongside railroad tracks for the convenience of their original guests. I've never been kept awake by the trains, but light sleepers will find earplugs helpful in coping with the noise. A few hotels supply these, but it's smart to bring your own.

- No night staff. A few of the smaller hotels are not staffed overnight. Guests are given emergency phone numbers, but if you need an extra pillow at 2 A.M., you're out of luck until the staff clock in again.
- Alarm clocks. Most small hotels do not offer wake-up calls. Some do not have alarm clocks. If you really must arise at a particular time, pack a travel alarm.
- No telephone. Travelers without cell phones will need to walk to the front desk to ask hotel staff questions and make requests. Hotels without in-room phones provide a phone for guests' use in the lobby or at another central location.
- Luggage handling. Many hotels of this size don't have staff assigned to carry your bags. But if you need assistance, don't hesitate to ask the innkeeper or the front desk clerk.
- Late-night arrival. If you plan to arrive late in the evening at a hotel in a small town, particularly during the early part of the week, it's best to eat dinner before you arrive. The town may offer few, if any, choices for late-night dining.

a healthy dose of collectibles, dried flowers, and table scarves à la your grandmother. At others the look can either be spare or have a designer's thoughtful touch.

The state's grander historic hotels often surround patrons with specially chosen antiques or contemporary furnishings and art, and their restaurants serve gourmet cuisine created by award-winning chefs. Fresh flower arrangements and background classical music fill the hotel's public areas. Some maintain an elegant atmosphere and require that guests lounging poolside cover up before entering the lobby. While a few of these hotels have fewer than fifty rooms, most offer hundreds of rooms and extensive meeting facilities.

Many hoteliers and hotel management companies work very hard to create a particular atmosphere at their establishments, with a professionally designed decor that aims for refined elegance, chic ultramodern, whimsical, rich Victorian, or classic cowboy. Some even offer themed guest rooms and suites along these lines. Background music, dramatic lighting, carefully selected color schemes or scents, and professional, attentive staff contribute to the overall mood. At some of the state's his-toric hotels, the ambience is created organically, through a combination of the warmth and personalities of the hosts, the homespun decor, and the flavor of both the community and the distinctive original features of the hotel building and its history.

NATIONAL AND STATE ORGANIZATIONS THAT PROMOTE HISTORIC HOTELS

Many of the hotels featured in this book are members of Hospitality Accommodations of Texas (www.hat.org). Member hotels, bed-and-breakfasts, inns, guesthouses, and ranches must pass an inspection by this statewide association. HAT promotes many historic lodgings through its Web site and printed directory.

A handful of the hotels in this book are members of Historic Hotels of America (www.historichotels.org). Membership in this organization, a program of the National Trust for Historic Preservation, has grown to more than two hundred hotels nationwide. Properties must be listed or eligible for the National Register of Historic Places and meet other National Trust standards to become members.

INDIVIDUALITY

A sample of some of the one-of-a-kind features found at historic Texas hotels:

- Standard guest rooms at the Queen Isabel Inn have full kitchens and bathrooms stocked with aspirin, razors, antacids, and toothbrushes.
- An expansive, artist-created rectangular light panel in the Alden Houston's ultramodern lobby changes color and the room's mood every few minutes.
- Guests at the Antlers Hotel in Kingsland on Lake LBJ find croquet and bocce ball equipment, a canoe, and fishing gear at their disposal.
- The mission/Spanish revival style Casa de Palmas in McAllen has a pool and two lushly landscaped courtyards featuring fountains, palm trees, and other exotic plantings.
- Many standard rooms at the Meyer Bed and Breakfast on Cypress Creek have modern gas fireplaces.
- The elegant lobby at The Adolphus in Dallas is filled with fine antiques and art, and its opulent French Room Restaurant features a hand-painted vaulted ceiling.
- The Bonnie and Clyde Suite in the Stockyards Hotel of Fort Worth displays writings by infamous Bonnie Parker, along with one of her pistols.
- Featured suites at The Fairmount in San Antonio have onyx and gold-leaf tile and mini chandeliers.
- The bar at the InterContinental Stephen F. Austin Hotel has Austin's only public terrace on Congress Avenue and great views of the state capitol four blocks away.
- Standard guest rooms at the Holland Hotel in Alpine come with mini fridges and microwave ovens.
- The Dome Bar at the Camino Real Hotel in El Paso is topped by a striking twenty-five-foot stained glass dome attributed to Tiffany Studios.
- Area locals and a few off-the-beaten-track tourists gather daily at the Hotel Blessing Coffee Shop for homemade southern-style favorites such as fried chicken, smothered steak, sweet potatoes, yeast rolls, and fruit cobbler.

Origins of Historic Hotels in Texas

Most Texas historic hotels can be identified as belonging to at least one of the following groups: stagecoach inn, railroad or drummer's hotel, resort or vacation hotel, hotels created from other businesses and homes, urban commercial hotel, community hotel, and apartment hotel. Some easily fit into more than one category.

The development of historic hotels in Texas generally has followed the development of transportation in the state. The earliest hostelries were located along stagecoach routes from the early nineteenth century, some even before Texas became a republic. Later in that century, when stagecoaches gave way to railroads, hotel development followed the tracks as they were laid. By the early 1930s, growing automobile travel further affected Texas communities and hotels. Over time, these changing modes of transportation led to the eventual demise of most early hotels.

Hotels were born where there was a demand for lodging. As people began to flock to parts of Texas for vacations or in search of healthful climates, new hotels were built and existing ones expanded to accommodate them. A number of early Texas merchants boarded customers overnight in their homes or stores. Wives prepared meals and tended to these lodgers, spreading a reputation of hospitality. As a matter of necessity, many of these business owners modified their properties to add hotel rooms for their growing clientele. Primarily in the early twentieth century, Texas cities gained hotels when town boosters and investors raised funds and sold stock in hostelries they thought would spur local commerce and improve the city's image. Developers also constructed apartment hotels to appeal to long-term lodgers who wanted spacious accommodations away from the city center while enjoying all the amenities of a fine hotel.

Hotels sprang up in rural boomtowns overrun by fortune seekers following the discovery of oil or in communities thriving from lucrative cotton and cattle markets. When the oil played out or the markets fizzled, many of these hotels declined and became cheap rooming houses before eventually closing.

STAGECOACH INNS

Texas pioneers in the early nineteenth century were known for warmly welcoming travelers. Settlers often provided bed and board free of charge, but according to Richard van Orman's *A Room for the Night: Hotels of the Old West,* poorer hosts charged a fee. As trails and stagecoach routes—such as the Old Spanish Trail, the San Antonio Road, the Overland Trail, and the Chisholm Trail—developed and the number of travelers grew, so did the need for lodging. Stagecoach inns, "stage stands," and "road ranches" appeared along these primitive highways. At these, stagecoaches could stop to change horses and drivers, and passengers could have a meal and get some rest.

The quality of accommodation at many stagecoach inns was quite poor, Kathryn Turner Carter writes in *Stagecoach Inns of Texas.* In fact the buildings were often crude with dirt floors and canvas roofs. Lodging was cramped, and it was not uncommon for guests to share not only a room but also a bed with strangers—and bedbugs. But these inns weren't all so primitive. Travelers arriving at the Nimitz Hotel in Fredericksburg found a combined theater-casino-dance hall and basement brewery. The Nimitz was reputed to have the cleanest beds on the Texas frontier. Guests at the Mansion House in Houston found washstands with mirrors in their rooms. The parlor had plenty of spittoons, chairs, a sofa, and an eight-day grandfather clock. For safety, the inn's kitchen was housed in a separate building and was outfitted with a cookstove and fireplaces for cooking wild game and cornbread.

The hostelries served fare that was usually unpretentious and frequently repetitious. Corn, pork, and coffee were often staples at all three meals. In 1853–54, Frederick Law Olmstead traversed the state on horseback, and in his account, *A Journey through Texas,* he describes his disgust for the meals at an unnamed Austin hotel: "Never did we see any wholesome food on the table. It was a succession of burnt flesh of swine and bulls, decaying vegetables, and sour and moldy farinaceous glues, all pervaded with rancid butter." Fresh food was particularly difficult to come by in the western part of Texas, and travelers on the Overland route had to get by on hardtack, dried beef, and beans. Where game was plentiful, guests dined on squirrel, turkey, buffalo, quail, or bear. Coastal travelers enjoyed oysters and fish.

By 1860 at least thirty-one stage lines crisscrossed the state, according to Carter. But at the same time, tracks were being laid that would eventually bring an end to the stagecoach era.

RAILROAD OR DRUMMER'S HOTELS

Railways expanded across Texas after the Civil War, carrying people and freight. Those communities lucky enough to be on a railway line sprouted hotels and other businesses and prospered economically. The hotels built in response to this transportation change are called railroad hotels or drummer's hotels, after the drummers, or traveling salesmen, who were often their primary customers. Railroad hotels were constructed near train depots and had restaurants or taverns. Many were also known as boardinghouses, because they offered guests meals, and some accommodated long-term lodgers.

The railroad companies sometimes constructed hotels in attractive destinations to encourage ticket sales for holiday excursions or at stops where there were no facilities for their customers. The Travelers Inn in Roaring Springs and the Antlers Hotel in Kingsland, both still operating, are two of these. Restaurateur Fred Harvey contracted with the Santa Fe railway to construct a Harvey House roughly every one hundred miles along its tracks. From the late nineteenth century into the early twentieth, Harvey Houses were known for their good food served promptly and courteously by "Harvey Girls." A few, such as the Harvey House at the Santa Fe Depot in Summerville, offered overnight accommodations.

The American Hotel Association made it easy for traveling salesmen and other rail passengers to locate hotels in North America. Copies of its "Official Hotel Red Book and Directory," which began publication in 1886, were available in all Pullman railcars in the United States and Canada. Notations next to each town listed its population and railway lines. Each hotel listing included the number of rooms, the rates, and the proprietor or manager's name.

These hotels often provided traveling salesmen with a "drummer's room," or showroom, where area merchants could browse a display of drummer's wares, from dresses and hats to hardware. Today, visitors to the Rogers Hotel in Waxahachie can see the freight elevator that once hauled drummers' merchandise and cotton samples harvested from county farms upstairs to two drummers' rooms. The rooms are now used for meetings and receptions.

As the railway brought new visitors to many small towns, some individuals made the most of their situations. A widow turned her Victorian home near the railroad depot in Calvert into a hotel to make ends meet. That hotel is now closed. The original proprietor of the Belle-Jim Hotel in Jasper, another widow, this one with four children, became well known among drummers for the complimentary feast she served them each January. After dining, many salesmen would reserve rooms at the Belle-Jim Hotel, which is open today, for the remainder of their trips that year.

These railroad hotels served other customers as well, of course. Some hotels still operating, such as the Texan Hotel in Panhandle and the Eastland Hotel in Eastland, opened when oil was discovered in their regions. Others, such as the Dabbs Railroad Hotel in Llano, served railroad workers who ate in the kitchen and spent the night before returning to Austin, at a time when trains were hauling cattle, cotton, and minerals mined from the area. In the early 1900s, hunters from as far away as the northeastern United States converged on boardinghouses in the Big Thicket to track its highly prized black bear.

RESORT AND TOURIST HOTELS

One special breed of hotel has historically catered to those seeking improved health and relaxation. Ye Kendall Inn in Boerne is one of those. By the late 1870s Boerne, in the Texas Hill Country, had become a famous resort known for its dry, healthful climate. Ye Kendall Inn, already serving those traveling by horse and stagecoach, handled the new influx of visitors by expanding its rooms and offering on-call doctors and a restaurant that accommodated special diets.

Hotel Limpia in Fort Davis is one of the last remaining hotels in West Texas that welcomed vacationers from Houston and the Gulf Coast. The humidity-averse would retreat each summer to the dry climate and higher altitude available in the Davis Mountains. By the 1940s this annual pilgrimage ended when the advent of air-conditioning made summering in Southeast Texas more palatable.

Local health industries grew up around mineral and hot springs flowing in parts of the state. The massive, now derelict Baker Hotel in Mineral Wells was just one of the many hotels to house guests who were attracted from across the country by the promise of the town's healing waters. In the 1880s the Springs Resort Hotel sat at the edge of a lake fed by several mineral springs in Sour Lake; the hotel has since burned. Hot Wells Hotel and Bath House in San Antonio, now in ruins, was also a well-appointed resort hotel in the early 1900s.

The 1911 Hotel Galvez in Galveston is the last remaining beach resort hotel of that era. Most guests arrived on one of the many trains that served the island, depositing vacationers from Texas, Louisiana, and across the country. A string of hotels along the Gulf Coast once welcomed vacationers and anglers, many of whom came to catch tarpon during the early 1900s. The Luther Hotel in Palacios, the Tarpon Inn in Port Aransas, and the Queen Isabel Inn and the Yacht Club Hotel in Port Isabel still cater to coastal visitors.

HOTELS CREATED FROM OTHER BUSINESSES AND HOMES

Many early Texas merchants and other business owners welcomed out-of-town customers at their tables and as overnight guests. Sometimes this led to the establishment of new hotels. French immigrant merchant Francois La Borde in 1917 modified his combined home and business in Rio Grande City to add hotel rooms to house his customers and others. Granbury pioneers Jesse, Jacob, and David Nutt added a parlor and twenty guest rooms to their mercantile in 1911 to accommodate the clients who had been staying with David and his wife.

Another businessman who expanded into innkeeping was San Antonio brewer William Menger. He and his wife began to accommodate their drinking customers overnight at their brewery. Then in 1859 they built the original fifty rooms of the Menger Hotel. It now has more than 300.

In the 1850s Captain William Perry rented rooms in his Jefferson home to cotton merchants, planters, and other business associates. The home quickly became well known for its hospitality in what was then Texas' largest inland port. After his death, new owners expanded the building and added rooms for traveling salesmen.

URBAN COMMERCIAL HOTELS

A number of historic hotels were born from a thriving economy and the dreams of Texas business leaders and investors. In 1910 Dallas' leading businessmen approached Adolphus Busch, who owned a brewery and hotel in Dallas, to seek his backing for the construction of a first-class hotel. The Adolphus was born two years later. At the time it was the tallest building in downtown Dallas. Fort Worth visionaries invested in the 1921 construction of the fourteen-story Hotel Texas, now the Hilton Fort Worth, with the goal of changing Fort Worth's rowdy cowtown image into one of a modern commercial and cultural center.

McAllen Mayor O. P. Archer, bank president R. E. Horn, and other town business leaders hatched the idea for the Casa de Palmas hotel, which opened in 1918. They believed McAllen should provide first-class accommodations for drummers, for those doing business in the area's growing

agricultural operations, and for visitors traveling to and from Mexico.

Many of these businesses opened shortly before or after the 1929 stock market crash that heralded the Great Depression. New Braunfels town boosters developed the Traveler's Hotel, which offered rooms with full private baths. Now known as the Faust Hotel, it opened only a few days before the crash and survived the Great Depression by serving drummers and the city's convention and tourism business. The Stephen F. Austin Hotel began as a dream of the Austin Chamber of Commerce. In 1924 it opened as the first high-rise hotel along Congress Avenue, a few blocks from the state capitol.

Many of these hotel deals came about through a similar arrangement: Leading investors would form a hotel company and front much of the funds for land purchase and construction. Additional financing came from loans and the sale of mortgage bonds or stocks.

COMMUNITY HOTELS

Community hotels were built with a more grassroots approach. Cities and towns across the country without deep-pocketed individual investors relied on door-to-door sales of hotel stock to residents. Volunteer sales teams competed against one another to support the hometown project, considering its success crucial to the future of their community. Nacogdoches jumped on the community hotel bandwagon in the 1950s. More than

1,100 individuals bought Community Hotel stock at $50 a share, contributing more than $500,000 toward the cost of the $1.3 million–dollar Fredonia Hotel. The Hockenbury Associates Company of Harrisburg, Pennsylvania, which had guided that city's fund-raising effort, later assisted Edinburg with a similar project to construct the town's Echo Hotel, which opened in 1959 with an architectural style and floor plan very similar to the Fredonia. Hockenbury helped dozens of communities across North America build such hotels. A company brochure from that period, *Why Build a Community Hotel?* is filled with testimonials from towns such as Bozeman, Montana, and Winfield, Kansas. Its prose states earnestly, "No community institution is more important to the growth and prosperity of a city than a modern hotel."

APARTMENT HOTELS

In the early 1920s, developers constructed apartment hotels away from city centers, often placing them alongside parks or along parkways, along major avenues or streetcar lines, and in quiet suburban neighborhoods. Residents could choose single-room apartments or multiroom accommodations with private bathrooms and kitchen. Many apartments featured the Murphy bed, which would fold upright and into a closet, granting more floor space. These establishments catered to permanent residents who sought hotel-type conveniences and didn't mind paying for them. The hotels generally supplied renters with all linen, cutlery, china, cookware, and appliances. They also provided janitorial, valet, and maid service.

Residents of the Melrose Court Apartments and Hotel in Dallas shopped at its on-site meat market and grocery store. The Stoneleigh Court Apartment Hotel, also in Dallas, featured an enormous ballroom on its eleventh floor. The Warwick Hotel in Houston, now Hotel ZaZa, also began as an apartment hotel. A February 1938 article in *Texas Hotel Review* says the hotel with its 153 "apartment-homes" offered "garage service and complete commissary, coffee shop, valet and beauty parlor service."

Over time, the attraction of apartment hotels faded, and these businesses altered their accommodations to lodge overnight guests.

THE BOUTIQUE HOTEL TREND

Many of the historic hotels that survive today have done so by adjusting to changes in the marketplace. Most recently, a handful of historic hotels have adapted to one of the more recent lodging trends—the boutique hotel. This concept was born in San Francisco in the 1980s. Boutique hotels feature tailor-made services, luxurious or quirky environments, guest rooms of individual design, and attention to detail. They market to a group of travelers who want more than a comfortable place to lay their heads. For these guests, a singular hotel stay with an enhanced level of service is very important, and they are willing to pay a premium for it.

Boutique historic hotels include the Alden Houston in Houston, with its spare but comfortable urban contemporary design, original art, and personalized service. The Hotel ZaZa, also in Houston, takes a more eclectic approach to its decor and offers guests extravagantly furnished suites and an on-site spa. The decor and ambience of the Warwick Melrose Hotel in Dallas aims for what the hotel literature calls "relaxed elegance," and its guests can order gourmet brown-bag lunches to take with them upon checkout. Hotel Indigo in Dallas uses a custom-designed line of furnishings, bright solid colors, and art and scents in the lobby that change with the season to create its own, more moderately priced take on the boutique concept.

Big Bend Country

Historic hotel locations in
the Big Bend Country region.
Drawn by Jon Michael Grant.

Holland Hotel

Alpine ⚜ 1928

Across from an Amtrak railway station, this Trost and Trost–designed hotel hosts travelers to West Texas' Trans-Pecos region and remains a favorite meeting place for those doing business in Alpine and with Sul Ross State University.

O N MARCH 16, 1928, the front page of the *Alpine Avalanche* announced the expansion and grand reopening of the "New Holland." The newspaper described the $250,000 hostelry, its restaurant, and large banquet hall as having "beauty, comfort, and convenience." This description still suits the Holland Hotel today.

Pioneer cattleman John R. Holland thought Alpine needed a "respectable" hotel to serve travelers drawn to the booming quicksilver mining industry in the Big Bend region and to encourage the Kansas City, Mexico and Orient Railway, intended to run from Wichita, Kansas, to Mexico, to include Alpine as a destination. Holland's desire led

to his opening the original Holland Hotel in 1912. Business boomed, and Holland's son Clay, who took over as owner, contracted with well-known Southwest architectural firm Trost and Trost and the H. T. Ponsford and Sons construction company of El Paso to build a forty-room, three-story addition west of the original hotel. That 1928 Spanish colonial revival building, with its lion's head friezes, now houses the current Holland Hotel. The 1912 edifice is no longer part of the hostelry.

The Holland declined during the 1950s and 1960s and hit a low point in 1969, when it was closed and all its furniture and fixtures, even the marble thresholds, were auctioned

Holland Hotel, Alpine. Photo courtesy Holland Hotel.

off. In 1972 a new owner completely renovated the reinforced concrete building, and the old hotel housed county and state government offices and local businesses. Although a few businesses still rent space on the first floor, all rooms on the second and third floors are now reserved for overnight lodgers.

Staff welcome arriving guests to the relaxed atmosphere with a letter describing amenities and with coupons for a free breakfast in the hotel's restaurant. Pet guests receive a greeting too (with treats for canines). My letter included directions to my room. Once inside, I found a room key, mints, and complimentary earplugs

ESSENTIALS

Contact: 209 W. Holland Ave., Alpine, TX 79830; 800-535-8040, 432-837-3844; fax: 432-837-7346; www .HollandHotel.net, info@HollandHotel .net

Rooms: 27 rooms and suites, all with private bath, in 1928 hotel building; tub/shower combinations and walk-in showers; twin, full, queen, and king beds; Crow's Nest room has multiple windows and private roof deck; 4 lofts located in historic Williams-Vogt building behind hotel.

Rates: $–$$$, includes full breakfast.

Room amenities: TV, coffee maker, phone, microwave, and refrigerator in most rooms; hair dryer, iron, and ironing board available upon request, free wired Internet; historic lofts have kitchenette or kitchen facilities.

Facilities: Edelweiss Restaurant and Brewery. 7 A.M. to 10 P.M. (brewery closes at midnight), daily; phone, free wi-fi available in lobby; guest laundry room; group space for up to 200.

Smoking: allowed in designated area of restaurant and outside.

Credit cards: V, MC, AE, D.

Parking: free parking in hotel lots and along street.

Accessibility: some rooms are on ground floor, elevator.

Pets: welcome; $30 fee, must inform hotel in advance; dog treats at check-in.

Author's tips:—Front Street Books, 121 E. Holland, has an extensive collection of general interest titles as well as Texana and specializes in books on travel, natural history, and regional history in the Big Bend.—Railroad Blues, 504 W. Holland, serves beer and wine and hosts performances by popular Texas musicians like Asleep at the Wheel, Pat Green, and Toni Price.—Ivey's Emporium, 109 W. Holland, offers unusual gifts and collectibles.

National Register of Historic Places: no

Texas historical marker: yes

Texas Heritage Trails Program: Texas Mountain Trail Region, www.texasmountaintrail.com

Visitor information: Alpine Chamber of Commerce, 106 N. 3rd St., Alpine, TX 79830; 800-561-3735; 432-837-2326; www.alpinetexas.com, chamber @alpinetexas.com

(to block the noise of the nightly trains across the street).

The main hotel building has twenty-seven guest rooms that feature either carpet, tile, or Pergo laminate floors. Each is individually decorated. Some have antiques, and others are furnished with more up-to-date pieces. All rooms have a private bath. Multiple adjoining rooms can be rented in combination to create suites, which would work well for families.

Four loft-style suites with partial or full kitchens are also available in the historic Williams-Vogt building (1908–12) off the alley behind the hotel. These share a secluded courtyard and sport a decor best described as modern with a touch of West Texas. Floors are of Pergo laminate, linoleum, and Saltillo tile covered with the occasional wool or sisal rug. The ceilings are pressed tin.

Using paint scrapings and early photographs, former owner Carla McFarland recently refurbished the portion of the lobby now used as the hotel's dining room to match the original Trost and Trost design. Plaster walls above the original light brown and blue–tiled wainscoting are painted a light golden yellow. The "meringue pie" textured ceiling is white, and the massive cast concrete and wood beams are painted dark brown and covered with decorative stenciling and painted flourishes. The original wrought iron light fixtures that had been auctioned off were re-hung, two returned all the way from Kansas. The Holland crest reigns over the room's gas fireplace. McFarland also had the Edelweiss Restaurant's furnishings custom-made to match pieces that were used in architect Henry C. Trost's El Paso home around the time the hotel was constructed.

The Holland has a prominent, convenient location on Holland Avenue (State Hwy. 90) across the street from the train station, which is served by Amtrak's Texas Eagle passenger service. For years the Holland has been a community gathering place for socializing and for holding business, civic, and political meetings. Cattle deals were sealed with a handshake in the hotel's tiled lobby. Area residents and hotel guests used to share conversations in the hotel coffee shop. Now they converse over German food and beer in the hotel's Edelweiss Restaurant and Brewery, billed as the highest-altitude brewery in Texas. Groups ranging from wedding parties and Alpine's civic clubs to students and faculty from Sul Ross converge in the hotel's banquet room.

While in Alpine, visitors may tour the Chihuahuan Desert Research Institute's cactus garden and exhibits at the Museum of the Big Bend on the Sul Ross campus. Some plan their stay around the annual spring Cowboy Poetry Gathering and outdoor summer theater staged by Sul Ross's Theater of the Big Bend. Alpine's downtown has a number of antique and collectibles stores, bakeries, coffee shops, and restaurants, all within easy walking distance from the hotel.

Camino Real Hotel

El Paso ⚜ **1912**

The original lobby of this hotel, designed by Southwest architects Trost and Trost, is now one of the country's most beautiful hotel bars, with a gemlike stained-glass dome, gold-trimmed coffered ceiling, and marbleized columns.

When the ten-story Paso Del Norte Hotel opened one mile from the Mexican border in 1912, Texas' southern neighbor was embroiled in the Mexican Revolution. Roughly three-fourths of the population of El Paso's Mexican sister city, Juarez, fled to El Paso for safety. The Juarez post office and two of its banks moved their assets into El Paso. And revolutionary Pancho Villa sought ref-

uge in the community, after bribing his way out of prison in Chihuahua City, Mexico.

During the revolution, it was popular to watch skirmishes in Juarez between revolutionaries and Mexican soldiers from the hotel's rooftop terrace. In a photograph from the time, well-dressed men stand on chairs and crane their necks southward. The lamp posts and light fixtures evident

Camino Real Hotel, El Paso. Photo by J. Griffis Smith/TxDOT.

in the photo are still in place, having survived stray bullets, but the terrace is now closed.

Guests today have to settle for the view out their windows. I had an impressive, almost 180-degree panorama from my room in the hotel's seventeen-story addition. I could see from the Franklin Mountains at El Paso's northern edge south across the city's downtown to the Rio Grande and into Juarez. The two cities appear as one. Combined, they form a metropolis of almost two million people.

Spanish explorers christened Juarez "El Paso del Norte" (the Northern Pass) in the seventeenth century. When Zach T. White and his group of El Paso investors constructed the original hotel for their community, they adopted the name. Trost and Trost designed the hotel in the Chicago and beaux arts styles. Henry C. Trost moved to El Paso in 1903 to join his brother Gustavus and became the city's foremost architect. The firm of Trost and Trost is credited with designing more than two hundred structures in El Paso and is famous for defining modern Southwest architecture through hundreds of buildings throughout West Texas, Arizona, New Mexico, and northern Mexico.

Trost designed the hotel at the corner of West San Antonio and North El Paso streets with two towers surrounding a central light court, which ensured every guest room an outside window. The seventeen-story addition constructed in 1986 on the north side of the original hotel adjoins and overshadows it.

The master craftsmanship showcased in the hotel's original lobby survived remodeling and expansion projects and provides the predominant link to the hotel's past. Now dubbed the Dome Bar, the two-story room is crowned by a gorgeous multicolored glass dome attributed to Tiffany Studios. The twenty-five-foot artwork depicts green, brown, and pink foliage stretching up to a sky of blues, violets, and tans as it arcs over a circular bar. Rose-colored columns, which at first glance also appear to be marble, are actually gypsum from White Sands, New Mexico. Italian craftsmen are said to have performed this transformation. I took the hotel's original stairway to the mezzanine level for a close-up look at the room's coffered ceiling, elaborately molded gold cornices, and capitals featuring stylized plumage and stalks of corn.

In admiring the splendor, I almost missed the Trost-designed crest, which hangs at the northern end of the bar and depicts a Spanish friar, an American Indian, and the Spanish royal crest, symbolic of El Paso's past. A closer look at the plaque revealed Henry Trost's signature. This is supposed to be the only sculpture Trost signed.

The adjacent Dome Restaurant, with its four large crystal chandeliers, still has the original stained glass windows made in the geometric patterns similar to those of Frank Lloyd Wright; these grace the southern walls of both the Dome Restaurant and Bar. While the bar and restaurant recall the hotel's past, the hotel's adjacent lobby, the remaining public areas, and its guest rooms have the look and feel of other modern, urban hotels.

The hotel lost some of its luster in the late 1960s and 1970s. After the White family sold it in 1971, it changed hands a number of times. The hotel was expanded and remodeled in 1986 and in 2004 underwent a $4.2 million renovation, when it was renamed Camino Real by new owners.

The Camino Real attracts business and leisure travelers and has hosted a number of famous guests from politicians and entertainers to sports figures. Almost every weekend, the hotel hosts local wedding parties. The city's convention center, the El Paso Museum of Art, and the renovated Plaza Theater are across the street.

ESSENTIALS

Contact: 101 E. El Paso St., El Paso, TX 79901; 800-769-4300, 915-534-3000; fax: 915-534-3024; www.caminoreal .com/elpaso_i, elpaso@caminoreal .com.mx
Rooms: 359 rooms and suites, all with private bath; modern tub/shower combinations; king, queen, full beds; the Presidential Suite is the largest of 3, two-bedroom luxury suites.
Rates: $$–$$$$
Restaurant: Dome Restaurant, Tues.–Sat. 5 P.M.–11 P.M.; Azulejos Restaurant, 6 A.M.–9 P.M. daily; Dome Bar, 3:30 P.M.–1 A.M. daily.
Room amenities: phone, TV, coffee maker, hair dryer, iron and ironing board, free wi-fi, room service.
Facilities: outdoor heated pool, gym, gift shop, business center; can accommodate groups up to 1,300.
Smoking: outdoors only.
Credit cards: V, MC, AE, DC, D, CB.
Parking: self-park in hotel garage, $5; valet, $8.
Accessibility: disabled access, elevator.

Pets: not allowed.
Author's tips:—Self-guided historic walking tours of both downtown El Paso and Juarez available from the El Paso Convention and Visitors Bureau.—Downtown El Paso is quiet at night, and most restaurants close, but local favorite Café Central is open across from the hotel. Mesa Street, west of downtown, also has a string of restaurants.—Take the Border Jumper trolley for a guided loop tour across the border and through Juarez with hop-on and -off stops.
National Register of Historic Places: yes
Texas historical marker: yes
Texas Heritage Trails Program: Texas Mountain Trail Region, www.texasmountaintrail.com
Visitor information: El Paso Convention and Visitors Bureau, One Civic Center Plaza, El Paso, TX 79901; 800-351-6024, 915-534-0601; www .elpasocvb.com, info@elpasocvb.com

Hotel Limpia
Fort Davis ⚜ 1913

Forty rocking chairs on the expansive porches of this homey hotel provide lots of encouragement to relax after a day of birding and hiking in the Davis Mountains or an evening of stargazing at McDonald Observatory.

The Union Trading Company built the Hotel Limpia, named after a nearby creek, to accommodate not only the West Texas ranching families who came to town for supplies, but a variety of semipermanent residents—including health seekers and tourists enjoying the scenic area's dry climate and mountain air. Tourism continues to bring most guests to the two-story Hotel Limpia, a landmark built of locally quarried pink granite in Fort Davis's small downtown.

The hotel is adjacent to the quiet town square, which seems barely changed since the early 1900s. Just south of the hotel are the historic Jeff Davis County Courthouse, the Union Trading Company Building (now the county library), and the Fort Davis State Bank, which was built by the same construction company, Campbell and Bance, that built the hotel. An earlier Limpia Hotel was Fort Davis's first hotel, built in 1884 of red brick, but it was used only a few years and had no connection to the current facility.

Hotel Limpia, Fort Davis. Photo by Victoria Lowe.

ESSENTIALS

Contact: P.O. Box 1838, 101 Memorial Square, Fort Davis, TX 79734; 800-662-5517, 432-426-3237; fax: 432-426-3983; www.hotellimpia .com, frontdesk@hotellimpia.com

Rooms: 31 rooms and suites, all with private bath in main hotel and 2 annexes; shower/tub combination; queen and king beds; refrigerators and kitchenettes available; hotel also operates 12 suites and guesthouses in old Fort Davis homes.

Rates: $$–$$$

Room amenities: TV, coffee maker, hair dryer, iron and ironing board.

Facilities: Hotel Limpia Dining Room, 5:30 P.M. to 9 P.M. Tues.–Sun.; Sutler's Club, 5:30 P.M. to 9 P.M. Tues. –Sun.; lobby phone available to guests; free wired Internet, heated outdoor pool, meeting space for up to 50.

Smoking: outdoors only.

Credit cards: V, MC, AE, D.

Parking: free parking along street and in hotel lot.

Accessibility: several rooms are on ground floor.

Pets: welcome, $10 fee.

Author's tips:—Room 34 on the first floor of the original hotel building has a private screened porch.—The Chihuahuan Desert Nature Center and Botanical Gardens, just a few miles south of Fort Davis, offers beautiful hiking trails and gardens and an informative interpretive center, which includes a mining heritage exhibit.

National Register of Historic Places: no

Texas historical marker: yes

Texas Heritage Trails Program: Texas Mountain Trail Region, www.texasmountaintrail.com

Visitor information: Fort Davis Chamber of Commerce, Box 378, No. 4 Memorial Square, Fort Davis, TX 79734; 800-524-3015, 432-426-3015; www .fortdavis.com, info@fortdavis.com

Hotel stationery printed in the 1920s boasts that the Limpia sits at the highest altitude of any hotel in Texas, one mile above sea level. This high desert climate attracted "summer swallows," travelers from Houston and Galveston who would take the train to Alpine or Marfa and continue the short distance north to Fort Davis. In West Texas they could escape the mosquitoes and humidity of back home. Early business was good, prompting the construction of an addition to the hotel building and an annex built in 1917 to its northeast. But when air-conditioning became widely available in the 1940s, many folks stopped making the trek west.

The hotel fell into disrepair, and in 1953 a fire gutted the building. J. C. Duncan was a Fort Davis native with an interest in historic preservation. He purchased the remains and rebuilt the hotel. It was hard making it profitable, but the enterprise received a boost when staff from the Harvard Radio Astronomy Station needed residences and office space. Duncan leased the entire building to them. The group collected data on solar radio wave activity from a radio telescope northwest of Fort Davis.

When the Harvard crew departed in 1978, Duncan remodeled the building further, adding private bathrooms and central heating and air-conditioning. Tourism in the area has grown, and the Limpia is once again a thriving business, now operated by Duncan's son Joe and his wife, Lanna.

The comfortable, carpeted rooms have 12-foot pressed tin ceilings. Furniture is a mixture of modern pieces, antiques, and reproductions in the style of the 1930s and 1940s. Most of the rooms are painted in cool pastel colors, which, combined with their tall, double-hung windows, make the accommodations light and airy.

The furnishings and decor give the main hotel building and its two annexes a very homey feeling. This suits the patrons, who are mostly nature lovers or outdoors enthusiasts. Area attractions include hiking, mountain biking, or birding at Davis Mountains State Park; horseback riding or hunting on local ranches; stargazing at McDonald Observatory; or cycling or motorcycle touring along West Texas' scenic highways.

While more serious birders can track acorn woodpeckers and canyon wrens in the nearby state park, the large number of birds flitting around the hotel's grounds makes even a low-energy approach to birding productive. I chatted with guests from Michigan as we listened to chirping cardinals and watched the swallows circle the eaves. The hotel's common areas are well stocked with board games, jigsaw puzzles, a piano, and local newspapers. Rocking chairs and clusters of furniture on several porches invite guests to sit with a good book. For those who must be in contact with home or work, free Internet access is provided.

Veranda Historic Inn

Fort Davis 🏛 **1883**

Sunny rooms filled with antiques, lovingly landscaped grounds, and plenty of shady spots to relax outdoors are prime features of this adobe hotel, where the home-cooked breakfasts are a delicious bonus.

When the Hotel Lempert opened in 1883, its guests likely included relatives of soldiers stationed at the nearby Fort Davis military post and stagecoach passengers traveling along the Overland Trail one block away.

Lodgers probably found this adobe-style building a secure shelter on the Texas frontier. Its sturdy walls

Veranda Historic Inn, Fort Davis. Photo by Kathie Woods.

are almost two feet thick, and the hotel was laid out in an E shape with its outbuildings, including a carriage house and horse barn, at the back of the property.

A few years after W. S. Lempert built the hotel, he sold it to James Stewart, and it became the Stewart Hotel. By 1927 the building was sold again, and it operated as the Clark Apartments through the 1980s. The current owners purchased the property, which occupies an entire city block, in 1989. They undertook two years of work, which included restoring the eighty-five original wood-framed windows, all of which open. The exterior stucco was also painstakingly restored over the course of one year.

The atmosphere at the Veranda offers plenty of opportunity for quiet relaxation in the comfortable rooms or on its grounds. Guests usually spend much of their time exploring attractions around the Fort Davis area. But when the weather permits, many can be found in either of the two courtyards or on the grounds behind the building enjoying an early morning cup of coffee or a late afternoon libation. The larger of the two enclosed courtyards offers shady seating in rocking chairs on two covered porches. The second, more intimate courtyard features a covered porch. Courtyard landscaping includes honey locust and redbud trees, and lilac bushes. More rocking chairs await on the Veranda's covered front porch.

Behind the hotel, the grounds are planted with lantana, autumn sage, cosmos, and rose bushes. Shady seating is provided under the peach, apricot, and fig trees. Adding to the compound's already cloistered feel is a fence made of two thousand spires cut from native sotol plants, historically a favorite fencing material of this area.

This is a low-key retreat from the electronics- and communication-filled world. The hotel provides one phone for guests' use and has no televisions. But for those who must remain connected, wi-fi is available in the hotel's eastern courtyard and in the rooms in its eastern wing. Cell phones work in Fort Davis, but connections can be spotty in the surrounding area.

Of the hotel's interior spaces, the most striking is its 145-foot-long main hallway with an oak floor, its tall ceiling punctuated by skylights added in the 1920s. Pine bead board is used for hallway wainscoting and on most of the hotel's 12-foot ceilings.

Each morning lodgers wake to a full breakfast served in the hotel's dining room. Typical dishes include ham, crepes, French toast, and homemade muffins.

The Veranda's ten guest rooms and suites all have private baths and are each unique in their size and furnishings. Guests can pick rooms with views of either of the courtyards or of the Davis Mountain foothills. The rooms' stucco walls are painted ivory, pale aqua, or peach. They have a light, airy feel, and the floors are either hardwood or carpeted. Antique furniture found throughout the hotel is an eclectic, mostly European mix. The hotel's former adobe bathhouse is now a cozy guest cottage, and its adobe carriage house has been converted into a two-bedroom guesthouse with a kitchen.

The Veranda sits two blocks west of Fort Davis's Main Street, the north-south thoroughfare through town. It's in a neighborhood whose northern edge is nestled at the base of Sleeping Lion Mountain, a picturesque spot near the towering columns of volcanic rock that form the mountain. Homes a few blocks away have been built amid car-sized boulders that long ago rolled down the mountain.

Flashlight-toting guests stroll the quiet neighborhood streets and enjoy stargazing free from glaring street-lights. The community's concern about light pollution is well founded, as the University of Texas' McDonald Observatory is only sixteen miles away. More than 100,000 people a year travel there for celestial viewing at its regular star parties.

Tourists make the Veranda their headquarters for trips to McDonald Observatory, visits to the Fort Davis National Historic Site, or for hiking, birding, and mountain biking in nearby Davis Mountains State Park. The large artesian spring swimming pool at Balmorhea State Park also beckons.

ESSENTIALS

Contact: 210 Court Ave., P.O. Box 1238, Fort Davis, TX 79734; 888-383-2847, 432-426-2233; www.theveranda.com, info@theveranda.com

Rooms: 10 rooms and suites, all with private bath; tub/shower combination, claw-foot tub, walk-in shower; king, queen beds; room 1 is extra large and has a working gas fireplace; suite 4 has a private entrance, living room, and bedroom; a guest cottage and guest-house are also available on the hotel grounds.

Rates: $$, includes full breakfast.

Room amenities: hair dryer, iron and ironing board available upon request.

Facilities: morning coffee in dining room, fridge available to guests, free wi-fi in part of hotel, meeting space for up to 25.

Smoking: outdoors only.

Credit cards: V, MC, D.

Parking: free parking on street.

Accessibility: all rooms are on ground floor.

Pets: welcome, no fee; arrangements must be made with owner in advance.

Author's tips:—The hotel's gardens are at their best in August, September, October, and November.—The hotel welcomes well-supervised children.

*National Register of Historic
   Places:* no

Texas historical marker: no

Texas Heritage Trails Program: Texas Mountain Trail Region, www.texasmountaintrail.com

Visitor information: Fort Davis Chamber of Commerce, Box 378, No. 4 Memorial Square, Fort Davis, TX 79734; 800-524-3015; 432-426-3015; www.fortdavis.com, info@fortdavis.com

Gage Hotel
Marathon ⚜ 1927

This hotel at the gateway to Big Bend National Park pampers guests in rooms that feature museum-quality art and artifacts from cowboy, Mexican, and Native American cultures.

The Gage Hotel has long been a meeting place and a scene of respite in the rugged Chihuahuan Desert of West Texas' Trans-Pecos region. Today guests at this Marathon institution enjoy spa treatments or a glass of wine with an expertly prepared meal while experiencing the ambience of the old West.

Alfred S. Gage built the two-story hotel in 1927. He was a Vermont native who came to Texas in the 1870s, picked up cowboy skills in the Texas Panhandle, and then headed south to supervise his half-brother Edward's ranching enterprise, the Alpine Cattle Company. This operation included land in what were then known as

Gage Hotel, Marathon. Photo by Jeff Carmack.

ESSENTIALS

Contact: P.O. Box 46, 102 U.S. Highway 90 West, Marathon, TX 79842; 800-884-4243, 432-386-4205; fax: 432-386-4510; www.gagehotel.com, welcome@gagehotel.com

Rooms: 37 rooms and suites, most with private bath; twin, full, queen, and king beds; walk-in showers; 3 guesthouses in Marathon also available.

Rates: $$–$$$$, includes continental breakfast.

Room amenities: original hotel rooms have robes; Las Portales rooms have phones, coffee makers, satellite radio—some have fireplaces.

Facilities: Café Cenizo, 6 P.M. to 9 P.M. Sun.–Thurs., 6 P.M. to 10 P.M. Fri.–Sat.; White Buffalo Bar., 5 P.M. to 11 P.M. Sun.–Thurs., 5 P.M. to midnight Fri.–Sat.; phone and TV in parlor, complimentary coffee in lobby, heated pool, outdoor fire pit, spa, gym, meeting space for up to 200.

Smoking: outside only.

Credit Cards: V, MC, AE, D.

Parking: free parking on property and along street.

Accessibility: disabled access, several rooms are on ground floor.

Pets: welcome, $10 fee.

Author's tips:—Be prepared for noise from passing trains on tracks across the street from the hotel. Complimentary earplugs and special treats welcome guests to their rooms.—Check with the Marathon Chamber of Commerce about guided tours of local ranches.—The Marathon Historical Museum, 3rd St. North and Ave. E, includes exhibits on early ranching, railroads, Fort Pena Colorado, and Marathon's early schools and mercantiles.

National Register
    of Historic Places: no

Texas historical marker: yes

Texas Heritage Trails Program: Texas Mountain Trail Region, www.texasmountaintrail.com

Visitor Information: Marathon Chamber of Commerce, 105 U.S. Hwy 90 West, Marathon, TX 79842; 432-386-4516; www.marathontexas.com, info@marathontexas.com

---

Presidio and Pecos counties. When Edward died in 1912, Alfred Gage took over the company and eventually became one of the largest land owners and ranchers in the Trans-Pecos area.

Gage soon moved his headquarters to San Antonio and built the Gage Hotel to provide himself a second home in Marathon and area ranchers a place to meet and discuss business.

Gage hired noted Southwest architects Trost and Trost and building contractors H. T. Ponsford and Sons of El Paso for the project. Although Gage died soon after the hotel opened, his legacy served as a business and social center in this sparsely populated region for decades as it changed ownership several times and eventually closed in the 1960s.

Art and artifacts collected by the owners, who rescued the boarded-up hotel in 1978 to remodel and reopen it, now fill the building and its comfortable guest rooms. Standouts include a painting of a stagecoach under Indian attack by western artist Robert Pummill, a framed poster of Buffalo Bill's Wild West Show, a variety of saddles from the early 1900s, and a collection of paintings by Alfred Gwynne Morang.

Mexican and Indian blankets and rugs, hand-carved wooden furniture, and wrought iron fixtures are used extensively throughout both the original building, built with tan bricks from Corsicana, Texas, and the hotel's mission-style adobe addition, Los Portales. Added in 1992, this hotel extension is called "the porches" in Spanish for good reason. The twenty rooms, which all have private baths, open onto a lushly landscaped courtyard. Outside each room are leather and wooden chairs from Guadalajara, Mexico, which allow guests to enjoy a semiprivate oasis of blooming plants amid the peaceful sounds of a gurgling fountain. Most of the seventeen guest rooms in the original hotel building have private baths, but nine share separate men's and women's bath facilities.

The hotel buildings are connected by two courtyards that feature a heated pool and a fire pit. My favorite pastime was reading poolside under the shade of a ramada roofed with sotol stalks. For the more energetic, the hotel gym occupies the historic Richey Brothers Building a short walk across the railroad tracks. The building also houses facilities to host weddings, receptions, and conferences. The hotel's Desert Moon Spa sits around the corner and offers everything from seaweed wraps to hot rock massages.

Café Cenizo and the White Buffalo Bar are in the former hotel manager's adobe home adjacent to the hotel. The cozy bar has a fireplace and six tables and attracts locals as well as hotel guests, 90 percent of whom are Texans. It takes its name from the mounted head of a white bison the owners acquired in Wyoming. Dinner patrons of Café Cenizo can choose to dine indoors or alfresco. Diners should make reservations and be prepared to splurge on dishes such as roasted game or buffalo ribeye.

Quiet Marathon is the community closest to the northern entrance of Big Bend National Park, making the Gage an ideal place to indulge before venturing into or after emerging from the vast park. It's also a popular visit for those touring the region's wide-open spaces by motorcycle.

Hotel Paisano

Marfa ⚜ **1930**

Best-known as headquarters for the filming of Giant *in 1955, this grand example of noted architect Henry C. Trost's work greets pilgrims drawn by Marfa's alluring desert setting, the Marfa Mystery Lights, and the town's growing arts scene.*

The legendary Hotel Paisano has been a hangout for deal-making cattlemen, 1950s movie stars such as James Dean, and most recently artists and moneyed urban art lovers who think Marfa is West Texas' answer to Santa Fe. The hotel was built for $175,000 in 1930 by C.N. Bassett and Associates and the Gateway Hotel Chain of El Paso to attract tourists to the tiny community of Marfa, a locus for the Trans-Pecos area's ranching and mining activities.

Now Marfa is a growing haven for artists and art lovers, a trend that has its roots in the 1980s establishment of the Chinati Foundation, spearheaded by minimalist sculptor Donald Judd. Today visitors arrive at this small, high desert community from around the world to attend art openings or seminars. Urbanites from Houston to New York City have renovated old adobe homes into West Texas weekend retreats.

These artsy newcomers join the

Hotel Paisano, Marfa. Photo by Victoria Lowe.

ESSENTIALS

Contact: Box Z, 207 N. Highland, Marfa, TX 79843; 866-729-3669, 432-729-3669; fax: 432-729-3779; www.hotelpaisano.com, info@hotelpaisano.com

Rooms: 41 rooms and suites, all with private bath; queen and king beds; tub/shower combinations; many rooms have private patios and kitchenettes; room 211, Rock Hudson's room during the filming of *Giant,* has been expanded into a suite with a rooftop patio. Liz Taylor's room, 212, has also become a suite. James Dean's room, 223, remains its original size and is the least expensive of the three.

Rates: $$–$$$

Room amenities: TV, hair dryer, iron and ironing board; coffee maker in suites.

Facilities: Hotel Paisano Restaurant, 5:30 P.M. to 9 P.M. daily; Hotel Paisano Bar, 5:30 P.M. to 9 P.M. daily; lobby phone available to guests, morning coffee in lobby, heated indoor/outdoor pool, meeting space for up to 100, free wi-fi in lobby.

Smoking: outdoors only.

Credit cards: V, MC, AE, D.

Parking: free along street.

Accessibility: mezzanine rooms are five steps up from the lobby.

Pets: welcome, $10 fee.

Author's tips:—Tours of the Chinati Foundation's permanent and temporary art installations are given Wednesday through Sunday. Reservations are recommended, www.chinati.org.—Marfa Book Company, 105 S. Highland, is a combined art gallery, wine and coffee bar, and bookstore with an extensive collection of art and architecture books.

National Register
  of Historic Places: yes

Texas historical marker: yes

Texas Heritage Trails Program: Texas Mountain Trail Region, www.texasmountaintrail.com

Visitor information: Marfa Chamber of Commerce, 207 N. Highland Ave., Marfa, TX 79843; 800-650-9696, 432-729-4942; www.marfacc.com, info@marfacc.com

other pilgrims who've been trekking to Marfa for years to see the Marfa Mystery Lights between Marfa and Paisano Pass on clear evenings and take in the outdoor wonders at nearby Big Bend National Park and Davis Mountains State Park. The hotel's resurrection and reopening in November 2001, after decades of being closed, came just in time to serve the growing crowds drawn to Marfa's desert charms.

Local hoteliers Joe and Lanna Duncan, who own the Hotel Limpia in Fort Davis, decided on a whim to watch Presidio County auction off the shuttered Hotel Paisano in March 2001. Two minutes before the event began they decided to sign up as bidders. Within five minutes the stunned Duncans had placed the winning bid of $185,000.

The two-story, Spanish revival–style Paisano was designed by celebrated Southwest architect Henry C. Trost of Trost and Trost. It has an embracing courtyard entrance and rates among the most beautiful of the hotels designed by the firm. According to the National Register of Historic Places, the Paisano's architecture is a blend of Southwest regional styles (mission, pueblo, and Spanish colonial) with Chicago and prairie school influences.

Despite operating its first years during the Great Depression, the hotel survived on the business of area ranchers, who played poker and brokered many a cattle deal there. Traveling salesmen and tourists seeking Marfa's dry desert air arrived by rail at the depot only two blocks away. During World War II, officers at the Marfa Army Air Field and nearby Fort D. A. Russell held parties in the hotel's ballroom, then called the Spanish Room. And regular Saturday night dances filled the courtyard as couples spun around its centerpiece fountain.

In the summer of 1955, the three hundred cast and crew members of the Warner Brothers movie *Giant* started filming on a set eighteen miles from Marfa and made the hotel their headquarters for six weeks. Dailies, the scenes filmed during that day's work, were shown each night in the hotel's ballroom. Elizabeth Taylor, Rock Hudson, and James Dean stayed at the hotel for one week before moving to more private accommodations at local homes. The hotel remained full with the remaining cast and crew. The hotel pays tribute to that defining time in its history by displaying *Giant* memorabilia, including autographed photos of the stars and a framed 1956 issue of *Life* magazine that features the making of the movie.

In July 2005 Marfa and the hotel held a one-day celebration of the fiftieth anniversary of *Giant*. More than seven hundred people gathered to welcome a handful of returning stars, including Jane Withers, for an outdoor screening of one of the three original prints of the film. Joe Duncan predicts the next *Giant* celebration may occur on the movie's sixtieth anniversary in 2015.

During the 1960s and 1970s, the hotel landed on hard times, barely staying open. In the late 1970s El Paisano Properties Corp. turned the Paisano's sixty-five rooms into nine time-share condominiums. Eight hundred individuals bought time-shares, but the building's owners eventually abandoned the business, and Presidio County subsequently foreclosed on the property and held the auction in 2001 to pay back taxes.

During my visit, I hung out in the large, sparsely furnished lobby and took time to examine the ornate wrought iron light fixtures with mica panels inset around glass globes—remnants from the hotel's past. Luckily, the original tan and brown tile floor and wainscoting have also survived the years. The hotel's original built-in phone booth still holds a working telephone. Issues of *Esquire* and *Town & Country Magazine* share table space alongside *Livestock Weekly* in the sunny, two-story lobby. Much like the hotel's early days, retail shops and the offices of the Marfa Chamber of Commerce occupy adjacent space on one wing of the ground floor. On the other side, guests enjoy a plush, comfortable sitting area that opens into the large ballroom and the hotel restaurant and bar.

The forty-one carpeted guest rooms and suites are comfortably furnished with modern pieces and period reproductions. The decor leans toward the 1930s and 1940s with a touch of Spanish influence. Some of the hotel's old radiators have been transformed into bedside tables, and the owners incorporated original tile and bathroom fixtures as much as possible during the renovation.

Many rooms have a private patio or a balcony overlooking the hotel's courtyard and indoor swimming pool. Rooms on the mezzanine floor are small, but each has its own private patio and outdoor fireplace and are only five steps up from the hotel lobby.

Hotel guests and locals patronizing the Paisano's restaurant in the summer enjoy patio dining in the courtyard. Bands play in the courtyard until 11 P.M. on Friday nights in the summer, which prompts noise-conscious guests to request a room at the back of the hotel.

Hotel Paisano sits one block from the 1886 brick and stone Presidio County Court House designed by San Antonio architect Alfred Giles. It's just a few blocks from Marfa's downtown restaurants, the well-known Marfa Book Company, and art galleries.

Gulf Coast

Houston

10

45

Galveston

35

77

Blessing

Palacios

181

37

Port Aransas

361

77

Port Isabel

100

Historic hotel locations in
the Gulf Coast region.
Drawn by Jon Michael Grant.

Hotel Blessing
Blessing 🏛 1907

The highlight of this simply appointed hotel is its restaurant, where the area's farmers and ranchers join Gulf Coast visitors for delicious, home-cooked southern meals served in a friendly atmosphere.

In-the-know travelers who find themselves anywhere near Blessing make it a point to arrive at the Hotel Blessing Coffee Shop during lunch, where they can partake in its bountiful southern-style buffet and soak up the atmosphere.

This rustic hotel has been a community gathering place and source of respite for travelers to Matagorda County since 1907. Built by cattleman Jonathan E. Pierce to lodge land seekers settling the region, it has also housed traveling drummers hawking their wares and the sweethearts and wives of World War II troops stationed at Camp Hulen in nearby Palacios.

Today's hotel visitors may be construction workers or temporary employees at the South Texas Nuclear Project, a Texas couple on a weekend retreat, or tourists from around the globe taking an off-the-beaten-path route through the state.

The mission revival–style hotel, a two-story wooden structure designed by Jules Leffland of Victoria, is a striking landmark in this small community and stretches the length of an entire block. The twin towers that flank the hotel's front entrance resemble the

Hotel Blessing, Blessing. Photo by J. Griffis Smith/TxDOT.

bell towers of a Spanish colonial mission, but instead of being constructed with adobe, they are built of pine with cypress siding.

Pierce, Blessing's founder, originally wanted the town's name to be Thank God in gratitude for the arrival of the Galveston, Harrisburg, and San Antonio Railway in 1903, for which he and others granted rights of way. The Post Office Department rejected the name, and as a compromise, the community was named Blessing.

This hotel's facilities are quite basic, and its atmosphere is small-town friendly. Most guest rooms share bathroom facilities with one other room. Guests in the remaining rooms use a toilet, community bathtub, or community shower down the hall. Lodgers should bring their own toiletries. Rooms on both floors have not only solid wood doors but also their original screen doors, which allowed summer breezes to circulate in Blessing's subtropical climate before the window air-conditioning units were installed in guest rooms. The hotel is simply furnished and features mostly well-used originals from the early

ESSENTIALS

Contact: P.O. Box 142, 817 F.M. 616, Blessing, TX 77419; 361-588-9579; www.hotelblessing.com, reservations@hotelblessing.com.
Rooms: 25 including 1 suite; 2 rooms have private bath, the rest share either a semiprivate bath or a bath down the hall; bathtub, walk-in shower; full-size beds.
Rates: $
Room amenities: TV
Facilities: Blessing Coffee Shop, breakfast and buffet lunch, 6 A.M. to 2 P.M. daily except Christmas; guest phone available in lobby.
Smoking: designated rooms.
Credit cards: cash and check only.
Parking: free parking on the street.
Accessibility: some rooms and one accessible shared bathroom on ground floor.

Pets: not allowed.
Author's tips:—If you're planning to dine at the popular restaurant on Mother's Day or Thanksgiving, be prepared to join an overflow crowd that spills into the hotel's parlor and onto its front porch.
National Register
    of Historic Places: yes
Texas historical marker: yes
Texas Heritage Trails Program:
Texas Independence Trail Region, www.texasindependencetrail.com
Visitor Information: Bay City Convention and Visitors Bureau, P.O. Box 768, 201 Seventh St., Bay City, TX 77404-0768; 800-806-8333, 979-245-8333; www.baycity.org, irenebishop@ visitbaycity.org

decades of the hotel's operation, including mission-style chairs and iron bedsteads.

The hotel's early fire hose is folded neatly and hangs on a second-story wall, an aging conversation piece collecting dust. Each second-story room once had its own fire escape—a rope tied to a metal ring installed near each window. But when Able Pierce, Jonathan Pierce's grandson, and his wife, Ruth, renovated and reopened the hotel in the late 1970s, they installed a metal fire escape from an old school building.

Reopening the hotel was a labor of love for the couple. To ensure its preservation as a Blessing landmark, the Pierces donated the building to the Blessing Historical Foundation, which operates the hotel to this day.

The original double screen doors hang at the hotel's front entrance, which opens into a wide hallway that has a sixteen-foot-high ceiling, original pine floors, and dark wood wainscoting. A strip of linoleum in a decades-old pattern stretches down the center of the first floor like a worn carpet, leading to the heart of the hotel—its coffee shop.

This restaurant, which seats fifty at several wooden tables, is an informal community gathering place. Here, rice- and turf-grass farmers, ranchers, grain haulers, business owners, and the occasional tourist share tables amid mounted deer heads and exposed pipes from the hotel's original steam heating system. The crowd congregates for the homemade favorites at breakfast and lunch and to catch up on family and community news. Early bird regulars show up first thing most days, choosing their favorite mug from the selection hanging next to the dining room coffee pot.

The typical lunch buffet features home-prepared selections including fried chicken, smothered steak, cornbread dressing, green beans, pinto beans, greens, sweet potatoes, yeast rolls, salad, and pie and cobbler. Chief cook Helen Feldhousen, who has managed the restaurant since 1977, recalls when she used to let diners into the kitchen to help themselves to the steaming pots on her stove—until the early 1980s, when health officials intervened. Now the piles of food are kept hot in the dining room on old wood-burning stoves outfitted with water heaters.

The 1907 Blessing State Bank across the street from the hotel is one of the few commercial buildings in Blessing from the turn of the century and is a Texas Historic Landmark.

Hotel Galvez

Galveston ⚓ 1911

This Queen of the Gulf exudes Old World sophistication while making its guests, whether here for a surf-side vacation or an extravagant wedding, comfortably at home in the last of Galveston's grand beach hotels.

The surf seekers in flip-flops and Bermuda shorts strolling through the elegant Hotel Galvez lobby barely disturb the gracious atmosphere. Uniformed doormen usher in beach bag–toting vacationers, while classical music plays quietly in the background. Patrons dressed for fine dining, a business meeting, or sightseeing sit in cushioned wicker chairs underneath the lobby's gold, aqua, and brown coffered ceilings adorned with dark mahogany.

The Hotel Galvez, called the Queen of the Gulf, has made holiday makers' A-list since 1911 on this island resort forty-five miles from Houston. Its parlors, Terrace Ballroom, and chandeliered Music Hall have been the scene of innumerable business, civic, and political gatherings and social celebrations. Even today, the hotel hosts up to six wedding parties a month, some back-to-back. It's not unusual to see a bridesmaid in silk and organdy sharing an elevator with a swimming pool–bound ten-year-old in Hawaiian print.

Business leaders and city benefactors dreamed of building the Hotel Galvez as a replacement for the massive four-story Beach Hotel, which

Hotel Galvez, Galveston. Photo by Jeff Carmack.

was destroyed by fire in 1898, just blocks down the beach. Before the project could take shape, a devastating hurricane hit Galveston in 1900. Called North America's worst natural disaster, it killed six thousand citizens and practically wiped out the community. Only twenty years earlier Galveston had been Texas' largest city and one of the country's leading ports.

The construction of a new hotel was then even more important to draw vacationers back to the island and help rebuild its economy. Key hotel investors included Ike and Dan Kempner, Bertrand Adoue, John Sealy, and H. S. Cooper of the Galveston Electric Company. In addition, the Galveston Hotel Company sold hotel stock to individuals at one hundred dollars a share.

The Galvez, designed by St. Louis architectural firm Mauran and Russell in mission/Spanish revival style, opened in June 1911 at a cost of about $1 million. It was called one of the most well-appointed seaside hotels in America, a distinction that it maintains today.

Early guests could lounge in the sun-drenched loggia and take in southerly views of the seawall promenade and crashing surf while being serenaded by the hotel's orchestra. Up to eight hundred diners at a time could use custom-made silver while tucking into Gulf oysters, crabs, fish, and wild game prepared by the hotel's

ESSENTIALS

Contact: 2024 Seawall Boulevard, Galveston, TX 77550; 877-999-3223, 409-765-7721; fax: 409-765-5623; www.wyndham.com

Rooms: 226 rooms and suites, all with private bath; tub/shower combination; king, queen, full beds.

Rates: $$–$$$$

Room amenities: phone, TV, coffee maker, hair dryer, iron and ironing board, robe, room service, wi-fi and wired Internet for a fee.

Facilities: Bernardo's Restaurant, 6 A.M. to 10 P.M. Sun.–Thurs., 6 A.M. to 11 P.M., Fri.–Sat.; Hotel Galvez Bar, 2 P.M. to midnight daily; outdoor heated pool, hot tub, spa, business center, group space for up to 500.

Smoking: outdoors only.

Credit cards: V, MC, AE, DC, D.

Parking: free self parking, valet parking, $12.

Accessibility: disabled access, elevator.

Pets: not allowed.

Author's tips:—Top off a weekend stay with the hotel's extravagant Sunday champagne brunch.

*National Register
   of Historic Places:* yes

Texas historical marker: yes

Texas Heritage Trails Program: Texas Independence Trail Region, www.texasindependencetrail.com

Visitor information: Galveston Island Convention and Visitors Bureau, 2027 61st St., Galveston, TX 77551; 888-425-4753 ext. 144, 409-763-4311; www.galveston.com, sgilbert@galvestoncvb.com

chefs. Room rates began at two dollars a night, and guests had a candy shop, drugstore, barber shop, and soda fountain at their disposal.

A brochure circa 1915 includes photographs of hundreds of modestly clad bathers wading in the surf in front of the hotel. These crowds mostly arrived by rail. Special trains ran from all parts of Texas and Louisiana to Galveston, and Houston pleasure seekers could catch regularly scheduled trains running from the city to the seaside resort.

Patrons had to be turned away from the popular hotel for two years during WWII while the Galvez served as the residence and offices for the U.S. Coast Guard. Galveston businessman W. L. Moody's company, Affiliate National Hotels, owned the hotel at the time. During the years between the world wars, Galveston had become known for its free-flowing liquor, gambling, and prostitution. Stars like Frank Sinatra, Jack Benny, and Bob Hope appeared in the famous Balinese Room nightclub on the pier across from the Galvez, and many celebrities joined the long list of famous guests to stay at the hotel.

In 1957 the Texas attorney general and a group of Texas Rangers shut down illegal activities at the Balinese Room and other Galveston establishments, putting a temporary crimp in the city's tourism receipts. The slowdown didn't last forever. Galveston native developer and philanthropist George Mitchell purchased the hotel in the mid-1990s and has spent several million dollars restoring the public spaces to their historic beauty and renovating the 226 guest rooms and suites. During the restoration, paint was carefully peeled to reveal 1911 color schemes, which were recreated in the lobby, Terrace Ballroom, and hotel parlors. The hotel is operated by Wyndham.

The south-facing rooms have a view of seagulls and pelicans soaring over the Gulf and of more than fifty swaying palm trees ringing the hotel's semicircular drive and lush, landscaped lawn. All rooms have private baths and feature crown molding, cherry wood furnishings, and fabrics, carpets, and wallpaper in verdant greens, gold, and sepia tones. Baths have Carrara marble tile, etched glass panels, scalloped sinks, and porcelain faucets.

Despite the view and comfortable room, I was lured outdoors to the hotel's walled patio and the pool that meanders through it. Soothing reggae, jazzy oldies, and riffling palm fronds quashed all traffic noise from nearby Seawall Boulevard. Tropical plantings offer areas where adults can visit and sip a cool one while children play nearby. At the swim-up bar I ordered a margarita before I realized I could have had a Mudslide, a chocolate milk shake with a kick.

Other options for fun include renting an umbrella at the front desk for a day of lounging surf-side, or catching a ride on the Galveston Island Trolley, which stops right outside the hotel. The trolley tours the city's historic architecture and the attractions in the Strand Historic District.

Tremont House
Galveston 🏛 1870

A rooftop terrace and a location in the heart of Galveston's Strand Historic District make this cheery hotel a popular base during Galveston's Mardi Gras and Dickens on the Strand festivals or for touring museums, shops, and other attractions.

The Tremont House embodies the spirit of the two fine nineteenth-century Galveston hotels that are its namesake. The original Tremont House opened in 1839 at the corner of Post Office and Tremont streets. The "San Jacinto Ball" kicked off the grand-opening celebration with tickets priced at fifty dollars in Republic of Texas currency, or twenty-five dollars in specie. The hotel entertained dignitaries including Texas presidents Sam Houston and Anson Jones, and the foreign ministers of England and France. In 1865 a raging fire that burned for days destroyed the hotel along with much of what is now the city's Strand Historic District.

A second Tremont was constructed in 1872, and it, too, built a reputation as a fine hostelry while Galveston, the largest city in Texas and a significant North American port at the time, recovered from the Civil War and a yellow fever epidemic. But after the catastrophic hurricane of 1900 that killed six thousand Galvestonians and left the community's economy in shambles, the Tremont fell into ruin. It was razed in 1928.

In 1985 Galveston native developer and philanthropist George P.

Tremont House, Galveston. Photo by Jeana Lungwitz.

ESSENTIALS

Contact: 2300 Ship's Mechanic Row, Galveston, TX 77550; 877-999-3223, 409-763-0300; fax: 409-763-1539; www.wynndham.com, Tremont@ Galveston.com

Rooms: 119 rooms and suites, all with private bath; tub/shower combination; king, queen, full beds.

Rates: $$–$$$$

Room amenities: phone, TV, coffee maker, hair dryer, iron and ironing board, robe, wi-fi and wired Internet for a fee, room service.

Facilities: The Merchant Prince, 6:30 A.M. to 2 P.M., 5:30 p.m. to 10 P.M. daily; Toujouse Lounge, 3 p.m. to 10 P.M. Sun.–Thurs.; 3 P.M. to 11 P.M. Fri.–Sat.; fitness center, group space for up to 600.

Smoking: outdoors only.

Credit cards: V, MC, AE, DC, D.

Parking: valet only, $12.

Accessibility: disabled access, elevator.

Pets: not allowed.

Author's tips:—Midsummer Books, across from the hotel, is the perfect place to shop for books about the city's history and architecture.

National Register
of Historic Places: no

Texas historical marker: no

Texas Heritage Trails Program: Texas Independence Trail Region, www.texasindependencetrail.com

Visitor information: Galveston Island Convention and Visitors Bureau, 2027 61st St., Galveston, TX 77550; 888-425-4753 ext. 144, 409-763-4311; www.galveston.com, sgilbert@galvestoncvb.com

Mitchell and his wife, Cynthia, unveiled the Tremont House's third incarnation in the restored and renovated Leon and H. Blum Building. Leon Blum, known as the Merchant Prince of Texas, had constructed the 1879 building as his import and wholesale dry goods headquarters.

In the late 1980s, the Mitchells expanded the Tremont into the former Belmont Hotel next door. The building, constructed in 1870, became the Royal Hotel in 1906 and was operating as the Belmont Hotel when it closed in 1983. The decor of today's Tremont House ties the two buildings together with emphasis on clean lines

and bold use of bright white with dark accents.

While there, I spied a few interior clues to their differing pasts. The former Belmont Hotel building retains its original wooden staircase and has a four-story, oval atrium topped by a skylight. The pressed tin ceilings are new but were manufactured by the same company that produced the original tin tiles. The millwork throughout and the ceramic tile on the first floor were recreated to match originals. The woodwork, tile, and ceilings are painted white.

A redbrick wall with high arched openings forms the front of the hotel's

Merchant Prince Restaurant in the former Leon and H. Blum Building. This is the only significant internal feature that ties the building to its history as a warehouse. The remaining first floor space is a bright, airy lobby and bar, crowned by a four-story atrium. Patrons relax in white wicker furniture with palm tree–patterned cushions shaded by three-story-high palms. The hotel's fourteen-foot rosewood bar and its ornately carved and mirrored bar back were crafted in 1872 and are leased from the Galveston Historical Foundation.

While visiting with a local resident one afternoon, I learned the bar is popular with Galvestonians. She discreetly pointed out several well-known individuals who regularly stop in to socialize during happy hour or for afternoon tea. When the weather permits, the crowd gathers on a rooftop terrace. The decked space on top of the former Belmont has a shady arbor and wooden park-style benches for taking in the view of downtown Galveston.

The hotel's 119 rooms and suites all have private baths and hardwood floors. They feature high ceilings, tall windows, and antique reproduction furnishings. Most rooms are decorated in white and black with touches of dark blue and complementary wallpaper, lacy curtains, and bright white bedspreads. Bathrooms feature hand-painted Italian tiles and towel warmers. The hotel is operated by Wyndham.

When the Mitchells resurrected the Tremont House they revived Galveston's annual Mardi Gras festivities as well. The city began to partake in the event in 1867 but discontinued it after 1941. Now for the two weeks preceding Lent, the city is awash in parades, masked balls, live music, sporting and art events, and general revelry. Ship's Mechanic Row in front of the hotel becomes the premier parade route, and the hotel's lobby and bar are turned into a dance floor with live entertainment. Guests who want to take advantage of the special packages offered during this time must book months in advance.

The Tremont is inside the Strand Historic District, an area with more than forty historic buildings, many of which are marked by plaques describing their significance to the city. The Strand is also well known for its annual Dickens on the Strand, the recreation of an English Victorian Christmas during the first weekend in December.

Restaurants, bars, museums, shops, and art galleries are within a short walk. The Galveston Island Trolley takes passengers to the beachfront and other attractions. The hotel is a few blocks from the commercial and cruise ships that dock at the Port of Galveston, the Texas Seaport Museum, and the 1877 tall ship Elissa.

Alden Houston

Houston ⚓ 1924

Once known as the venerable Sam Houston, this hotel now provides boutique accommodations in a sleek, chic atmosphere near downtown Houston's sports arenas and convention center.

The Alden Houston tips its hat to its former namesake, Texas statesman Sam Houston, but today this upscale boutique hotel is a far cry from its past as no-frills, moderately priced lodging for business travelers. Panels of tooled leather, in the style of a western belt, cover the walls behind the hotel's dark chocolate front desk, which is made of African wenge wood. Instead of standing while they handle formalities, guests checking in can plop down in cowhide-backed chairs with pinstripe cushions. A row of pears, arranged by degree of ripeness, create a minimalist centerpiece atop the otherwise bare desk.

The brown and white lobby is spare and ultramodern. Its long, low-backed sofas and mahogany-stained cherry coffee tables are very twenty-first century, but an observant guest can still spot clues to this building's past as the Sam Houston Hotel. The 1924 granite staircase, which leads up to second-floor meeting space, lands near the entrance to the hotel restaurant. A rectangular recessed light fixture featuring a geometrically patterned screen of dark wood is

Alden Houston, Houston. Photo courtesy Alden Houston.

ESSENTIALS

Contact: 1117 Prairie St., Houston, TX 77002; 877-348-8800, 832-200-8800; fax: 832-200-8811; www.aldenhotels.com.

Rooms: 97 rooms and suites, all with private bath; walk-in showers, bathtubs; king beds.

Rates: $$$–$$$$

Room amenities: phone, TV with DVD player and access to DVD library, hair dryer, iron and ironing board, robe, free wi-fi, room service.

Facilities: 17 (the restaurant), 6:30 A.M. to 10:30 A.M., 11 A.M. to 2:30 P.M., 5:30 to 11 P.M. Fri.–Sat.; 5:30 to 10 P.M. Sun.–Thurs. ; a+ (the bar), 2:30 P.M. to 2 A.M. Fri.–Sat.; 2:30 P.M. to midnight Sun.–Thurs.; fitness center, group space for up to 200.

Smoking: designated rooms.

Credit cards: V, MC, AE, D, DC.

Parking: valet only, $25.

Accessible: disabled access, elevator.

Pets: allowed, free up to 25 lbs.; $150 deposit for pets over 25 lbs.

Author's tips:—Check out the fading sign painted on the back of the hotel advertising rooms from $2.00 to $2.50 per night.—The Franklin Street Coffeehouse, 913 Franklin Street, offers pastries, light lunches, coffee, wine, and beer in cozy quarters a few blocks from the hotel.

National Register of Historic Places: yes

Texas historical marker: no

Texas Heritage Trails Program: Texas Independence Trail Region, www.texasindependencetrail.com

Visitor information: Houston Convention and Visitors Bureau, 901 Bagby, Suite 100, Houston, TX 77002; 800-4-HOUSTON, 713/437-5200; www.visithoustontexas.com

installed above the lobby. This new piece was modeled after the hotel's original skylight.

When the hotel was the Sam Houston, a large sepia-toned mural of the 1836 Battle of San Jacinto dominated the lobby. The hotel's original namesake, Sam Houston, led soldiers in the decisive battle of the Texas revolution. He was the first regularly elected president of the Texas Republic, and when Texas became a state he represented it in Congress and later

became governor. In the mural's place today hangs a contemporary light installation by New York designer David Lander. The large rectangular panel of colors changes every few moments (from cool blue and violet to warm red and orange), altering the room's mood accordingly.

The Sam Houston Hotel Company constructed this ten-story building during the city's post-WWI building boom. The hotel was marketed to the budget-minded business traveler and was only a few blocks from Union Station (now part of Minute Maid Park). It offered comfortable, moderately priced rooms without the frills found at pricier establishments. Each room had a private bath, but the hotel's decor was plain.

The prominent Texas architectural firm of Sanguinet, Staats, Hedrick, and Gottlieb designed the hotel to be a lower-budget version of the more expensive hotels they had designed for clients in other Texas cities, such as the Texas in Fort Worth and the Stephen F. Austin in Austin. The L-shaped building was praised for being well ventilated, and it had screened double-hung windows, transoms, and guest room doors with louvers. Air-conditioning didn't arrive until the late 1930s.

The hotel operated until the mid-1970s. It sat empty and unused until 2002, when it reopened after an extensive, multimillion-dollar renovation by new owners. For a time, it kept its original name, but when the owners realized customers outside Texas didn't recognize or appreciate who Sam Houston was, they changed it to Alden Houston, which in Old English translates to "old friend."

The hotel's ninety-seven rooms and suites have clean, modern lines, ergonomic desk furniture, fluffy duvets, ironed European bed linens, and padded leather headboards. Next to more pedestrian items like Sprite and Snickers in the room mini bar, I found a small bottle of Bailey's Irish Cream and a can of San Pellegrino Aranciata orange soda.

When I entered the bathroom, it was like stepping into a Starbucks mocha grande with a floor made of Hershey chocolate bars. The walls were coffee- and chocolate-colored Labrador granite with iridescent flecks of blue. The shelf in the large glass-enclosed shower was piled with fluffy white towels. A container of cotton balls and individually wrapped swabs sat on a curved glass vanity next to the funnel-shaped, rippled porcelain sink.

Well-dressed locals and hotel guests patronize the Alden's sophisticated bar, a+, and its lauded restaurant, 17, which occupy space once held by shops on the hotel's ground floor. The restaurant, which features regional, in-season delicacies, was named for the number of railroads that converged in Houston in the early 1900s.

The Alden's plethora of amenities, personalized service, and chic urban charm attract business clients with expense accounts and celebrating couples indulging themselves in luxury. Those celebrating a special occasion take advantage of weekend packages, some of which include breakfast and a three-course prix fixe dinner in 17.

The hotel is near the Houston Astros' Minute Maid Park, the Houston Rockets' Toyota Center, the George R. Brown Convention Center, and the dozens of bars, clubs, and restaurants in Houston's Main Street/Market Square Historic District.

Hotel ZaZa
Houston ❀ 1926

Once a stately host to world-famous guests and home to Houston's rich, this hotel has been transformed into modish lodging that promises guests a new "ZaZa" experience.

A 1938 article in *Texas Hotel Review* describes the Warwick Hotel lobby as "Swank with a capital S" and its Crystal Dining Room as providing the elite with an "atmosphere of quiet dignity and beauty." This former apartment hotel, which opened in 1926, has over the years been home to the city's rich as well as to visiting world leaders, business tycoons, and entertainers—from the Duke of Windsor and the Queen of Sweden to Bob Hope and Arnold Schwarzenegger.

The classic, stately Warwick has been transformed into the chic, hip Hotel ZaZa, a boutique property offering its own take on high-class

Hotel ZaZa, Houston. Photo courtesy Hotel ZaZa.

accommodations presented in a sophisticated atmosphere. Long-time Houstonians might have trouble recognizing their Old World friend with its new, eclectic decor and youthful ambience. The antique European furnishings and artwork for which the Warwick was once known, installed in the 1960s by former owner and Houston oil wildcatter John Mecom, are long gone except for the lobby's intricately carved wooden panels from eighteenth-century France. Among the pieces sold at auction prior to the ZaZa metamorphosis was a nineteenth-century marble sculpture of Eve that brought $46,000. That wasn't the first time Warwick treasures had been liquidated before a major renovation. Bidders walked away with everything from oil paintings to 25-inch

ESSENTIALS

Contact: 5701 Main Street, Houston, TX 77001; 888-880-3244, 713-526-1991, fax 713-526-0359

Rooms: 315 rooms and suites, all with private bath; walk-in shower, tub-shower combination, oversized tub; king, queen, full beds; some luxury suites include full kitchens and private entrances.

Rates: $$$–$$$$

Room amenities: phone, TV and DVD, DVD library available, hair dryer, iron and ironing board, free wi-fi, robe, room service; morning coffee and pastries served in butler's pantry on each floor.

Facilities: Monarch restaurant, 6 A.M. to 11 P.M.; Monarch lounge, 5 P.M. to 2 A.M.; outdoor pool with private cabanas, fitness center, spa, concierge, group space for up to 500.

Smoking: outdoors only.

Credit cards: V, MC, AE, D, DC.

Parking: valet only, $16.

Accessibility: disabled access, elevator.

Pets: welcome; individualized treats at check-in.

Author's tips: Don't be afraid to ask the ZaZa staff for their help to make your visit extra special. They've been known to hang 100 long-stemmed red roses from the ceiling of a suite as a surprise for a guest's wife and to hire Marilyn Monroe or Austin Powers impersonators to spice up a birthday party or anniversary celebration. (Any costs will be added to your bill, of course.)

National Register of Historic Places: no

Texas historical marker: no

Texas Heritage Trails Program: Texas Independence Trail Region, www.texasindependencetrail.com

Visitor information: Houston Convention and Visitors Bureau, 901 Bagby, Suite 100, Houston, TX 77002; 800-4-HOUSTON, 713-437-5200; www.visithoustontexas.com

RCA televisions during a five-day auction in 1989, when the hotel became the Wyndham Warwick.

ZaZa facilities include a 10,000-square-foot spa, a 1,400-square-foot fitness center, and the Monarch restaurant and bar. True to the ZaZa "brand," the hotel uses dramatic lighting and has a professionally crafted decor that's a blend of antiques, reproductions, and modern pieces collected from around the world. The pulsing, steady groove of down-tempo background music sets a sensuous mood in the hotel's public spaces, including the Urban Oasis—an outdoor pool/patio with a resort feel. Guests can hang out by the pool while enjoying their privacy or share an intimate dinner in one of six cabanas with comfortable lounging areas, individual sound systems, and flat-screen TVs.

ZaZa has 315 rooms, including 75 individualized suites. All have private baths. Some suites have one or two bedrooms, and the largest has multiple bathrooms, full kitchens, and private access—accommodations akin to high-end condominiums. This hotel is twice as large as the original (and only other) Hotel ZaZa, which is in Dallas. Rooms are filled with comfortable furnishings and feature special touches such as Italian linens and down comforters. The "Far East" suite I stayed in at the Dallas property (while the Houston ZaZa was undergoing renovation) was filled with Chinese art and had bamboo-patterned wallpaper and carpeting. Smooth black river rocks were inset into the floors of the foyer and the large walk-in shower. The more than two-dozen items in the mini bar included a split of merlot, Chex Mix, and M&Ms as well as teeth whitener and Oxia, a personal-sized can of oxygen purported to relieve stress and boost energy.

Each guest room floor in Houston has a butler's pantry, where guests help themselves to complimentary morning coffee and pastries. During my evening at the Dallas ZaZa, the turn-down service staff lit bedside votives and left gourmet chocolates accompanied by a quote to contemplate while drifting off: "Myths are public dreams. Dreams are private myths."

With all this trendy sophistication, Houston's Hotel ZaZa could be intimidating to some. But like the Dallas ZaZa, the Houston hotel is friendly and welcoming, part of the company's aim to create a warm, albeit posh, atmosphere.

The hotel occupies a prized location across the street from Hermann Park and its zoo, Japanese gardens, the Miller Outdoor Theater, and the Museum of Natural Science. It is also smack-dab in Houston's Museum District and adjacent to the Houston Museum of Fine Arts. The city's light-rail stops just outside the hotel on Main Street and runs north into downtown and south toward Rice University, Texas Medical Center, and Reliant Sports and Convention Complex. The hotel is also near Midtown and the Kirby and Montrose districts.

Lancaster Hotel

Houston ⚓ 1926

This hotel, with its refined decor that recalls an English manor, is a favorite of the corporate crowd, theater patrons, and performers because of its location near the city's commercial towers and Houston's Theater District.

When the Auditorium Hotel opened in 1926 on Texas Avenue, Houston's economy was flourishing, and a local newspaper called the newly paved and widened avenue a "canyon of commerce." Italian immigrant and real estate investor Michele DeGeorge built his hotel directly across from the Municipal Auditorium and named it for the facility, playing up the hotel's prime location. He chose his friend, Houston architect Joseph Finger, to design the twelve-story brick building. When the

Lancaster Hotel, Houston. Photo by Liz Carmack.

ESSENTIALS

Contact: 701 Texas, Houston, TX 77002; 800-231-0336, 713-228-9500; fax: 713-223-4528; www.hotelvalencia.com, lwilliams@valenciagroup.com

Rooms: 93 rooms and suites, all with private bath; tub/shower combination; king and queen beds.

Rates: $$–$$$$

Room amenities: phone, TV, video player with video library available, hair dryer, iron and ironing board, free wi-fi, robe, room service.

Facilities: Bistro Lancaster and Bistro Bar, 6:30 A.M. to 11 P.M. Mon.–Fri.; 7:30 A.M. to 11 P.M. Sat.–Sun.; group space for up to 150, fitness center, business center, complimentary car service within downtown.

Smoking: designated rooms.

Credit cards: V, MC, AE, D, DC.

Parking: valet only, $25.

Accessibility: disabled access, elevator.

Pets: not allowed.

Author's tips:—Visit the Calpine Building, 717 Texas, next door to the hotel and descend into Houston's extensive downtown tunnel system, which is filled with shops, restaurants, and other businesses.

National Register of Historic Places: no

Texas historical marker: yes

Texas Heritage Trails Program: Texas Independence Trail Region, www.texasindependencetrail.com

Visitor information: Houston Convention and Visitors Bureau, 901 Bagby, Suite 100, Houston, TX 77002; 800-4-HOUSTON, 713-437-5200; www.visithoustontexas.com.

two-hundred-room facility opened, its up-to-date amenities included private baths, ceiling fans, and ice water in every room.

The Auditorium Hotel aided the growth of Houston's early arts and entertainment industry, accommodating theater patrons and performers alike. Everyone from professional wrestlers, with names like Whisker Savage and The Angel, to vaudeville players and symphony musicians roomed here. A DeGeorge family member once recalled that the hotel even impounded the clothes of fledgling actor Clark Gable for an unpaid bill.

The hotel had its own performance space for a time, a circus-themed basement cabaret. The club served free soft drinks and food and featured live shows for servicemen and -women during WWII. Gene Autry once rode his horse, Champion, downstairs into the venue to serenade its patrons.

By the 1970s, the hotel had begun to show its age. After an extensive, multimillion-dollar renovation in the early 1980s, it reopened as the Lancaster, billing itself as Houston's first small luxury hotel.

A photo from the hotel's early days

shows electric fans mounted on the lobby's columns to help guests cope with Houston's summer heat. The generously sized room was originally adorned with hand-painted frescoes, a tile floor, stained glass, and walnut wainscot. Today the carpeted, somewhat smaller lobby has the refined yet comfortable look of an English country manor. The room displays a collection of eighteenth-century English paintings and antiques, comfortable sofas and chairs, and brass chandeliers.

The hotel's ninety-three rooms and suites are decorated with plaids and floral-patterned English fabrics. Much of the furniture is antique reproduction. The private baths feature wraparound mirrors, brass fixtures, and white Italian marble tile floors, walls, and vanities. The hotel prides itself on individualized service and personal touches—a room service tray is strewn with rose petals, a CD player comes stocked with classical music (including a recording by the Houston Symphony).

Conveniently located near commercial centers such as the Pennzoil Place and JP Morgan Chase Tower, the hotel is a weekday home to corporate clientele. But weekends mostly belong to tourists and the theater crowd. The hotel's cozy Lancaster Bistro and Bar are popular stops for patrons before and after a show.

The Lancaster's full-time concierge keeps a running tally of celebrity guests, which, since the hotel's reopening, has included Edward Albee, Beverly Sills, Placido Domingo, Whoopi Goldberg, and Jon Voight.

The Jesse H. Jones Hall for the Performing Arts now stands where the City Auditorium once was. To the east of the Lancaster are numerous theaters and other performance halls, as well as the Bayou Place Entertainment Complex. According to the city's Convention and Visitors Bureau, Houston now has almost thirteen thousand theater seats, ranking second only to New York City. The Houston Arts District south of downtown is a short ride away on the city's light-rail, which runs north and south along Main Street. The train stops a few blocks from the hotel.

Luther Hotel
Palacios ⚓ 1903

Views of Tres Palacios Bay and unpretentious rooms in the quiet setting of tiny Palacios make this hurricane survivor a peaceful seaside getaway for birders, anglers, and laid-back sightseers.

The sprawling three-story Luther Hotel has been the crown jewel of Palacios on Texas' mid-coast for more than a century. Its rooms, many of which have views of Tres Palacios Bay, are comfortable and homey, suiting the relaxed, friendly atmosphere.

D. D. Rittenhouse constructed this three-story building of longleaf pine and cypress for the Palacios Townsite Company. In 1905 the owners undertook the incredible task of having it cut into three sections and moved by mules one-half mile west to its current location overlooking Tres Palacios Bay. Early accounts say the hotel was originally called the Bay View but renamed Hotel Palacios upon its move.

The hotel first accommodated early settlers arriving in the new coastal town and inland residents who came by train to enjoy a seaside holiday. Many visitors now come to the area for birding along the Great Texas Coastal Birding Trail or to visit historic sites on the Texas Independence Trail, both of which are nearby. Outdoor enthusiasts enjoy quiet fishing off Palacios' numerous piers or walk for miles along the town's seawall, which is just across the street from the hotel.

Luther Hotel, Palacios. Photo by Richard Stockton.

The Luther is carpeted throughout. Its furnishings, which are mostly from the 1960s through the 1980s, and the genial charm of managers Dolly and Billy Hamlin made me feel as if I were visiting a relative's home. Some of the winter Texans who spend months at the Luther practically become family, passing peaceful evenings playing cards and sharing potluck meals with the Hamlins.

Rooms are available on three floors, and many have views of the bay. The two-room penthouse, the hotel's most expensive suite, is the only room on the third floor. It has a kitchenette and private balcony, but guests have to climb three flights to enjoy the seclusion.

The building originally had a 300-foot covered gallery that extended across its front and wrapped around its two wings. The hotel's owners added a grand ballroom and dining room after the 1905 move, which helped turn it into a social center for the community. The gallery, ballroom, and dining room are gone, but

ESSENTIALS

Contact: 408 S. Bay Boulevard, Palacios, TX 77465; 888-585-7067, 361-972-2312; fax: 361-972-3525.

Rooms: 31 rooms and suites, all with private bath; tub/shower combination, walk-in shower; full, queen, and king beds.

Rates: $–$$, includes continental breakfast.

Room amenities: TV; some rooms have kitchenettes or full kitchens; suites have coffee makers.

Facilities: phones in lobby available for guest use; group space for up to 25.

Smoking: outside only.

Credit cards: MC, V.

Parking: free in hotel lot.

Accessibility: disabled access, some guest rooms on ground floor, no elevator.

Pets: not allowed.

Author's tips:—It's best to call ahead for a reservation, even in the winter. The hotel can fill up for six weeks at a time when out-of-town contractors arrive to work at the South Texas Nuclear Project near Bay City.—Palacios Mexican Restaurant, 511 Main, offers tasty meals three blocks from the hotel.

National Register
of Historic Places: no

Texas historical marker: yes

Texas Heritage Trails Program: Texas Independence Trail Region, www.texasindependencetrail.com

Visitor information: Palacios Chamber of Commerce, 420 Main, Palacios, TX 77465; 800-611-4567, 361-972-2615; fax: 361-972-9980; www.palacioschamber.com, palcoc@tisd.net

the remaining building, with its wide expanse and ample front porch, is still an impressive structure, difficult to photograph without a wide-angle lens.

The hotel changed hands several times and fell into disrepair until 1936, when buyer Charles Luther, a local car dealer, and his wife refurbished and modernized it. The couple added tile bathrooms to each room and also built motor courts adjacent to the hotel. Reopened in 1941 as the Luther Hotel, it began serving visitors to National Guard units at adjacent Camp Hulen, which trained thousands of troops in antiaircraft maneuvers during World War II. A photograph of a smiling Rita Hayworth signing an autograph at the hotel in 1942 hangs in the small living room–like lobby. The actress was in town entertaining soldiers.

The walls in common areas are dotted with framed newspaper articles about the Luther and the historic Palacios Pavilion, which juts into the bay across from the hotel and has hosted many traveling orchestras and wedding parties. Photos of the Luther family and Texas politicians hang behind the front desk and in the breakfast room, where guests help themselves to a complimentary continental breakfast of sweet rolls and cereal and to afternoon coffee. Charles Luther was active in politics, and his collection of political biographies fills the breakfast room's shelves.

A loaner from the Luther library and a cup of coffee are the perfect accompaniments on the hotel's front porch, where rocking chairs and wrought iron furniture offer an unspoiled view across the hotel's semicircular drive and expansive lawn to Tres Palacios Bay.

Port Aransas ⚓ 1925

Guests find individually decorated rooms, a pool, and wireless Internet one-half mile from the beach at this hotel, which once offered simple lodging for Gulf Coast anglers.

Tarpon Inn, Port Aransas. Photo by Reba Graham-Clough.

Visitors from around the world drop by to see the seven thousand tarpon scales lining the walls of the Tarpon Inn's sunny lobby. The hotel collected the scales, which are dated and signed by each lucky angler, when tarpon fishing along the Gulf Coast was at its peak, from the 1920s to the 1940s. President Franklin D. Roosevelt fished off the Port Aransas coast in 1937, and his signed and framed tarpon scale hangs alongside photos of him and his companions. The fish was so important to the early life of this island community that Port Aransas was known as Tarpon until 1911.

The original Tarpon Inn was built in 1886 by Frank Stephenson using lumber from a former Civil War barracks. That hotel, which is said to have resembled a barracks itself, was destroyed by fire in 1900. Two new buildings replaced it, and the larger of the two was destroyed by a hurricane in 1919.

In 1923 James M. Ellis bought the property. In 1925, with the help of

J. B. Earl of Waco, Ellis used cypress to construct the existing two-story hotel building with its long covered galleries. No architect was hired to assist with the design, but Ellis recreated the two-story, horizontal barracks style. To bolster the construction, dozens of pine logs were soaked in creosote and anchored into twenty feet of concrete throughout the hotel. They extend up into the hotel's attic and are credited with helping the inn survive more than one nasty storm. Today, in some guest rooms, a careful eye can discern where wood paneling in the corners covers them.

In 1936 Duncan Hines and his bride brought Port Aransas national attention when they spent their honeymoon at the Tarpon. Following the trip, Hines recommended the inn's restaurant in his guidebooks.

When tarpon fishing dwindled along the Gulf Coast, the inn fell into disrepair and changed owners a number of times. It served as headquarters for the Salvation Army, the Red Cross, and military units until a new owner

ESSENTIALS

Contact: P.O. Box 8, 200 E. Cotter, Port Aransas, TX 78373; 800-365-6784, 361-749-5555; fax: 361-749-4305; www.thetarponinn.com, info@thetarponinn.com

Rooms: 24 rooms and suites with private bath; claw-foot tub with shower attachment, walk-in shower, shower/tub combination; king, queen, full, and twin beds.

Rates: $–$$$

Room amenities: hair dryer, iron and ironing board available upon request; wi-fi for a fee.

Facilities: morning coffee in lobby, TV and phone for guests in lobby, outdoor pool.

Smoking: outside only.

Credit cards: V, MC, AE.

Parking: free in hotel lot.

Accessibility: some rooms are on ground floor.

Pets: not allowed.

Author's tips:—Gallery-sitting guests bothered by Cotter Street traffic find there is less noise on the second floor gallery.—Locals toss back longnecks at Shorty's Place, 821 Tarpon, which brims with personality one block from the hotel.

National Register
   of Historic Places: yes

Texas historical marker: yes

Texas Heritage Trails Program: Texas Tropical Trail Region, www.texastropicaltrail.com

Visitor information: Port Aransas Chamber of Commerce, Tourist and Convention Bureau, 403 W. Cotter, Port Aransas, TX 78373; 800-45-COAST; 361-749-5919; info@portaransas.org, www.portaransas.org

made repairs and reopened the inn in 1975. The Tarpon became popular once again among anglers and hunters, offering basic accommodations. A writer in 1982 described the hotel's decor as "seaside tacky."

Today, the inn is far from tacky. Hand-picked antiques, wicker chairs, and hand-crafted iron furniture are used throughout the individually decorated rooms, which feature coordinated designer fabrics on beds and windows. Guests often offer to buy particular pieces of furniture, such as a rolled-iron sleigh bed and a century-old rocking chair with dovetail and wood peg construction.

Each of the twenty-four guest rooms and suites has a private bathroom and polished pine floors. A few of the rooms have been painted, but most have their original pine paneling. Some of the rooms are very small, with just enough space for a bed, small dresser, and chair. The inn's more spacious rooms have sitting areas.

The hotel's featured accommodation is the FDR Suite. Although the president never stayed at the inn, this plush, three-room corner suite was named in his honor. It is the only room in the hotel with a television and full kitchen. Formerly the hotel manager's quarters, it has its own private balcony overlooking the pool and grassy courtyard, a favorite spot for weddings. Across the courtyard sits the building that survived the 1919 hurricane. It has been used as a restaurant for years but is now closed.

The tourists and business travelers who make up the majority of the Tarpon Inn's guests these days can relax poolside under the shade of a small palm frond–covered palapa. Dozens of pastel rocking chairs and benches also await them on the hotel's two long, covered galleries facing busy, and sometimes noisy, Cotter Street.

The front of the hotel is lined with more than a dozen palm trees, and just outside its white picket fence is the trolley stop for rides to the beach, one-half mile away.

A dock with fishing and sightseeing tour boats and a number of restaurants and bars is a few blocks from the hotel. Wildlife viewing is available at the Leonabell Turnbull Birding Center a short drive away. The center has a boardwalk and observation tower over shallow, brackish water, where visitors can see alligators, turtles, and many birds, including roseate spoonbills, cormorants, and pelicans.

Queen Isabel Inn
Port Isabel ⚓ 1906

A bayside gem with a beautiful pool and patio overlooking the Queen Isabella Causeway and South Padre Island, this small hotel offers a laid-back ambience that encourages long stays.

The oldest remaining seaside resort hotel in the Rio Grande Valley, the Queen Isabel Inn has hosted anglers, hunters, and tourists at the southern tip of Texas on the Laguna Madre for more than one hundred years. During the hotel's lifetime, hurricane winds have ripped its wide verandas and lashed at its roof, but the hotel has withstood these onslaughts. How? Its three-brick-thick walls sit solidly on pyramid-shaped brick piers sunk deep into Port Isabel's soil.

At the turn of the twentieth century, the Rio Grande Railway delivered cargo and passengers to the small fishing village of Port Isabel (then called Point Isabel) from Brownsville, one hour away. The railroad owned bayfront property on the point, where it had a depot and a rail line that extended on trestles 1,500 feet into the Laguna Madre. Small vessels would shuttle cargo between the pier and ships anchored outside Brazos Santiago Pass. The point was a popular destination for tourists who chartered fishing boats and rode ferries across the bay to undeveloped Padre Island for fishing, swimming, and beachcombing.

Caesar Kleberg, a wildlife promoter and rancher associated with the King Ranch and the Rio Grande Railway, opened this hotel in 1906, calling it the Point Isabel Tarpon Fishing Club. The hotel took its name from the popular sport fish caught in abundance along the Gulf Coast at that time. The inn was ideally located just across from the railway.

Queen Isabel Inn, Port Isabel. Photo by Jeff Carmack.

ESSENTIALS

Contact: 300 S. Garcia Street, Port Isabel, TX 78578; 800-943-1468, 956-943-1468; fax: 956-943-3574; www.queenisabelinn.com
Rooms: 8 rooms, all with private bath; shower/tub combinations, walk-in showers; most rooms are suites with separate kitchen/sitting area; queen beds.
Rates: $$–$$$
Room amenities: phone, TV, DVD/video player with DVD video library, hair dryer, iron and ironing board, free wi-fi, full kitchen, ice chest.
Facilities: outdoor pool, barbecue grills, shuffleboard, boat ramp, boat slips on Laguna Madre, laundromat, meeting rooms for up to 20.
Smoking: outdoors only.
Credit cards: V, MC, AE, D.

Parking: free in hotel lot.
Accessible: disabled access, some rooms are on ground floor.
Pets: not allowed.
Author's tips:—A great time to visit Port Isabel is September/October when temperatures are moderate and the crowds abate.
**National Register
  of Historic Places:** no
Texas historical marker: yes
Texas Heritage Trails Program: Texas Tropical Trail Region, www.texastropicaltrail.com
Visitor information: Port Isabel Chamber of Commerce, 421 Queen Isabella Blvd., Port Isabel, TX 78578; 800-527-6102, 956-943-2262; www.portisabel.org, info@portisabel.org

An early photo of the H-shaped hotel shows its two stories ringed with wide, covered verandas. These wooden porches provided shade and directed breezes into rooms. The verandas covered 8,200 square feet, almost as much area as the 8,580-square-foot hotel itself. Drinking water collected from the roof flowed into three cisterns at the western side of the hotel, where the main entrance is today.

Hurricanes in 1933 and 1967 damaged the hotel's verandas and peaked roof. When repairs were made, owners chose a more wind-resistant design. The verandas weren't replaced, and the roof is now flat, but the bay-facing portion of the hotel has a second-floor balcony. The old veranda foundations have become borders for the planters that surround the hotel perimeter.

The Texas Historical Commission presented the inn its Texas Treasure Business Award in 2006. Over the years the hotel has had numerous owners and has operated under various names, including the Point Isabel Hotel, Jefferson Inn, Red Arrow Hotel, Hotel Alder-Deck, Hotel Brazos, and Coastal Hotel. It became the Queen Isabel Inn in 1958.

The inn, its grounds, and its once-popular dining room (which closed for good in the 1960s) have been the scene of numerous school proms, wedding receptions, and local civic club events. The Port Isabel Rotary Club was founded here in the 1930s.

Hotel manager Dr. James A. Hockaday founded the Rio Grande Valley Fishing Rodeo in Port Isabel in 1934, and the hotel served as the tourney's headquarters. (Now called the Texas International Fishing Tournament, it is the largest competitive saltwater fishing event in the state.) An amusing 1930s photo publicizing the event shows an attractive fisherwoman sitting beside what's labeled as a can of "Texas Sardines": a box spring with springs removed and packed fin to fin with a dozen five-foot-long silvery tarpon.

Photos such as this one are hung throughout the Queen Isabel Inn, each accompanied by its historical information. Through these, guests can see Port Isabel and the inn as they were thirty, seventy, and ninety years ago, sometimes immediately following a hurricane. John Haywood, the inn's owner since 1978, tracked down the photos, dug through records, and interviewed past owners and guests to piece together the hotel's past. He gladly shares details about the hotel and the area. Upon my arrival, he told me the best place to access the beach on South Padre Island and offered his recommendations for local restaurants.

Accommodations at the Queen Isabel Inn are comfortable enough to encourage long stays. All of its eight two- and three-room suites are outfitted with full kitchens and small dining areas. A building adjacent to the inn was initially a stable; in 1945 it became the area's first motel units, and the building is now configured as six cottages.

All guest rooms have modern furniture and white painted walls. Solid-color fabrics of mostly blue and green are employed throughout. Thoughtful details help make the inn feel more like a home than a hotel. Bathrooms are stocked with aspirin, antacids, razors, and toothbrushes. A wide selection of loaner DVDs and tapes are available for the players in each room. Gas and charcoal barbecue grills stand ready for a burger or the day's catch. Ice chests in each room can be taken on day trips to the beach.

At any one time, several of the inn's guests will have been lodging there for several weeks or months. Most of the remaining patrons are child-free couples seeking a more intimate seaside getaway than that offered by the condominium towers lining South Padre Island's busy beach.

I spent a fall afternoon on the hotel's tidy patio accompanied only by the sound of two-dozen palm trees buffeted by the sea breeze. The cabana, the rippling water in the Esther Williams pool, and the neatly arranged chairs and lounges were a study in cool blues and white. My view to the southeast extended across the hotel's lush lawn and on to the causeway, which curves across the water to the cityscape of South Padre

Island. To the north I could catch the top of the century-old Port Isabel Lighthouse, which is part of the Museums of Port Isabel complex.

Just a few miles north of Port Isabel is the Laguna Atascosa National Wildlife Refuge, which offers hiking and wildlife viewing. A variety of birds, from green jays and chachalaca to cactus wren and roadrunners, can be spotted there. It's also easy to spot the occasional osprey and innumerable soaring pelicans from a poolside perch at the inn.

Yacht Club Hotel
Port Isabel ⚓ circa 1928

Originally built as a private club for the Rio Grande Valley's wealthy, this hotel features verandas, views of a marina, and a private patio and pool.

The Rio Grande Valley's wealthiest families opened the Port Isabel Yacht Club in the late 1920s as a private retreat for members only. Now the private-club-turned-hotel welcomes all vacationers who come for the area's surf, sand, and fishing.

Prohibition was in full swing when the Yacht Club opened, and Port Isabel was a small, remote fishing community. Some speculate that the club was a speakeasy and that smugglers used its "lookout" tower to watch for the law as their boats were loaded with alcohol at the marina across the street. Today the tower, which extends above the two-story Mediterranean-style building with its red terra-cotta tile roof and white-painted stucco, is being renovated so guests can take in a view encompassing Port Isabel, Laguna Madre, and South Padre Island.

The Yacht Club's intimate walled patio at the back of the hotel has a tropical feel, with white patio furniture, a swimming pool rimmed with colorful tiles, and lush, well-established plantings. Several species of palm, including some trees that are taller than the hotel, also beautify the small landscaped areas in front and along the edges of the building's two wings. Beds filled with yellowbells and oleander, and large terra cotta pots displaying tropical plants, help shade

Yacht Club Hotel, Port Isabel. Photo by Jeff Carmack.

ESSENTIALS

Contact: 700 N. Yturria St., Port Isabel, TX 78578; 956-943-1301; fax: 956-943-1301

Rooms: 24 rooms and suites, all with private bath; tub/shower combination, walk-in showers; king, full, and twin beds.

Rates: $$

Room amenities: TV; iron, ironing board, and hair dryer available upon request.

Facilities: meeting space for up to 300; outdoor pool.

Smoking: outdoors only.

Credit cards: V, MC.

Parking: free in hotel lot.

Accessibility: disabled access, some guest rooms on ground floor.

Pets: not allowed.

Author's tips:—Boat-owning guests can rent a slip at the Anchor Marina a few blocks from the hotel, www.anchormarinapark.com, 956-943-9323.

National Register
   of Historic Places: no

Texas historical marker: no

Texas Heritage Trails Program: Texas Tropical Trail Region, www.texastropicaltrail.com

Visitor information: Port Isabel Chamber of Commerce, 421 Queen Isabella Blvd., Port Isabel, TX 78578; 800-527-6102, 956-943-2622; www.portisabel.org, info@portisabel.org

---

the hotel's Saltillo-tiled porch and deflect heat from a semicircular drive and parking area.

Guests walk under a central portico to enter the lobby. The mounted silvery tarpon and the photograph of a boy straddling a six-hundred-pound Kemp's Ridley sea turtle in 1929 speak to early amusements that are no longer allowed. Fishermen now must release any tarpon they catch, and the Kemp's Ridley is an endangered species.

The Yacht Club once had a private dock across the street, and boating was a favorite pastime of its early members. More than fifty motorboats registered for the club's first regatta in 1929. An article in the *Port Isabel Pilot* shortly before the event said spectators were expected to arrive by train from Texas, Louisiana, and Florida. The club offered more than $1,000 in cash prizes.

The club's first regatta was also to be its last. Later that year came the stock market crash that heralded the Great Depression. Valley citrus magnate John Shary, one of the club's initial investors, bought out the rest of the group and opened the club to the public. Shary operated the business until the mid-1940s and is said to have hosted such famous guests as Charles Lindbergh, Andrew Carnegie, and members of the Rockefeller family.

The Yacht Club Hotel and Restaurant became "the" fine dining spot in the Rio Grande Valley during the 1980s and 1990s, when it was run by Ron and Lynn Speier. Locals and regular visitors to Port Isabel talk wistfully about its fabulous meals. The most recent owners purchased the hotel in 2003, after it had been closed for a year, and have renovated it room by room. The hotel's kitchen now serves catered events only.

In trying to capture a touch of 1920s opulence, floral-patterned wallpapers and rich fabrics have been used throughout. Guest rooms have either hardwood or marble floors. Furnishings are a mix of mostly antiques with a few modern pieces. Each room is individually decorated with custom-made bedding and drap-eries with pleated swags in floral patterns and shimmery solid fabrics. Several of the private bathrooms feature hand-painted Mexican tile in bright blue, gold, and green. Just outside the door of each room are covered verandas lined with tables and chairs, offering views of what is now the Anchor Marina across the street, the original site of the club's private boat dock.

Guests, who range from hunters, birders, and motorcyclists to winter Texans, often strike up conversations around the pool, in the lobby, or in the adjacent sitting area, which has two fireplaces.

The hotel is a short drive from the Queen Isabella Causeway that crosses the Laguna Madre to South Padre Island. At the foot of the causeway are Port Isabel's museums, the Port Isabel Light House State Historic Site, shops, restaurants, and the Pirate's Landing fishing pier.

Hill Country

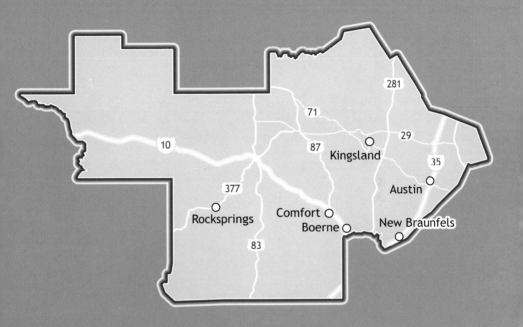

281

71

10

87   Kingsland

29

35

377

Austin

Rocksprings

Comfort

Boerne

New Braunfels

83

Historic hotel locations in the
Hill Country region.
Drawn by Jon Michael Grant.

Driskill Hotel
Austin 🏛 1886

This Texas cattleman's dream hotel has entertained heads of state, hosted many a Texas governor's inaugural ball, and barely escaped demolition to survive as a grand retreat amid Austin's downtown entertainment districts.

In 1886 guests at the newly built Driskill Hotel could watch the sun set behind Austin's undeveloped rolling hills and enjoy views of the Colorado River. While dining in its Grande Salon, they could monitor construction of the Texas capitol building five blocks away. More than 120 years later, amid condominium towers and multimillion-dollar glass and steel skyscrapers, this Richardsonian Romanesque hotel stands as a link to nineteenth-century Austin.

In the 1880s, Pecan Street (now Sixth Street) was the main route from the east into Austin and led into the city's budding business center. Cattleman Col. Jesse L. Driskill chose this thoroughfare on which to build his luxurious hotel—the traveler's last refuge in Texas' westernmost metropolis.

The carved busts of Jesse Driskill and his two sons, Will and Tobe, are perched upon the four-story pressed brick and limestone building. They overlook its covered balconies, gargoyles, and a thirty-five-foot arched entrance onto Sixth Street, once called the largest arched doorway in Texas.

Driskill Hotel, Austin. Photo courtesy Driskill Hotel.

ESSENTIALS

Contact: 604 Brazos St., Austin, TX 78701; 800-252-9367, 512-474-5911; fax: 512-474-2214; www.driskillhotel.com

Rooms: 189 rooms and suites, all with private bath; tub/shower combination, oversize tub, Jacuzzi tub, walk-in shower; queen; king beds; Lyndon B. Johnson Presidential Suite has one bedroom and a 10-foot stained glass window featuring bluebonnets and a Texas star; Cattle Baron Suite includes two bedrooms, an entertainment center, and a Jacuzzi tub and spa shower; Yellow Rose Bridal Suite includes separate dressing room with floor-length mirrors, four-poster canopy king bed, large picture window.

Rates: $$$–$$$$

Room amenities: phone, TV, coffee maker upon request, iron and ironing board, hair dryer, free wi-fi, robe, room service.

Facilities: Driskill Grill, 5:30 P.M. to 10 P.M. Tues.–Sat.; 186 Café and Bakery, 7 A.M. to 10 P.M. Sun.–Thurs., 7 A.M. to midnight, Fri. and Sat.; Driskill Bar, noon to midnight, Sun.– Thurs., noon to 2 P.M. Fri. and Sat.; fitness center, business center, concierge, group space for up to 350.

Smoking: outside only.

Credit cards: V, MC, AE, D, DC.

Parking: valet only, $18.

Accessibility: disabled access, elevator.

Pets: yes, $50 fee, 20 lb. weight limit.

Author's tips:—Contact the hotel's concierge to join a fact-filled tour of the Driskill led by a local historian. —Stop by the Austin Visitors Center at 209 E. Sixth Street for information about self-guided historic walking tours of Austin's downtown, or call about the free guided tours, 800-926-2282, 512-583-7233.

National Register of Historic Places: yes

Texas historical marker: no

Texas Heritage Trails Program: Texas Hill Country Trail Region, www.txhillcountrytrail.com

Visitor information: Austin Convention and Visitors Bureau, 301 Congress Ave., Suite 200; 866-GO-AUSTIN; www.austintexas.org

---

The hotel, designed by the Austin firm Jasper N. Preston and Son, took two years to build. The year "1885" carved in limestone tops the building, but the hotel actually opened in December 1886. Driskill spent $400,000 to construct and furnish the then sixty-suite hostelry, an incredible sum at a time when a plate lunch cost fifteen cents. Ten suites even had private baths. Velvet carpets, brass hardware, and solid walnut and leather furniture acquired by Driskill on a trip back east adorned its interior. Upon its opening, writers dubbed the Driskill the finest hotel west and south of St. Louis. A special edition of the *Austin Statesman* called it the "palace hotel of the south" where "all the traveling world may be assured of an elegant and comfortable home." The Missouri Pacific Railway touted the Driskill to its customers, promoting Austin as a winter tourist destination. Hotel guests paid from $3 to $5 for a room on the American plan, which included three meals a day. Shortly after its opening, the Driskill's ballroom and parlors became the venue of choice for celebrations and other gatherings. Students at the newly established University of Texas chose it for their dinner dances, tea dances, and graduation receptions. And a number of Texas governors, starting with Sul Ross in 1887, have staged elaborate inaugural balls at the Driskill.

Despite its grand start, the Driskill's first few decades were rough. Colonel Driskill, who had made a fortune selling beef to the Confederate army, lost three thousand head of cattle in an 1888 blizzard and was forced to sell his hotel. The Driskill changed hands several times before 1900 and was even closed for awhile before a single owner and consistent management brought stability.

Beginning in 1908 and continuing for many decades, national election returns were projected by stereopticon from a balcony at the Driskill onto a building across Sixth Street. Politics is a sport in Texas' capital city, and a century later, the Driskill is still home to election watch parties and

political strategy sessions. President-elect George W. Bush leased the hotel's entire mezzanine for two weeks in 2001 for cabinet selection meetings. President Lyndon B. Johnson and his family held the most famous election returns party ever at the Driskill in 1964 when they occupied the Jim Hogg Suite. Johnson, who thirty years earlier had had his first date with future wife Lady Bird in the Driskill's dining room, was elected by a landslide that night, and the Driskill made international headlines.

Five years later the city almost lost its world-famous institution to the wrecking ball. In 1969 the hotel's owners announced they would tear the building down because their business wasn't profitable. They intended to temporarily keep open the Driskill's twelve-story 1930 addition to the north, designed by Henry Trost, but even its fate wasn't certain. The hotel shut its doors in June, when Texas politicians and lobbyists who had been staying there left at the end of the 1969 legislative session.

Almost immediately, concerned Austin architects, attorneys, and the newly formed Heritage Society of Austin created the Driskill Hotel Corporation and rallied to save the icon. Texas legislation and editorials in state and local papers voiced support for the Driskill. After a tense few years of hard work, the corporation raised $900,000 by selling $1 stocks and secured financing to save and refurbish the hotel to the tune of $2 million. It reopened with great fanfare in 1972 and hasn't closed its doors since.

Most of today's visitors are oblivious to this tumultuous past as they walk off the busy sidewalks into the lobby's refined atmosphere. Carpeted sitting areas are situated among black, gold, and white marble walkways and thirty-four cast iron columns with embellished capitals that are original to the hotel. Subdued lighting and a warm, rich color scheme of deep burgundy, black, cream, and gold make this a gracious, intimate space despite its 22-foot coffered ceilings. Presiding over the lobby is Colonel Driskill himself, in a life-size portrait by William Henry Huddle that has hung in the hotel since 1890. A colorful, inverted stained glass dome tops off an area where the hotel once had a four-story rotunda and skylights.

Over the past decade, the hotel's corporate owners have spent tens of millions of dollars and used old photographs, written descriptions, and paint painstakingly matched to old remnants to restore the Driskill to its original grandeur. The 1886 building's public rooms have artisan-painted frescoes and light fixtures, draperies, and furnishings that are either from the turn of the twentieth century or else finely crafted reproductions matching original pieces.

Despite numerous renovations over the years, including one that enclosed the rotunda to allow for more guest rooms, a number of the hotel's original features have been preserved. The American National Bank's vault door stands open in the lobby. The bank established an office here in 1890, and now the vault door is used to secure guests' safe deposit boxes.

The original white Italian Carrara marble spans the large mezzanine floor. The mezzanine also has its original 18-foot high iron columns, stained longleaf yellow pine wainscoting, and two balconies overlooking Sixth and Brazos streets. The former Grande Salon is now the Driskill Ballroom. Its Capitol view was obscured by the 1930 addition.

The Maximilian Room is the most famous of the public rooms off the mezzanine. It takes its name from the eight large mirrors hanging in it. These mirrors, said to be backed with silver and diamond dust, and secured in frames covered in gold leaf, were crafted in Europe and destined for the castle of Emperor of Mexico Ferdinand Maximilian and his wife, Carlotta. Maximilian's rule was short lived, and in 1867 he was shot before the mirrors could be delivered to their Mexico City destination. In 1930 the Driskill's owner purchased them when the pristine, eight-by-six-foot works of art turned up in the hands of a San Antonio antique dealer.

The older building's guest rooms, called historic rooms, and those in the 1930 tower, called traditional rooms, are comfortably furnished with quality fabrics, bedding, and antique reproduction furniture. All have private baths. The historic rooms lean toward the Victorian, and their bathrooms have brass fixtures and black Brazilian marble. The traditional rooms have a hint of art deco style, and their facilities are outfitted with stainless and porcelain fixtures and white and gray tile. Each room features a custom-made wrought iron bed whose headboard displays a prominent *D*. This monogram appears throughout the hotel, an artful reminder to guests that they are in the one and only Driskill.

Other small touches throughout the hotel add to its distinctive feel. An ornate brass medallion covers the peephole in each guest room door; it must be swung aside before the occupant can spy into the hallway. The nightly turndown service includes a gourmet chocolate accompanied by a freshly printed card with Roy Rogers' "Cowboy's Prayer" and Austin's weather forecast. On the walls of each guest room are individual arrangements of old photographs, prints, and shadowboxes. Many of the framed collections have an Austin or Texas bent, such as the shadowbox in my room, which included a silhouette of a Texas longhorn made of square nails, a withered rose, and a postcard of the University of Texas campus from the 1930s.

The gallery-like hallways are lined with original oil paintings whose subjects range from a bouquet of peonies and a pastoral landscape to a portrait of a young girl. Only the occasional bluebonnet-covered pasture can be found. This extends to the hotel's overall atmosphere, which is elegant with a subtle Texas touch.

The Driskill Bar, on the other hand, has the not-so-subtle feel of a cattle baron's ranch house, with its leather sofas near the limestone fireplace, mounted longhorn, and cowhide-backed bar stools. The night I visited, a couple at one table celebrated over champagne while locals shared a bowl of jalapeno potato chips with a New York television producer in town to tape Willie Nelson. The bar makes a nice staging area for dining next door in the hotel's award-winning Driskill Grill, which features contemporary American cuisine such as hot smoked Bandera quail. The hotel's 1886 Café and Bakery is a favorite spot for morning business meetings over poached eggs with chorizo gravy.

Although the hotel doesn't mention it, ghost hunters say that restless spirits roam the Driskill's halls—those of a four-year-old girl who died on the hotel's grand staircase, a young woman who killed herself after being jilted by her fiancé, and Colonel Driskill himself.

The Driskill is situated on the western end of the Sixth Street entertainment district, a few blocks from several downtown restaurants, museums, bars, coffee shops, upscale shopping, and music venues concentrated in the Warehouse District and the Second Street District. The state capitol building is a short walk away.

InterContinental Stephen F. Austin Hotel

Austin ⚓ 1924

The first high-rise hotel on Austin's Congress Avenue, this brainchild of city business leaders has a wraparound terrace and beautiful views of the Texas capitol in the thick of downtown.

Austin business leaders in 1920 began to envision a new hotel in the Texas capital to host conventions and accommodate the increasing number of travelers visiting the growing city for business and pleasure. Their dream was realized in May 1924, when the ten-story Stephen F. Austin opened as the city's first high-rise hotel on Congress Avenue. It had taken four years of perseverance, a public subscription of $600,000 in mortgage bonds, and a deal struck by the city's Chamber of Commerce with Fort Worth's Baker Hotel Company, but the Stephen F. Austin was now

InterContinental Stephen F. Austin Hotel, Austin.
Photo courtesy InterContinental Stephen F. Austin Hotel.

a reality. Grand opening festivities included a lavish dinner and dance for more than six hundred guests in the Longhorn Garden atop the hotel. The *Austin Statesman* said the beaux arts–style hotel was a "keystone to Austin's future development" and called the Stephen F. Austin a "palatial hostelry."

The Fort Worth architectural firm of Sanguinet, Staats, and Hedrick designed the brick building with a granite base, a second story of ornamental white stone, and a wrap-around terrace. The hotel was to be called the Texas, but the Business and Professional Women's Club of Austin and other local groups successfully petitioned the Baker Hotel Company to change its name to Stephen F. Aus-

ESSENTIALS

Contact: 701 Congress Ave., Austin, TX 78701; 800-327-0200, 512-457-8800; fax: 512-457-8896; www.austin.intercontinental.com, Austin@ichotelsgroup.com
Rooms: 189 rooms and suites, all with private bath; tub/shower combinations; king and queen beds. Governor's Suite includes Jacuzzi tub and wraps around three corners of the hotel's top floor. Yellow Rose Suite has a spacious open floor plan with living area and includes a marble bar.
Rates: $$$–$$$$
Room amenities: phone, TV, hair dryer, iron and ironing board, wired Internet for a fee, robes, room service.
Facilities: Café Julienne, 6:30 A.M. to 11 A.M. Mon.–Fri., 6:30 A.M. to 2:30 P.M. Sat. and Sun.; Roaring Fork, 11:30 A.M. to 10 P.M. Mon.–Thurs., 11:30 A.M. to 11 P.M. Fri., 4:30 P.M. to 11 P.M. Sat., and 4:30 P.M. to 9 P.M. Sun.; Stephen F. Austin Bar and Terrace, 2:30 P.M. to 1 A.M. Mon.–Thurs., 2:30 P.M. to 2 A.M. Fri. and Sat., 2:30 P.M. to 11 P.M. Sun.; fitness center,

heated lap pool, business center.
Smoking: designated rooms.
Credit cards: V, MC, AE, D, DC, JCB.
Parking: valet only, $21, $25 for oversized.
Accessibility: disabled access, elevator.
Pets: not allowed.
Author's tips:—The best Texas capitol views are on the eighth floor and above in the one-bedroom suites on the northwest corner of the building.—Use the city's free 'Dillo bus service to a number of Austin landmarks, shopping areas, and other attractions in and around downtown and central Austin.
National Register of Historic Places: no
Texas historical marker: yes
Texas Heritage Trails Program: Texas Hill Country Trail Region, www.txhillcountrytrail.com
Visitor information: Austin Convention and Visitors Bureau, 301 Congress Ave., Suite 200; 866-GO-AUSTIN; www.austintexas.org

tin, in honor of the "father of Texas." The hotel is said to be the first building named for the state's leading colonist and statesman.

The hotel building made historic changes to downtown Austin's skyline. The structure was the first with a lighted roofline, a feature now employed by a number of the city's other high-rise buildings. Its rooftop Longhorn Garden was ringed with 125 multipaned windows and transoms. This popular space, which was removed when the hotel added five floors in 1938, had a polished wood floor and offered sweeping views of the Texas capitol and the city's growing downtown. In a photo from the hotel's early years, hundreds of ladies in hats and men in linen suits and ties dine at long tables in the sunny, breezy room. Rustic log beams draped with greenery stretch above tables dotted with fresh flowers.

Numerous, sometimes dramatic remodeling projects transformed the hotel over the years. In the 1950s the interior was updated to reflect contemporary tastes and its mezzanine reconfigured, perhaps to accommodate the fifteen Austin service organizations that regularly met there. As a result, the hotel removed the two main elements that gave the lobby its grandeur—a large, marble staircase and the room's two-story opening to a mezzanine.

By the early 1980s new owners from Minneapolis/St. Paul undertook another round of changes that rubbed Austinites the wrong way. For a start, the hotel was renamed the Bradford.

Owners intended salmon pink paint for the exterior and wanted to replace the building's original wood-framed, six-pane-over-six-pane windows with single panes of glass. Instead, in a compromise reached with the Austin Historical Landmark Commission, they nixed the paint color and installed two-pane windows instead, the windows the hotel has to this day.

The Bradford closed in 1987, when Austin had a glut of hotel rooms. The city considered turning the hotel into an upscale apartment community, but the idea never came to fruition. Its fixtures and furnishings were sold, and the building sat empty except for a few vagrants camped out in its rooms. In the late 1990s, InterContinental Hotels purchased the building and, using research collected from photographs and text descriptions, spent two years and millions of dollars returning it to its original beauty. The "Stephen F.," as locals call it, reopened in 2000.

Today the lobby once again has its marble double staircase, whose landing is an ideal setting for bridal portraits. The lobby is open to the mezzanine, and the balcony is rimmed with ornamental plaster and a railing of geometric designs that match the original details. The decorative plaster capitals atop the room's four pillars feature five-pointed Texas stars. The columns' capitals are re-creations based on a single piece salvaged from the hotel.

A painting of Stephen F. Austin, a copy of his portrait in the state capitol, hangs over one of the lobby's sitting areas. The modern furnishings in plush gold, cream, and black fabrics are grouped near the entrance to the Roaring Fork Restaurant and Saloon. This establishment serves gourmet western cuisine and leases space from the hotel that was initially occupied by the Austin Pharmacy upon the hotel's 1924 opening. Austinites who club-hopped in the 1980s remember this same spot as the Hippopotamus lounge and piano bar.

The hotel's 189 comfortable guest rooms and suites have a classic look with modern furniture and a cream, gold, and black color scheme. Fluffy duvets cover the beds, which are stacked with down pillows. Colorful prints of Texas wildflowers in gold frames adorn the walls. The private bathrooms throughout feature gold-tone fixtures, tan marble, pedestal sinks, and gold-framed mirrors. Some have separate marble vanities.

During its first week of business in 1924, the hotel hosted the Texas Bankers Association's annual meeting. The bankers still patronize the hotel, whose mostly corporate clients also include law firms and high-tech companies. In addition, the state capitol crowd has always favored the Stephen F. Austin. The building is only four blocks from the capitol, and a few state senators and representatives used to live at the hotel while the legislature was in session. In 1937 Lyndon Johnson set up his congressional campaign headquarters here. Although these days no legislators call the hotel home, politicos frequent the Stephen F. Austin's meeting rooms, restaurants, and bar.

The hotel's bar, with its over-stuffed chairs, mounted longhorn, and modern decor with a light Texas touch, is popular with locals and offers outdoor seating on the wraparound terrace. This is the only publicly accessible terrace on Congress Avenue, where patrons find an impressive view up the avenue to its crown, the capitol building. In typical Austin fashion, it's not unusual for the bar to be filled with a mix of local political and business types, Texas Longhorn fans, and visiting musicians and filmmakers.

The terrace is also the perfect spot for parade viewing. The hotel occasionally will book part of the terrace to groups during events, but a portion is always kept open for public access. Both the historic Paramount Theater and the State Theater are next door. The Arthouse at the Jones Center is across the street, and the Austin Museum of Art is a short walk away.

Ye Kendall Inn

Boerne  1859

New American cuisine, spa treatments, and facilities for weddings and conferences attract guests to this large native limestone hotel and its expanded facilities.

The National Register of Historic Places calls Ye Kendall Inn one of the last remaining nineteenth-century resort hotels in Texas. At the turn of that century, the hotel was one of five in Boerne that hosted tourists traveling by train or stagecoach to enjoy the Hill Country's "healthful climate," which was considered ideal for those with respiratory ailments. The hotel restaurant accommodated special diets, and a staff of local doctors remained on call for guests.

More than one hundred years later, Boerne is bustling with vacationers and retirees who like the small-town feel combined with an abundance of antique and specialty shops, restaurants, and outdoor attractions. Consequently, the modern Kendall clientele seek a slightly different set of amenities. The hotel has a spa, a conference center, and an award-winning restaurant that hosts monthly wine dinners. Nowadays guests are touring the Hill Country by motorcycle, hunting for retirement property, or attending business meetings in the hotel's conference center.

The first lodgers at the 1859 inn were the guests of Erastus and Sarah Reed, who built a two-story home of native limestone facing south on Boerne's main square. Like many

Ye Kendall Inn, Boerne. Photo by Liz Carmack.

ESSENTIALS

Contact: 128 W. Blanco, Boerne, TX 78006; 800-364-2138, 830-249-2138, fax: 803-249-1724; www.yekendallinn.com, info@yekendallinn.com

Rooms: 9 rooms and suites, in original hotel; 27cottages, cabins, and suites; all accommodations have private bath; claw-foot tubs with shower attachment, modern tub/shower, walk-in showers; king, queen, and full beds.

Rates: $$–$$$

Room amenities: phone, TV, hair dryer, iron and ironing board, free wi-fi.

Facilities: Limestone Grille, 7:00 A.M. to 2:30 P.M. Mon., 7:00 A.M. to 9 P.M. Tues.–Sat.; 7:30 A.M. to 2:30 P.M. Sun.; Tavern 128, 3 P.M. to close, Tues.–Sat.; complimentary morning coffee available from restaurant; fitness center, outdoor hot tub, spa, business center; group space for up to 400.

Smoking: outdoors only.

Credit cards: V, MC, AE, D.

Parking: free parking on street and in hotel lot.

Accessibility: disabled access, most rooms are on ground floor.

Pets: not allowed.

Author's tips:—The claw-foot tub and toilet in each of the four guest rooms in the original 1859 building are behind a louvered wooden partition in the guest room, not behind a solid door in a separate bathroom.—Boerne Market Days, held the second weekend of every month, features dozens of Texas vendors selling arts and crafts, antiques, collectibles, unusual items, and food.

National Register of Historic Places: yes

Texas historical marker: yes

Texas Heritage Trails Program: Texas Hill Country Trail Region, www.txhillcountrytrail.com

Visitor information: Boerne Convention and Visitors Bureau, 1407 S. Main St., Boerne, TX 78006; 888-842-8080, 830-429-7277; www.visitboerne.org

settlers of the time, the Reeds made room for overnight guests. Known as the Reed House, this original building is the heart of the inn, which was expanded in 1878 by C. J. Roundtree and W. L. Wadsworth. They added two flanking limestone wings, covered front and back galleries, and named it the Boerne Hotel. During these early days, stagecoaches, cattle drives, and army supply convoys congregated in the city square across from the inn, in what is now a city park lined with pecan trees just off Main Street. Guests included not only stagecoach passengers and trail bosses but, supposedly, Colonel Robert E. Lee, who was stationed at Fort Mason in the Hill Country before the Civil War.

An 1890 newspaper advertisement for the Boerne Hotel boasted "rooms large and spacious, fronting south, well ventilated, open fire places, fine scenery" for $2 a day, which probably included a meal. The inn offers thirty-four accommodations on its grounds in guest rooms, suites, historic cabins, and a chapel. All have private baths. Nine of these rooms are on the second floor of the original vernacular Greek revival–style building. Some of the original inn's rooms have been combined to make them more spacious, and all are decorated in plush Victorian style, each with a different color scheme and antique furniture, including large armoires and marble-topped sideboards. The rooms have wall-to-wall carpeting and fourteen-foot ceilings. Room doors open out onto the wide covered galleries, which offer a few seating areas. The fireplaces advertised more than one hundred years ago remain, but for safety reasons, only those in the hotel's restaurant and bar operate. A button inside an ornate, black metal box sits just inside each room's door. Guests could once use the button to communicate with front desk staff, who would see lights appear next to room numbers on a central display in the lobby.

The hotel's lobby has dark stained ceiling beams and wainscoting and a longleaf pine floor covered with Oriental-style rugs. The windows are covered with heavy drapes, and the room is filled with antique furnishings. This atmosphere is carried through to Tavern 128 and the Limestone Grille, whose wine selection has been lauded by *Wine Spectator* magazine. The Kendall Provisions Company off the lobby has a large selection of gifts, wines, health foods, and books on self-help and nutrition.

The hotel has a concrete courtyard, dotted with a few tables and chairs and a fireplace, but I think the prettiest part of the grounds is the native plant landscaping among the cluster of historic cabins and the small chapel that was moved to the property and is rented to overnight guests.

The hotel is not far from Boerne's numerous shops, antique stores, and art galleries. Nearby are the Cibolo Nature Center, known for its hiking trails, estuary, and birding opportunities, and the Agricultural Heritage Center, a museum of antique farm equipment, which has a working nineteenth-century blacksmith shop. Picnicking, fishing, and swimming are a short drive away at Guadalupe River State Park.

This hotel, built by one of Comfort's most prominent German pioneer families, features private cottage-style gardens and American country decor on a quiet, historic main street.

The frequent appearance of the name *Ingenhuett* on plaques marking historic buildings and homes in Comfort indicates the important role this family had in the town's early days as a community of "free-thinking" German immigrants. During the latter part of the nineteenth century, the Ingenhuett family established an opera house, saloon, livery stable, and mercantile business in Comfort. In addition, Peter Joseph Ingenhuett hired San Antonio architect Alfred Giles to design this two-story limestone hotel, which has 20-inch thick walls and covered galleries, on the city's main thoroughfare. Providing lodging and meals to stagecoach and rail passengers traveling between Fredericksburg and San Antonio was so profitable that in 1894 Ingenhuett had Giles plan a hotel expansion that doubled the number of rooms to sixteen.

The business stayed in the Ingenhuett family until 1909, when the Louis E. Faust family purchased it and operated it as the Faust Hotel until 1945. The building passed among numerous owners until the 1970s, when it sat empty for several years and was sold at auction to pay a lien. It was renamed the Comfort Common in 1985, and when interior designers and

Comfort Common, Comfort. Photo by Liz Carmack.

antique dealers Jim Lord and Bobby Dent became the new owners in the early 1990s, they kept the name. The property includes an 1894 gazebo and carriage house, a gift shop, and a historic cottage and cabins.

Guests can find homemade soaps, old-fashioned handkerchiefs, and Christmas ornaments in the gift shop that now occupies the L-shaped hotel building's downstairs parlor and former guest rooms. The rooms retain their original wood floors and pressed-tin ceilings, but the building no longer shelters guests; the second story, which until a few years ago still housed hotel rooms, is now one of the owner's living quarters and office.

Six accommodations, all with private bath, are available on the landscaped grounds behind the old hotel. Two guest rooms are in the 1894 building that once served as the hotel's carriage house. Next door, guests are served a full breakfast in a small dining room filled with a half-dozen linen-topped tables. The remaining accommodations are in historic cabins and cottages moved to the property.

Visitors enter the secluded grounds through the hotel building or by way of a private gate that leads

ESSENTIALS

Contact: P.O. Box 539, 717 High St., Comfort, TX 78013; 830-995-3030, fax: 830-995-3455; comfortcommon .com, comfortcommon@hctc.net
Rooms: 2 rooms in hotel's original carriage house, 2 historic cottages, and 2 historic cabins, all with private bath; tub/shower combinations, walk-in showers, claw-foot tubs with shower attachment; queen beds.
Rates: $$, includes full breakfast.
Room amenities: phone, TV, coffee maker; hair dryer, iron and ironing board available upon request; gas or wood-burning fireplaces in some rooms, kitchens available in some rooms.
Facilities: group space for up to 20.
Smoking: outdoors only.
Credit cards: V, MC, AE, D.
Parking: free on street.

Accessibility: rooms are on ground floor.
Pets: not allowed.
Author's tips:—Children 12 and older are welcome.—814 A Texas Bistro, 713 High St., serves freshly prepared fish, steaks and pasta Wed. –Sun. Reservations are recommended, 830-995-4990.
National Register of Historic Places: yes, as part of Comfort Historic District
Texas historical marker: yes
Texas Heritage Trails Program: Texas Hill Country Trail, www.txhillcountrytrail.com
Visitor information: Comfort Chamber of Commerce, P.O. Box 777, Comfort, TX 78013; 830-995-3131; www.comfortchamberofcommerce .com, info@comfort-texas.com

to a peaceful, country cottage garden. Stone patios show off potted begonias and rustic wooden benches. Hackberry, pecan, and elm trees shade folk art birdhouses, birdbaths, blooming coral vine, and four o'clock bushes. Chairs and citronella candles on porches throughout the facilities encourage visitors to idle away their time watching birds or the hotel's gecko-hunting cat.

Decor throughout is American country and includes rough-hewn wood furniture and accessories from the late 1800s as well as modern upholstered chairs and quilt-covered beds. Rooms have personal touches such as old aprons hanging from coatracks and ladies' gloves adorning dressers, and some feature a dose of whimsy, such as the hand-painted vine and footpath enlivening the walls and floor in one room. These adornments make each room unique and have brought national attention to the hotel, whose interior has been featured in *Country Living*, *Country Home*, and *In Style* magazines.

The hotel sits on Comfort's quiet, picturesque High Street, in the midst of a ten-block downtown historic district that claims almost one hundred buildings built before 1900. Comfort is a peaceful historic German town that welcomes tourists but hasn't been overrun by them. Today's hotel guests are mostly repeat visitors from Houston and Dallas, couples or groups of friends who appreciate the town's two dozen or so antique stores and specialty shops. Some visitors make this a stop on a multiday tour of the Texas Hill Country.

Meyer Bed and Breakfast on Cypress Creek

Comfort ❧ circa 1860s

Situated along Cypress Creek, this charmingly furnished hotel's numerous historic buildings and cottage-style gardens create intimate areas to relax in a peaceful setting.

In the 1860s this creek-side property offered a welcome respite for stagecoach passengers heading to and from San Antonio. Today the stagecoach stop, its half-timbered German Fachwerk walls since covered by stucco and wood siding, is the office for the extensive Meyer Bed and Breakfast compound.

German native and wheelwright Frederich Christian Meyer and his wife, Ernestine, operated the stage stop here until 1869 when Meyer built a two-story limestone residence just west of the original lodging. In 1872 Meyer further developed his property, constructing a two-story wooden building to accommodate midwife Ernestine's clients and other overnight visitors. With the arrival of the railroad in 1887, Frederich added a cottage and a two-story hotel that included a restaurant and dining room. The hotel began to accommodate city dwellers who found Comfort to be a healthful country retreat, thanks to its slightly higher elevation and proximity to the Guadalupe River.

This hotel has grown and now offers twenty-six rooms and suites, all with private bath. Many of these accommodations are in the Meyer family's historic buildings; others are in more recently built structures that extend west from the original lots

Meyer Bed and Breakfast on Cypress Creek, Comfort. Photo by Liz Carmack.

ESSENTIALS

Contact: 845 High Street, Comfort, TX 78013; 888-995-6100, 830-995-2304; www.meyerbedandbreakfast.com, info@meyerbedandbreakfast.com

Rooms: 26 rooms and suites, all with private bath; tub/shower combination, walk-in shower, claw-foot tub with shower attachment, Jacuzzi tubs; king, queen, full, and twin beds.

Rates: $$, includes full breakfast.

Room amenities: TV, coffee maker, hair dryer, iron and ironing board, free wi-fi, porch or screened porch, gas fireplaces in most rooms.

Facilities: guest telephone in Gast Haus building, outdoor pool and hot tub, Cypress Creek access, screened-in common areas.

Smoking: outdoors only.

Credit cards: V, MC, AE, D.

Parking: free on hotel property and on street.

Accessibility: disabled access, most rooms are on ground floor.

Pets: not allowed.

Author's tips:—The Creekside Cottage is the Meyer's most popular accommodation. It has a sitting area, queen bed, large bathroom, and private screened porch overlooking Cypress Creek.—The Welfare Café, 223 Waring Welfare Road between Comfort and Boerne, offers diners delicious entrees, fine wines, and imported beers in a former post office/general store.

National Register of Historic Places: yes, as part of Comfort Historic District.

Texas historical marker: yes

Texas Heritage Trails Program: Texas Hill Country Trail Region, www.txhillcountrytrail.com

Visitor information: Comfort Chamber of Commerce, P.O. Box 777, Comfort, TX 78013; 830-995-3131; www.comfortchamberofcommerce.com, info@comfort-texas.com

along Comfort's main thoroughfare. The hotel remained in the Meyer family until 1956 and then changed owners a number of times. In the 1960s it was known as the Casa de Cazador Motel, and a swimming pool and more rooms were added. In the 1980s and 1990s, new owners opted to focus on the hotel's German roots and operated under the name the Gast Haus Lodge.

Although the grounds are sprawl-ing, the cottage-style plantings create areas of intimacy. Guests can wander along shaded stone pathways, admire the fishpond or the doves caged underneath a historic gazebo, or relax in tucked-away seating with views of lazy Cypress Creek and its wildlife.

The kitchen is housed in the two-story 1887 hotel building, and guests are served a full breakfast in the original dining areas and on a new deck overlooking the creek. The original hand-dug well and block and tackle that lifted guests' trunks to the second story of the old hotel building sit near its entrance. The hotel's former screened summer kitchen is now an outdoor lounging area, complete with gas fireplace and willow furniture.

Rooms at the Meyer are comfortable and well appointed with obvious attention paid to details, including bedside chocolates to greet arriving guests. Accommodations are decorated with antique, wicker, and upholstered furniture. Most beds are antiques or antique reproductions, and most rooms are large and have new, but old-looking, freestanding gas fireplaces made of porcelain and cast iron. Floors are wood and have area rugs or wall-to-wall carpeting. Several rooms have separate sitting areas. Bathrooms have generous vanities, and most have updated fixtures. Some of the larger rooms feature glass cases filled with antiques and collectibles, including items from the owner's families, which follow a music, sewing, or hunting theme.

If you're like me, you appreciate lodging that offers outdoor seating. In addition to the numerous spots to relax around the grounds, all the Meyer's rooms have either a covered or a screened porch.

Some guests today come to attend reunions or weddings in the area or to participate in one of Comfort's many civic events, such as the annual Comfort Village Antiques Fair, held in October, or the community's Fourth of July celebration. Comfort is still appreciated by urbanites for its quiet, country charm; visitors, including many regular guests from Austin and Houston, arrive to enjoy a weekend retreat or stop off on their way to children's summer camps further west in the Hill Country.

Antlers Hotel
Kingsland ⚜ 1901

After seventy years as a private vacation retreat, this lakeside hotel again welcomes vacationers just as it greeted holiday makers arriving by rail during the early twentieth century.

The Austin and Northwestern Railroad built the Antlers as a resort hotel to encourage city dwellers to take rail excursions into the Texas Hill Country. When the two-story wooden building with its long covered galleries opened in 1901, it sat on the shores of Crescent Lake, which was formed by a lock on the Colorado River. Guests could see both the Colorado and the Llano rivers from the hotel's second story. Arriving rail passengers had only to walk across the street from the depot, now gone, to the hotel and Campa Pajama, its adjoining campground.

Kingsland in the early 1900s was a popular recreation destination for hunting, fishing, and swimming, just as this area is now. Overnight visitors also included cattlemen driving herds to the railhead for shipping, and traveling salesmen, or drummers. Travelers to this lively community joined locals at a pavilion, dance hall, and skating rink near the hotel.

When the automobile opened access to the countryside, it changed the way cattle were shipped to market and made traveling to larger towns for shopping easier; rail travel declined and so did Kingsland. The railroad sold the hotel, and Thomas Barrow, who had been a guest during

Antlers Hotel, Kingsland. Photo by Liz Carmack.

its heyday, purchased it in 1923. The Antlers then spent seventy years as the Barrow family retreat. Toward the end of that era it fell into disrepair.

Photos from the early 1990s show paint peeling on the gingerbread detailing, a faded and weather-beaten red metal roof, and weedy, unkempt grounds posted with a No Trespassing sign. The hotel was transformed during a three-year renovation by new owners and reopened in 1996. The ornately molded sink bowls that sit in a corner of each room—once covered with rust, now beautifully restored and working—are a decorative reminder of the hotel's past. Comfortable modern furnishings and hand-

ESSENTIALS

Contact: 1001 King, Kingsland, TX 78639; 800-383-0007, 325-388-4411; fax: 325-388-6488; www.theantlers.com, innkeeper@theantlers.com

Rooms: 6 rooms and suites, all with private bath; tub/shower combination, claw-foot tub, clawfoot tub with shower attachment, walk-in shower; king beds; accommodations are also available in cabins and train cars.

Rates: $$–$$$

Room amenities: phone; hair dryer, iron and ironing board available upon request; flashlight provided for wandering the grounds at night; cabins and train cars have full kitchen or kitchenette, grill, and picnic tables, some have screened porches.

Facilities: Chariot Grill, breakfast and dinner Thurs.–Sun., hours vary by season; Orange Blossom Café; 8:30 A.M. to 3:00 P.M. Mon.–Sat. (closed on Sat. during winter); morning coffee in hotel dining room or delivered to hotel rooms; TV, pool table available in hotel recreation room; access to Lake LBJ.

Smoking: outdoors only.

Credit cards: V, MC, AE, D.

Parking: free on hotel property.

Accessibility: disabled access, some rooms are on ground floor.

Pets: not allowed.

Author's tips:—Personal watercraft and ski boats can make this narrow portion of Lake LBJ rough during busy weekends.—Children under 16 can't stay overnight in the hotel building, but they are welcome in the hotel's other accommodations. The train cars' bunk beds and cupolas with seating are a favorite with kids.

National Register of Historic Places: included in Kingsland Historic Railroad District.

Texas historical marker: yes

Texas Heritage Trails Program: Texas Hill Country Trail Region, www.txhillcountrytrail.com

Visitor information: Kingsland/Lake LBJ Chamber of Commerce, 2743 FM 1431, P.O. Box 465, Kingsland, TX 78639; 325-388-6211; kingslandchamber.org

picked art and antiques decorate the themed rooms. I found the Texas Writers Suite had a serene, study-like atmosphere. It was stocked with Texas periodicals and a glass-front bookcase full of Texana hardbacks. The 1901 Suite has boldly patterned wallpaper reminiscent of that era. All hotel rooms have doors that open onto both the front and back galleries. Screen doors display their original decorative hinges.

Other original historic touches include the hotel's telephone booth, still tucked underneath the stairs in the sunny lobby, and the "Train Bulletin" blackboard behind the front desk, where faded chalk announces that Engine 253 will be arriving at 12:10 P.M., headed west. The hotel's old potbellied stove is in the former dining room, where guests gather for morning coffee. The hotel's huge wood-fired cookstove, manufactured in St. Louis, remains in its kitchen, retrofitted to electric. The kitchen once prepared meals for lodgers as well as campers who phoned in their orders from Campa Pajama's wood-floored tents.

White-painted rockers, cane benches, and porch swings used for decades encourage guests to relax on the hotel's covered galleries and listen to birds singing in the large pecan, elm, and crape myrtle trees. The veg-etation muffles traffic noise on Farm to Market 1431 two blocks away and the occasional personal watercraft or ski boat on Lake LBJ behind the hotel.

The Antlers' 15-acre grounds have 1,500 feet of lakefront and include a peach, apple, and pear orchard, three fishing docks, and granite outcroppings worthy of geology field trips. Boat-owning guests use an adjacent public boat ramp and the hotel's boat hoist. The hotel loans its paddleboat, canoe, and fishing poles for puttering around on the narrow lake. A mixture of thick woods and large manicured lawns between the hotel and the water make the grounds perfect for playing bocce ball or croquet with equipment stored in the hotel's former ice house. I used the combination flashlight/nightlight in my room to take an evening stroll through the orchard.

Several eclectically decorated historic cabins and train cars on the grounds also provide lodging. Most of these have kitchenettes, screened porches, grills, and picnic tables.

There are plenty of restaurants and attractions in nearby Marble Falls and Llano, but they have stiff competition from the Antlers' peaceful compound, which also includes two shops, a café/deli, and the Chariot Grill, housed in the lovely restored 1890 Victorian house used in the movie the *Texas Chainsaw Massacre*.

Faust Hotel
New Braunfels ✾ 1929

Visitors to this hotel in New Braunfels' downtown admire
a number of features from its Depression-eve beginnings,
including an artistically crafted tile floor in its expansive lobby.

At the gala thrown to celebrate the opening of the Traveler's Hotel on Oct. 12, 1929, partyers dined on an eight-course meal. Ironically, the Gloom Chasers Orchestra provided music for the event, which was held only weeks before the stock market crashed. The ensuing Great Depression and its economic malaise prompted the hotel's builders, the New Braunfels Hotel Company, to put the new business into the hands of city leader Walter Faust. Faust was president of the bank that financed the venture, and the hotel had been built on his family's homestead. A few years after Faust's death in 1933 the hotel was renamed in his honor. Guests might want to take a close look at his portrait, which hangs in

Faust Hotel, New Braunfels. Photo by Liz Carmack.

the lobby, just in case they run into his restless spirit. Some claim they've recognized Faust's smartly dressed figure moving in and out of rooms and manning the hotel elevator.

Harvey Partridge Smith of San Antonio designed this four-story hotel for New Braunfel's town leaders. When it opened it was one of the few hotels in Texas to offer full private baths and was called one the finest small hotels in the southern United States. It survived the Depression to serve the growing convention and tourism industry in New Braunfels and welcomed drummers, providing them with sample rooms to show their wares.

From its start, the hotel has hosted the city's service, business, and social organizations, and its Grand Ballroom, with its original chande-

ESSENTIALS

Contact: 240 S. Seguin, New Braunfels, TX 78130; 830-625-7791; fax: 830-620-1530; www.fausthotel.com, innkeeper@fausthotel.com.

Rooms: 61 rooms and suites, all with private bath; walk-in shower, tub/shower combination; full, king, and queen beds; two-room Ambassador Suite has a king bed, and a marble-topped wet bar; two-room Honeymoon Suite has queen bed and two full baths.

Rates: $–$$, includes continental breakfast.

Room amenities: phone, TV; hair dryer, iron and ironing board available upon request; free wi-fi.

Facilities: Faust Brewing Co., 4:30 P.M. to midnight Mon.–Sat.; group space for up to 250.

Smoking: outdoors.

Credit cards: V, MC, D, AE.

Parking: free in hotel lot.

Accessibility: disabled access, elevator.

Pets: not allowed.

Author's tips:—Naeglin's Bakery, 129 S. Seguin, is one block from the hotel and features German and Czech pastries such as sausage and cheese *kolaches* and flaky butterfly rolls stuffed with cinnamon apples.—The Sophienburg Museum, 401 W. Coll St., displays hundreds of artifacts from New Braunfels's past.—The Visit Historic Downtown New Braunfels walking tour brochure is available at the hotel and the city's chamber of commerce. The Faust and more than 40 homes, businesses, and other buildings are featured.

National Register of Historic Places: yes

Texas historical marker: yes

Texas Heritage Trails Program: Texas Hill Country Trail, www.txhillcountrytrail.com

Visitor information: New Braunfels Chamber of Commerce, P.O. Box 311417, New Braunfels, TX 78131; 800-572-2626, 830-625-2385; www.nbcham.org

liers, continues to be the scene of many weddings. During the 1940s it became known as the Honeymoon Hotel because many of its guests were newly wed soldiers stationed in San Antonio with their brides.

The hotel, built of reinforced concrete with ornamental stonework and brick, has experienced periods of neglect followed by renovation over the years. Luckily, the original features in its lobby and the ceiling fans and steel casement windows in the guest rooms survived through changing ownership. These appealing links to its past are complemented by the 1930s-era decor, which includes many antiques and features old family photos from the owners and photos of early New Braunfels.

For me, the hotel's single most impressive original feature is its colorful tile floor in the spacious lobby. The beautiful teal, rose, gold, and black tiles feature designs arranged to resemble a carpet. The floor is said to be the work of an unknown Mexican artisan from San Antonio. The black

iron ceiling fans and light fixtures, brass sconces, and built-in phone booth are also original to the lobby, which now includes a dining area serving the hostelry's complimentary continental breakfast. Visitors can also sit on the hotel's shady, small front patio next to a wall-mounted fountain.

The hotel is one block from the town square, in the heart of New Braunfels' downtown. The adjacent neighborhoods are filled with a number of Victorian homes featuring wraparound porches and gingerbread detail. A few miles away are several attractions, including the Gruene Historic District, the Museum of Texas Handmade Furniture, Natural Bridge Caverns, and Schlitterbahn Waterpark Resort. The town celebrates its German heritage during the annual ten-day Wurstfest, where German food and beer are the star attractions. But guests at the Faust can enjoy home-brewed German-style beer year-round at the hotel's micro-brew pub, the Faust Brewery.

Prince Solms Inn

New Braunfels ⚜ 1898

This hotel, named for New Braunfels' founder, holds true to its heritage with Victorian decor and offers guests a spa, home-cooked breakfasts, and a basement piano bar.

A number of New Braunfels hotels provided lodging to stagecoach and rail travelers arriving in this manufacturing and shipping center at the turn of the twentieth century. The town had flour mills and wool and cotton textile factories and was connected by telegraph and rail lines with Austin and San Antonio.

The Prince Solms Inn is the only hostelry that remains open from that era. Originally named the Eggeling Hotel, it was renamed the Comal Hotel after New Braunfels' Comal springs and river. German immigrant Christian Herry built the two-story brick building for hotelier Emilie Eggeling, who had owned the town's Plaza Hotel. Carriage drivers collected drummers and other travelers at the depot a few blocks away and delivered them to the hotel. It was common at that time for hotels to provide sample rooms for drummers to display their goods and take orders, and no doubt the Eggeling Hotel had such a room. The Eggeling family welcomed guests until 1919, when they leased the building for a time for use as a sanatorium and hospital. In the early 1950s, the family sold it, and the new owners reopened the

Prince Solms Inn, New Braunfels. Photo by Liz Carmack.

ESSENTIALS

Contact: 295 E. San Antonio St., New Braunfels, TX 78130; 800-625-9169; 830-625-9169; fax: 830-625-2220; www.princesolmsinn.com, princesolmsinn@msn.com
Rooms: 10 rooms and suites, all with private bath in main hotel; 3 rooms in historic feed store and guest cottage also available; claw-foot tub, walk-in shower, tub/shower combination; twin, full, queen, and king beds.
Rates: $$, includes full breakfast.
Room amenities: TV, iron and ironing board; hair dryer available upon request; some rooms include a kitchenette or full kitchen; one has a washer and dryer.
Facilities: phone in parlor; Uptown Piano Bar, 4 P.M. to midnight Mon.–Fri., 4 P.M. to 1 A.M. Sat., 7 P.M. to midnight Sun.; morning coffee in downstairs hallway, spa.

Smoking: bar and patio.
Credit cards: V, MC, AE, D.
Parking: free in hotel lot or on street.
Accessibility: rooms available on ground floor.
Pets: not allowed.
Author's tips:—Children must be 14 or older to stay in original hotel building.—Book early for lodging during New Braunfels' ten-day Wurstfest celebration, held each November.
National Register of Historic Places: yes
Texas historical marker: yes
Texas Heritage Trails Program: Texas Hill Country Trail, www.txhillcountrytrail.com
Visitor information: New Braunfels Chamber of Commerce, P.O. Box 311417, New Braunfels, TX 78131; 800-572-2626, 830-625-2385; www.nbcham.org

hotel as the Prince Solms Inn, named for New Braunfels' founder, Prince Carl of Solms-Braunfels, Germany.

Today the hotel's decor holds true to its turn-of-the-century roots and German heritage. Photographs of the Eggelings hang in the downstairs hallway. The wood-floored parlor features a portrait of Prince Solms, period settees, and an 1879 Stieff piano. The chandeliered entrance hallway has a cheery black-and-white diamond-patterned linoleum floor. Above is a glass cupola thought to be original to the hotel. Although

the Prince Solms has central heating and air-conditioning, the cupola's windows are opened on mild days to encourage breezes through the building, just as they were before the advent of air-conditioning.

Guests are welcomed to their rooms with packages of pretzels and cookies, and they share a full breakfast and conversation each morning at a long table in the formal dining room behind the parlor. The rotating menu of home-cooked dishes includes sausage pie, stuffed French toast, muffins, and cream cheese eggs.

All the Victorian-style guest rooms are filled with period antiques, and most are on the second floor. Two suites on the first floor are named for Prince Solms and his wife, Sophie, who some say may haunt the hotel. Some guests have claimed to see a ghostly female figure in Sophie's room. Each of the remaining rooms takes its name from the wallpaper pattern decorating its walls, such as Songbird, Rose, and Peony. Windows are dressed with shutters or mini-blinds and drapes.

In addition, the hotel also offers three ground-floor accommodations with private baths in a former feed store, circa 1860, across the hotel's shady brick patio and in the two-room 1852 Klein House behind the inn. Texas country style best describes the feed store rooms, which have pine paneling, floors, and furnishings accented by longhorn skulls, spurs, and other Texas-themed pieces. Each room has a private, simply furnished courtyard. The cottage features lace curtains, a quilt-topped bed, and a mixture of antique and modern furnishings.

The hotel's brick patio hosts wedding parties and receptions, and accommodates the overflow of guests and locals visiting the hotel's Uptown Piano Bar for its regular live music. This cozy basement venue, popular with locals, has seating at antique tables and a conversation nook outfitted with comfortable sofas.

The Great Escape Bath Haus Spa in the hotel's carriage house offers services ranging from facials and ear candling to massage therapy by appointment.

New Braunfels attractions include the Schlitterbahn Waterpark Resort, the Sophienburg Museum and Archives, and 196-acre Landa Park, site of Comal Springs. The town has a number of outfitters that provide tubes, canoes, and rafts for enjoying the Guadalupe River, and on the northern edge of town is Gruene Hall, billed as Texas' oldest operating dance hall.

Rocksprings Hotel

Rocksprings ⚜ 1916

This modest hotel in the Hill Country's highest town once sheltered the sick during the 1918–19 influenza epidemic and the homeless after a 1927 tornado, and today it serves deer hunters and wildlife watchers.

After a tornado ripped through Rocksprings in 1927, few of the town's buildings were left standing, but the Balentine Hotel was one of them. Although the storm damaged the hotel's second-floor galleries, the modest two-story structure on the Edwards County courthouse square survived to shelter some of the homeless until they could rebuild. Ninety years later, hunters, bat watchers, and other nature lovers are frequent guests at what is now dubbed the Rocksprings Hotel.

Jesse Walter Gilmer built the hotel in 1916. Originally called the Gilmer Hotel, its dining room served Rocksprings residents, a few of whom lived at the hotel, and short-term guests, such as drummers, who made regular monthly or weekly sales stops on their way through this sparsely populated county. Gilmer and his wife, Inez, housed influenza patients at the hotel during the 1918–19 epidemic, with Inez seeing to it that the sick remembered to take medicines prescribed by the town's doctor.

In 1918 the Balentine family purchased the hotel and owned it for several decades. Mildred Williams, a Rocksprings native, recalls that the Balentines served diners family style

Rocksprings Hotel, Rocksprings. Photo by Kevin Stillman/TxDOT.

ESSENTIALS

Contact: 200 W. Austin, Rocksprings, TX 78880; 830-683-4212; fax: 830-683-2695

Rooms: 10 rooms, all with private bath; claw-foot tub, tub-shower combo, walk-in shower; king, queen, full, twin beds.

Rates: $–$$

Room amenities: phones in some rooms, TV; hair dryer, iron and ironing board available upon request.

Facilities: group space for up to 20 people with one month's notice.

Smoking: designated rooms.

Credit cards: V, MC, AE, D.

Parking: free on street.

Accessibility: no, but several rooms on first floor.

Pets: yes, crated and with advance notice, $20 deposit.

Author's tips:—Stop by the Hen House Café, 105 W. Main, for soups, salads, and a slice of homemade pie.—It's best to make reservations a few months in advance for the week leading up to the community's popular Fourth of July Rodeo and the August Old Settlers Reunion in Camp Wood or during deer season.

National Register of Historic Places: no

Texas historical marker: yes

Texas Heritage Trails Program: Texas Pecos Trail Region, www.texaspecostrail.com

Visitor information: Visitor's Center for Devil's Sinkhole State Natural Area, 101 N. Sweeten St., Rocksprings, TX 78880; 830-683-2287; www.devilssinkholetx.com

---

around a single table that always included a heaping bowl of mashed potatoes at one end and a steaming bowl of beans at the other. Williams remembers that teachers lodged in the hotel in the 1930s, as did children from area ranches who would board during the school week to avoid the long round-trip into town each day. Youngsters who came into Rocksprings on Saturday to see a movie would use the hotel phone to call home for a ride. Today the hotel's built-in telephone booth remains off the lobby, sans phone.

New owners bought the hotel in 1999, about a decade after it had closed. Although the hotel was damaged by fire in 2000, today ten remodeled rooms are available. Two apartments are also available. All have private baths. Many of the hotel's original fixtures and furnishings have been lost, but a few of the cast iron bathtubs remain, as do the pressed-tin ceilings in the first and second floor hallways. The guest room doors still have their transoms. Accommodations are simply furnished and fairly utilitarian. Most furnishings are modern, and guest room floors are either painted hardwood or carpeted. Windows hold air conditioners and are covered by mini-blinds.

Offerings in the hotel's small gift shop off the lobby include colorful mohair scarves. Before Congress ended a long-standing mohair subsidy, Rocksprings was called the "Angora Goat Capital of the World." The hotel no longer operates a restaurant, but the managers will gladly describe Rocksprings' somewhat limited dining options.

During hunting season, the hotel is a popular headquarters for deer hunters with leases on area ranches.

Hunters can tote in unloaded guns if they are locked in a case. Guests cycling around this highest point of the Texas Hill Country (elevation 2,410 feet) are encouraged to wheel bicycles into guest rooms. From April to October, crowds arrive to visit the community's largest tourist attraction, Devil's Sinkhole State Natural Area, where roughly three million Mexican free-tailed bats take flight each evening. The hotel also often hosts those in town for family reunions and weddings or religious meetings at area churches.

Panhandle Plains

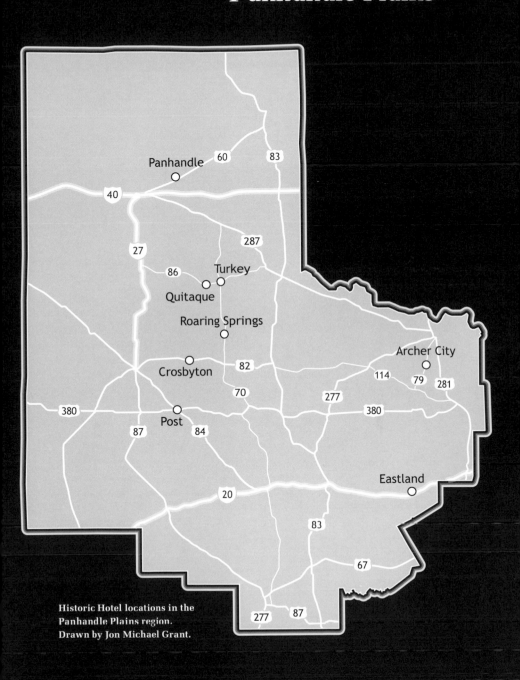

Panhandle 60 83

40

27

287

86 Turkey

Quitaque

Roaring Springs

Archer City

Crosbyton 82

114 79 281

70

380 277 380

Post

87 84

Eastland

20

83

67

Historic Hotel locations in the
Panhandle Plains region.
Drawn by Jon Michael Grant.

277 87

Spur Hotel

Archer City ⚜ 1929

Hunters of books and wild game, patrons of live music at the Royal Theater, and film buffs tracking scenes from The Last Picture Show *find this Depression survivor a convenient headquarters.*

The Spur Hotel originally opened for business on this windswept plain in 1929 as the Andrews Hotel, probably to serve travelers doing business at the area's cattle ranches and oil fields. In the mid-1920s more than four hundred oil wells were within a 13-mile radius of Archer City. The town also had two railroad lines and was a milling and market point for wheat and other grains.

Will Andrews, one of the largest landowners in Archer County, financed the three-story brick hotel's construction by Shamburger Lumber Company. Andrews had interests in cattle, oil and mining, and stock in the People's Exchange Bank in Archer City. Like many others, he was financially ruined after the stock market crashed the year the hotel opened.

The few details known about Andrews and his hotel have been passed along by area old-timers, since little documentation of the hotel's history exists. A framed black-and-white photo from the 1957 Archer County Rodeo Association Parade attests to a time when the hotel had a third name. Cowgirls on horseback carry flags, and band members in western shirts, hats, and boots march down Center Street past an "Archer Hotel" sign. By 1966, when it closed, it was

Spur Hotel, Archer City. Photo by Liz Carmack.

ESSENTIALS

Contact: P.O. Box 1207, 110 N. Center, Archer City, TX 76351; 940-574-2501; fax: 940-574-2506; www.thespur hotel.com, abby@abbya.com

Rooms: 11 rooms and 1 suite, all with private bath; tub/shower combination, sinks with separate taps for hot and cold water; queen, full, and twin beds.

Rates: $$

Room amenities: coffee maker; hair dryer, iron and ironing board available upon request, free wi-fi.

Facilities: phone and TV available for guests; group space for up to 24.

Smoking: outdoors only.

Credit cards: V, MC.

Parking: free on street.

Accessibility: all rooms are on second and third floors and accessed by stairs only.

Pets: not allowed.

Author's tips:—The view from rooms on the west and south sides of the hotel are the best, but these rooms are also the noisiest since they face the street.—Guests should book early to reserve a room on nights when there is a performance at the Royal Theater, www.royaltheater.com.—Wildcat Cafe, 107 N. Center St., serves breakfast and lunch across from the hotel. If the local fare doesn't satisfy, try Sevis Burritos, 907 Denver, in Wichita Falls.

National Register of Historic Places: no

Texas historical marker: no

Texas Heritage Trails Program: Texas Lakes Trail Region, www.texaslakestrail.com

Visitor information: Archer City Visitor Center, P.O. Box 877, 101 N. Center, Archer City, TX 76351; 940-574-2489; www.archercitytx.com

known as the Spur. During the next couple of decades the building was home to several businesses, including a domino parlor, a leather goods shop, and the *Archer County News.*

A local ranching family totally remodeled the Spur and reopened it with twelve guest rooms in 1991. About that same time, Archer County native and author Larry McMurtry moved his Booked Up bookstore from Washington, D.C., to Archer City. The four stores around the quiet Archer County courthouse square are filled with several hundred thousand vol-

umes on everything from anthropology and poetry to western pulp fiction. The inventory includes many rare and out-of-print volumes. The opening of Booked Up and the reopening of the Royal Theater in 2000, thirty-five years to the day after it burned down, have rejuvenated this quiet ranching community and brought visitors from around the world to stay at the Spur.

The Royal Theater was featured in the movie *The Last Picture Show,* which was based on McMurtry's novel of the same name. Only the box office and parts of the original stone walls still stand, but a new 245-seat theater is adjacent to the original building. The Royal Theater presents musical performances and plays throughout the year, including a summer musical and a one-act dinner theater featuring local talent.

The Spur is open mostly on weekends when hunters arrive in Archer City to stalk game on area ranches or track esoteric titles in McMurtry's bookstores. I was the only guest during a midweek visit and was given the key to the front door to come and go as I pleased. The hotel also hosts writers' conferences, family reunions, and other small events.

The Spur's twelve carpeted rooms are all on the second and third floors, and all have private baths. The decor is mostly contemporary western, with individual touches in each room, such as colorful quilts and black-and-white photographs of the area. Black iron headboards and ironwork on the front desk were handcrafted by the owner. None of the early hotel's furnishings remain, but the pressed-tin ceiling in the lobby and wood floors in the hallways are original. The scored concrete floor from the old coffee shop is still visible on the hotel's first floor.

Archer City businesses around the square close early, and many keep limited hours. If there is no show at the Royal Theater, the best bets for evening entertainment are settling into the hotel's small parlor, with its native sandstone fireplace, for reading or television watching. Larry McMurtry himself has lamented Archer City's lack of restaurants. The hotel provides a list of local eateries as well as those in Wichita Falls, twenty-five miles away.

Smith House

Crosbyton ❄ 1921

This south Panhandle Plains hotel is a well-kept secret, but guests who discover it return for the relaxed atmosphere, quiet surroundings, and the many features that remain from its past.

The Smith House looks like just another craftsman-style stucco home on a quiet street lined with houses one block from the Crosby County courthouse. But once inside, visitors see that this is instead a lovely hotel with a sunny parlor and expansive dining room floored in yellow pine. The hotel's kitchen was once well known for the delicious meals prepared by its long-time proprietors, J. Frank Smith and his wife, Minnie.

The Smiths had plenty of experience feeding and sheltering people. In 1901 they arrived in Crosby County to manage a ranch house and fed ranch hands in nearby Blanco Canyon for the C. B. Livestock Company, which operated the N–Ranch. They moved into town in 1919 to operate

the Crosbyton Inn until it was torn down. The Smiths then had Dave Weller build the wood shiplap Smith House as a combination boarding-house and hotel. It opened in 1921 and was later stuccoed and expanded with east and west wings. The town's teachers were long-term guests, and overnight lodgers included drummers and cotton buyers.

The Smiths' meals included produce from their garden and area farms, and their menu often featured pheasant, quail, and prairie chicken contributed by lodgers after a successful hunt. On weekends, chairs and tables were pushed aside, and area residents danced to a small orchestra or the $350 player piano the Smiths purchased on credit from

Smith House, Crosbyton. Photo by Liz Carmack.

Brook Mays & Co. in Dallas. The framed receipt for their last $25 payment, made in 1929, hangs in the hotel's stairwell. The piano sits in one corner of the parlor and, except for a broken bellows, is well preserved.

Across the room a hotel register from 1946 is cradled in an oak stand. Almost all the hotel's registers remain, and one is always available for guests to leaf through. Ads on the stand for area businesses include the matter-of-fact pitch for Dee's Barber Shop, which proclaims, "Sanitary expert barbers. Ask the hotel about us."

Mr. Smith died in 1953, and Mrs. Smith continued to operate the hotel until her death in 1961 at age eighty-four. Then a niece took over the operations for a time, and the inn eventually closed. The building was reopened briefly in the 1980s as a restaurant and teahouse.

New owners undertook a major renovation in 1989, turning several of the room's closets into private bathrooms. The former owners' first-floor quarters were also converted into what is now the Honeymoon Suite. The remaining ten rooms are all upstairs. Six have private baths with claw-foot tubs or walk-in showers.

ESSENTIALS

Contact: 306 W. Aspen, Crosbyton, TX 79322; 806-675-2178; smithhouse bnb.samsbiz.com, smithhousebnb@ valornet.com

Rooms: 11 rooms, including 1 suite; most have private bath; claw-foot tub, walk-in shower; king, queen, full, and twin beds; Honeymoon Suite has a private entrance.

Rates: $–$$, includes full breakfast.

Room amenities: hair dryer, iron and ironing board available upon request; Honeymoon Suite has TV.

Facilities: phone for guests; big-screen TV, videos, stereo in den; morning coffee in dining room; hotel kitchen serves lunch 11:30 A.M. to 2 P.M. on Wed., Thurs., and Fri.; meals for groups and special dinners for couples can be arranged in advance; group space for up to 35.

Smoking: outdoors only.

Credit cards: V, MC.

Parking: free on street.

Accessibility: one room is on ground floor.

Pets: not allowed.

Author's tips:—There aren't many choices for dinner in Crosbyton, but catfish and burgers with a view can be had at the White River Lake Marina, 20 miles south.

National Register of Historic Places: no

Texas historical marker: no

Texas Heritage Trails Program: Texas Plains Trail Region, www.texasplainstrail.com

Visitor information: Crosbyton Chamber of Commerce, 114 W. Aspen, Crosbyton, TX 79322; 806-675-2261

Each upstairs room has its original louvered door, which is only two-thirds the size of the room's solid door. Before air-conditioning, guests could open their windows and leave their solid door open and the louvered door closed, which maintained a bit of privacy while encouraging a breeze. Now central heat and air-conditioning are pumped through the original ductwork that moved hot air to rooms from a coal-fired basement boiler. The black ornamental iron grates over the air vents remain in most rooms.

Most of the hotel's original furnishings—dressers, chairs, and wooden four-poster and iron beds—are distributed throughout the neat rooms and common areas. The hotel is a thoughtfully arranged mix of old and new furnishings that keep guests' comfort in mind. Shelves for personal toiletries are provided next to the original wall-mount sinks, which have separate hot and cold taps, and next to the claw-foot tubs. Color-coordinated towels, bath salts, and bath gel are provided. Some of the rooms' bedspreads, paint, and curtains mix pastels and white for a more feminine look without being too frilly. Other rooms are decidedly more masculine and better suit the repeat guests who visit Crosbyton during hunting season. The hotel also hosts lodgers in town to visit family, attend a retreat, or enjoy a weekend escape.

The only key I received during my visit was to the front door. I locked myself in my room that night with the hook and eye lock on the louvered door and a chain lock on the solid room door—there are no other locks. Although the hotel's atmosphere felt safe, I was a little uncomfortable not being able to lock my room door when I left for an afternoon of sightseeing. The owners, a mother and daughter from Australia, say they've never had any trouble with this arrangement.

Owners Sande Smyth and Sue Bentley conduct mind-body retreats for pregnant women and weekend workshops such as Soul Connection, where attendees use meditation and dream work to improve self-awareness and clarify their life's purpose. Hotel packages include course registration, lodging, and meals.

Smyth and Bentley serve a tasty breakfast buffet of homemade biscuits, fresh fruit, eggs, and bacon or sausage each morning. Guests can help themselves to coffee and check out the tidy, roomy kitchen and its original stainless-steel countertops and white-painted bead board cabinetry.

Fishing is popular at nearby White River Lake, and hunters are welcome at many area ranches and farms. Exhibits at the Crosby County Pioneer Museum, a few blocks from the hotel, showcase some of its more than forty-five thousand artifacts. Guided tours are offered of the Mt. Blanco Fossil Museum nearby, which shows off ongoing fossil restoration and plaster casting work in addition to its exhibits.

Eastland Hotel
Eastland ⚜ 1918

This hotel, born of an oil boom, has been lovingly restored and makes an ideal headquarters from which to explore Eastland's beautiful historic town square, public art, and county history museum.

An impressively high 14-foot ceiling of beautiful pressed tin grabs the attention of those who call on the Eastland Hotel today. The tin dates to the 1918 building's opening, when the Stanley Café and the Princess Theater sat side by side on the ground floor and the Stanley Hotel occupied the second and third floors.

The hotel's current owners, a couple of former Navy pilots, found the tin when they removed a modern false ceiling during an extensive renovation in the mid-1990s. The overhaul took more than a year and included painstaking attention to detail, such as scraping old paint from the ceiling using flat-head screwdrivers and stripping paint from the hotel's knot-

Eastland Hotel, Eastland. Photo by Liz Carmack.

ESSENTIALS

Contact: 112 N. Lamar, Eastland TX 76448; 254-629-8397; fax: 254-629-8994, www.theeastlandhotel.com

Rooms: 8 rooms, all with private bath; tub/shower combination, walk-in shower, claw-foot tub, Jacuzzi tub; king beds; Dallas room has full kitchen.

Rates: $–$$, includes extended continental breakfast.

Room amenities: TV, coffee maker; hair dryer, iron and ironing board available upon request, free wi-fi.

Facilities: guest phone available in second floor sitting area; outdoor pool.

Smoking: outdoors only.

Credit cards: MC, V, AE, D.

Parking: free on street.

Accessibility: elevator.

Pets: yes, no fee.

Author's Tips:—The 1928 Connellee Hotel around the corner has been majestically restored to offer event facilities on its first floor and eighth-floor rooftop garden.—Café Rico, 1013 West Main St., offers tasty Mexican food in a friendly atmosphere.

National Register of Historic Places: no

Texas historical marker: no

Texas Heritage Trails Program: Texas Forts Trail Region, www.texasfortstrail.com

Visitor information: Eastland Chamber of Commerce, 209 W. Main, Eastland, TX 76448; 877-2-OLD-RIP, 254-629-2332; eastlandchamber.com, ecofc@eastland.net

less old-growth pine woodwork. The owners' efforts dovetailed with Eastland's goals to preserve and promote the community's historic architecture and heritage.

The discovery of oil in nearby Ranger in 1917 heralded an oil boom that dramatically affected the development of Eastland and area towns. Eastland's population increased fourfold between 1910 and 1920 to more than 3,300 people and peaked in 1930 with 4,600 inhabitants. Hoping to profit from the affluent times, local attorney Cyrus Frost hired architect and family member Snow Frost to design the building that houses the Eastland.

A panoramic photo of the town at the time the hotel was being built shows a number of office buildings under construction. Some speculate that Frost initially intended to open an office building and at the last minute decided it would be a hotel. One clue that this might be correct is the design of the original guest room doors. Each knotless old-growth pine door has a large glass panel, like those found on office doors of that era. The glass panels are etched with a frost-crystal design, perhaps a nod to the owner and architect's family name.

The hotel originally had thirty-four rooms with ten shared baths.

Over the years it's also been known as the Maverick Hotel, the Johnson Hotel, and the Rawson Building. For a time, a pool hall/recreation center occupied the former theater, and the city's Greyhound bus station operated out of the old café.

The small rooms were combined to create eight spacious guest rooms with private baths on the second floor. Each is named for a Texas town. The owners' living quarters occupy the third floor. Each guest room is carpeted and has an antique armoire stocked with hangers, but most of the furnishings are an eclectic mix of more modern pieces. The walls are dotted with old photos of the owner's family members. One of the owner's grandmothers sewed many of the floral print bed skirts and matching valances in the pastel painted rooms.

Two of the rooms on the second floor look out on the air shaft between the hotel and the Majestic Theater next door, but the facing wall has been enlivened with murals. The Austin room has five large windows and a large bathroom with both a claw-foot tub and a walk-in shower. The Dallas room is the biggest and has a full kitchen and Jacuzzi tub.

Guests help themselves to the fresh fruit, juices, milk, cereal, frozen waffles, and other breakfast items in the kitchenette off the second-floor hallway. The cupboards offer ice buckets and champagne glasses for those who bring their own bubbly.

The hotel's lobby features its original floor of small white hexagonal tiles and offers guests a number of sitting areas. Visitors can relax outdoors around a small pool in the hotel's private courtyard.

There is plenty to see within a few blocks of the hotel, starting with a visit to the Eastland County Museum in the beautifully restored First State Bank of Eastland building. Another of the community's many restoration projects, the Majestic Theater, is next door to the hotel. Originally opened in 1919 as the Connellee Theater by Eastland's founding father C. U. Connellee, it shows first-run films on weekends and hosts touring acts and local community theater performances. Guides to these and other historic Eastland buildings and to its public art are available at the city's chamber of commerce on the town square.

A visit to Eastland would not be complete without a stop by the tomb of Old Rip in the Eastland County Courthouse. The legendary horned toad was encased in the cornerstone of an earlier courthouse and, as the tale goes, was found alive when removed thirty-one years later in 1928. He toured the country, making headlines and visiting president Calvin Coolidge.

Texan Hotel

Panhandle ⚓ 1926

This hotel, built during an oil boom, provides homey accommodations in a small prairie town that takes pride in its more than twenty state historical markers and an award-winning county history museum.

Travelers passing through the small town of Panhandle might disregard the green and white Texan Hotel sign in front of this small two-story hostelry and instead search for the familiar signage and predictable accommodations of a national hotel/motel chain. But if they choose cookie-cutter comforts over taking a chance on the unknown, they'll pass up a memorable experience. The Texan Hotel is modestly appointed and feels like it hasn't changed much since it hosted wildcatters, oil field workers, cowboys, and traveling salesmen, but the accommodations are filled with personality.

C. B. and Margaret Downs opened Hotel Downs in 1926 after oil was discovered in the area. Panhandle quickly grew from a small farming and ranching community of a few hundred to an oil field boomtown of 40,000. Major oil field supply houses headquartered in Panhandle because the Santa Fe Railway established a major terminal there. Oil well freight was unloaded in town by the ton and trucked north to Borger. This hotel and seven others opened in Panhandle to provide needed rooms, shared baths, and meals to workers. The Downs lost their hotel during the Great Depression. A subsequent

Texan Hotel, Panhandle. Photo by Liz Carmack.

ESSENTIALS

Contact: P.O. Box 216, 117 E. Broadway, Panhandle, TX 79068; 806-537-3372.
Rooms: 5 rooms, 3 share facilities with shower down the hall, 2 share adjoining facilities with claw-foot tub; full-size beds.
Rates: $, includes continental breakfast.
Room amenities: TV.
Facilities: house phone available in lobby, small refrigerator and microwave in upstairs hallway.
Smoking: outdoors only.
Credit cards: cash and check only.
Parking: free on street.
Accessibility: all rooms are on second floor, accessible by staircase only.
Pets: not allowed.

Author's tips:—Light sleepers might benefit from earplugs since trains pass two blocks from the hotel.—Take Texas 207 south from Panhandle for a scenic drive across Palo Duro Canyon.—The Buffalo Grass Steak House, 200 Main Street, is next door and offers sirloin, catfish, and sandwiches in an area where there are few options for eating out.
National Register of Historic Places: no
Texas historical marker: yes
Texas Heritage Trails Program: Texas Plains Trail Region, www.texasplainstrail.com
Visitor information: Panhandle Chamber of Commerce, P.O. Box 1021, Panhandle, TX 79068, 806-537-3517.

owner renamed it Texan Hotel in 1935, and as times changed after World War II, some of its rooms were remodeled to accommodate the need for furnished apartments. The hotel still rents apartments but continues to keep a handful of hotel rooms available to overnight lodgers.

Patrons staying here now use some of the same wooden furniture—a dresser here, a rocker there—from the early days of the hotel. Current owner Betty Rhynehart bought it in 1973 with her husband. She has supplemented the original furnishings with other period pieces, some of which came from one of Panhandle's closed old hotels. The Texan Hotel is

the only hostelry from the boomtown days still operating. The hotel has never shut its doors, and its owners have worked to retain its good reputation and old-fashioned feel, which is a source of pride for the community.

When I arrived in the small, wood-paneled lobby for my complimentary breakfast of sliced fresh fruit, a cinnamon roll, coffee, and juice, the hotel cat was dozing on the front desk next to a bowl of chocolates. Around the corner I found several Hotel Downs skeleton keys with their large room number tags hung next to portraits of Indians and prairie landscapes, one of which was painted on a saw.

The hotel's five wallpapered guest

rooms are all upstairs, toward the front of the brick building. While they are not plush, they are comfortable and clean. Three of them share a shower and toilet down the hall, while the other two rooms share a claw-foot bathtub and toilet. Most of the rooms have their original sinks, with separate hot and cold taps. Framed copies of the original Hotel Downs "Rules and Regulations" advise guests not to drink, gamble, or spit on the floor.

In an ingenious arrangement, the hallway ceiling has been lowered and ductwork installed to provide central heat and air-conditioning through the old transoms above the room doors. I controlled the temperature of my room by using the original hardware along the door trim to raise and lower the transom.

Most overnight guests today are en route to a destination other than Panhandle, but the town's Square House Museum around the corner from the hotel is a good excuse to change travel plans. This facility has been amassing its collection of historic buildings and exhibits since 1967. The American Association of Museums cited it as one of the best small museums in the country. Visitors can learn about area wildlife and early farm and ranch life, see a homesteader's dugout home, and view exhibits displaying early Panhandle businesses.

Hotel Garza

Post ⚜ 1916

Lubbock residents retreat to this railroad hotel and take advantage of its dinner-theater packages in a town that was founded at the turn of the century by cereal magnate C. W. Post.

Before its rebirth as a popular destination in the early 1990s, this two-story building, then known as Matt's Hotel, had become derelict. It was so spooky that neighborhood kids dared each other to enter the building and snatch a book of hotel matches. It is a miracle the building didn't burn to the ground during its low point in the 1970s and '80s. A few permanent residents claimed the first floor, but its rooms were largely unoccupied. The state fire marshal had declared the upstairs, strewn with extension cords, off-limits.

Amid the detritus and spray-paint-covered walls, Janice and Jim Plummer saw the building's potential and undertook a painstaking renovation after purchasing it in 1991. Since its rehabilitation by the Plummers, the Hotel Garza has become a popular getaway for Lubbock residents and a pleasant surprise for travelers seeking an overnight rest stop in the sparsely populated Panhandle.

Michigan industrialist and cereal magnate C. W. Post's purchase of more than 200,000 acres in the Panhandle during the early 1900s and his subsequent colonization and founding of Post is a fascinating story, one the town is proud to tell. Until his suicide in 1914, Post was involved in virtually every aspect of this town's development, from installing its wa-

Hotel Garza, Post. Photo by Liz Carmack.

ter and sewage systems to building homes and surveying, outfitting, and selling area farms to settlers. The hotel is just one reminder of the town's ambitious founder, who, even after his death, was connected to its construction.

In 1915, when J. D. Hume and his wife, Annie Bell, wanted to construct a commercial building on the town's Main Street, they had C. W. Post's architect, identified in records only as Gilmore, design it. Post's contractor, U U Company, built the building, and the Scottish stonemasons who'd worked on numerous Post buildings laid the tan brick that clad the hotel's exterior.

The Hume Building opened in 1916, with guest rooms upstairs and a variety store, post office, and dining room on the first floor. After the 1930s, as ownership changed hands, the hotel slowly declined until the Plummers rescued it and renamed it Hotel Garza, the name it carried during the 1940s and '50s.

The hotel's wood-floored lobby merges with a large dining room. Hanging from the 14-foot-high pressed-tin ceiling are two massive turned wood and brass antique

ESSENTIALS

Contact: 302 E. Main Street, Post, TX 79356; 866-495-2880, 806-495-3962; fax: 806-495-3962; www.hotelgarza.com, info@hotel garza.com

Rooms: 11 rooms and suites, all with private bath; bathtub, walk-in shower, tub/shower combination; king, queen, and twin beds.

Rates: $$, includes full breakfast on weekends and extended continental breakfast on weekdays.

Room amenities: phone, TV, hair dryer, iron and ironing board, free wi-fi, DVD/video player upon request.

Facilities: complimentary refreshments, microwave, and refrigerator available on each floor; facilities for groups up to 25.

Smoking: outdoors only.

Credit cards: V, MC, AE, D.

Parking: free on street.

Accessibility: disabled access, rooms on ground floor.

Pets: not allowed.

Author's tips:—Bring earplugs for night trains passing a few blocks from the hotel.—Holly's, 615 S. Broadway, is an authentic drive-in restaurant that also has a dining room.—Ruby Lane Books, 127 E. Main St., carries new and used books, including rare titles.

National Register of Historic Places: no

Texas historical marker: no

Texas Heritage Trails Program: Texas Plains Trail Region, www.texasplainstrail.com

Visitor information: Post Commerce and Tourism Bureau, 104 S. Broadway, Post, TX 79356; 806-495-3461

chandeliers that the stunned owners bought at auction for ten dollars. Antiques are placed throughout the hotel, and collectibles such as old hardback books, porcelain figurines, and old photographs adorn walls and surfaces.

The eleven individually decorated guest rooms and suites have private baths. One room's bath is situated across the hall. Bathroom night-lights add a comforting touch. Some guest rooms have a simple country decor, including patchwork quilts and antique dressers, tables, and beds from the hotel's early days. Other rooms feature a bold designer's touch. The Victorian Suite was designed around a circa 1929 bathtub, pedestal sink, and toilet—all in matching purple and rescued from a local 1920s-era home. The bedroom features heavy curtains, lace sheers, and deep purple wallpaper. A chandelier adds unexpected drama to the large bathroom. The hotel is filled with original art, including a desert scene in oils hanging in one guest room that, according to legend, was an artist's payment decades ago for his lodging.

The Hotel Garza's Theatre Package combines one night's stay, a home-cooked dinner from its kitchen, tickets to a show at the Garza Theater, and breakfast the next morning. The hotel offers dinner only on these nights or if arranged in advance for groups.

Guests can relax on the hotel's private patio to the sounds of a waterfall and Post's regular trains. Or they can curl up with a book, play a board game, or watch TV in a small mezzanine sitting area overlooking the dining room.

Post attractions include the Garza County Historical Museum, where the story of C. W. Post, his family, and the founding and development of this town are told through impressive exhibits. The O. S. Ranch Art Museum rotates exhibits from a private collection.

Arts and crafts lovers and antique hunters converge on the town one weekend a month for Post's Old Mill Trade Days. The event is held at the former Postex Cotton Mills, which closed in the 1980s. In 1923 the mill turned out 1.2 million sheets and pillowcases and employed hundreds of Post residents.

Sportsman Lodge

Quitaque ⚜ 1929

This former railroad hotel has a colorful Tex-Mex style decor and serves hunters, outdoorsy types, and lovers of western swing in this tiny Panhandle community.

When it was sold at auction in 2002 for $1,500, the two-story Sportsman Lodge had a large hole in its roof, collapsed ceilings, and was filled with debris. It was a deteriorating eyesore one block north of Main Street in this tiny farming and ranching community.

The hotel's new owners, a pair of cousins from Amarillo, recruited the help of relatives and spent weekends and vacations working to restore the redbrick hotel. Out came piles of dirt, books, plaster, and old draperies. They replumbed the gas lines and patched the roof. By 2005 the partially renovated hotel reopened to patrons of the annual Bob Wills Day Festival in nearby Turkey. The hotel is now open intermittently as restoration continues. Fifteen guest rooms are available, but guests must be prepared to share three bathrooms until the remaining facilities are replumbed.

The work has turned Sportsman Lodge into a simply appointed hostelry whose Tex-Mex decor mixes bright colors with hunting and cowboy themes. The walls are hung with a mishmash of prints acquired from antique and collectible shops, a few

Sportsman Lodge, Quitaque. Photo by Liz Carmack.

ESSENTIALS

Contact: 100 Jones, Quitaque, TX 79255; 806-455-1200, 806-676-8352; sportsmanquitaque@yahoo.com
Rooms: 15 rooms, all either share an adjoining bath or a bath down the hall or downstairs; deep iron tub, tub/shower combination, walk-in shower; queen, full, twin beds.
Rates: $
Room amenities: hair dryer, iron and ironing board available upon request.
Facilities: TVs in guest lounge and lobby, morning coffee in kitchen; group facilities for up to 25.
Smoking: designated.
Credit cards: cash and check only.
Parking: free on street and in hotel lot.

Accessibility: some rooms are on ground floor.
Pets: yes, but must make arrangements in advance; no fee.
Author's tips:—Sportsman Restaurant, 114 W. Main, is well known for its steaks, hamburgers, and chicken fried steaks.
National Register of Historic Places: no
Texas historical marker: no
Texas Heritage Trails Program: Texas Plains Trail Region, www.texasplainstrail.com
Visitor information: Quitaque Chamber of Commerce, P.O. Box 487, Quitaque, TX 79255; 806-455-1456; www.quitaque.org

pieces of original western art, and mounted fish and game. Flashy red, periwinkle blue, and a shade called Margarita Yellow enliven the hotel's kitchen and two small dining rooms. Lodgers are treated like extended family and are welcome to use the kitchen's old International Harvester refrigerator and Detroit Jewel stove.

The hotel retains its original hardwood floors throughout. Most have not been refinished, and some rooms' floors have been painted, adding to the hotel's rustic feel. The lobby has rough-textured plaster walls painted an adobe red and features a bearskin rug. Guests can relax in a small

parlor, which has one of the hotel's two TVs, or meditate in one of the two swings on the front porch. Porch sitters might have to make room for local amateur musicians, who have been known to drop by for an impromptu outdoor jam session.

Each of the hotel's fifteen guest rooms, named for a different member of the innkeeper's family, has a different, often bold, color scheme—from burgundy or red to tan or steel blue. Many of the walls have faux paint finishes or a rough plaster finish. Mexican blankets serve as curtains on some of the double-hung wooden windows. Individual touches such as handmade iron lamps and headboards, hand-embroidered pillows and quilts made by family members, and galvanized tin pails filled with guest towels add to the country feel. The well-worn antique dressers and brown iron beds used in most of the guest rooms were in the hotel at auction and are thought to be part of its original furnishings.

When the hotel opened in 1929, the local paper reported that the new eighteen-room hotel was modern and beautifully furnished. Each guest room had hot and cold running water, and six rooms had private baths. C. G. Higgins and his wife operated the hotel, originally called the Hotel Quitaque (pronounced "kitty kway"). A few months earlier, the first train had arrived in Quitaque. The community, which had existed since the turn of the century, was officially incorporated in 1927 on land that was once part of legendary cattleman Charles Goodnight's Quitaque Ranch. The train brought traveling salesmen, and although Quitaque already had at least one hotel, more accommodations were probably needed for the drummers and other travelers.

Local historian Robert W. Brown recalls living in the hotel when his parents managed it during the early 1960s. At that time the hotel housed a few locals in addition to overnight guests. Residents included a twelve-year-old boy who boarded while attending school and two women who waited tables at Cochran's Restaurant.

The rails that brought the initial customers to the hotel have since been removed, and a 64-mile stretch of former railway has been turned into the Caprock Canyons State Park Trailway. The trail passes a few blocks from the hotel and runs through a number of small communities and the 742-foot-long Clarity Tunnel, once the longest railroad tunnel in Texas.

Other patrons find the hotel convenient to local ranches that allow hunting and nearby Caprock Canyons State Park, where birding, hiking, biking, and horseback riding are popular. Cyclists can wheel their rides into rooms. Music lovers find the Sportsman Lodge one of the few hotels available in the area during the Bob Wills Day Festival, which is held the last Saturday in April in neighboring Turkey.

Travelers Inn
Roaring Springs ⚘ 1913

American cherry, walnut, maple, and oak floors and home-cooked breakfasts show off the owners' skills at this small former railroad hotel.

In 1912 the Quanah, Acme, and Pacific Railroad platted a town site on land that had originally been a camp on the Matador Ranch and then sold lots in anticipation of the arrival of rail service. The trains arrived the following year, bringing drummers, settlers, and other travelers to this small farming and ranching community, named Roaring Springs for the rushing waters to its south, site of an ancient camping ground. Although there is little documentation about the Travelers Inn's beginnings, it was likely built by the Q, A, & P to accommodate the new influx of visitors to Roaring Springs. The two-story brick

hotel was heated with coal-burning stoves. An early photograph of the box-shaped inn shows at least four tall chimneys punctuating the roof.

In 2000 the old hotel had been sitting empty for three decades. Plywood covered the windows, and the elements had taken their toll. The ambitious new owners said it was in such bad shape that they could stand on dirt where the first floor should have been and see sky through the damaged second floor and roof. The Herculean task of repairing the building included completely replumbing and rewiring the hotel and hanging new drywall. The owners, who once

Travelers Inn, Roaring Springs. Photo by Liz Carmack.

ran a hardwood floor installation and refinishing business, replaced all of the inn's floors with a beautiful mixture of oak, American cherry, maple, and walnut. The differing colors and grains form colorful mosaics in the hotel.

The original coal stoves are long gone, but the large well-worn oak kitchen cabinet with its tin countertop and built-in produce and flour bins is now a conversation piece in the hotel's kitchen. In the dining room, guests are treated to a filling breakfast of bacon, sausage, potatoes, eggs, biscuits, and gravy as part of their stay. Lodgers may find that they're sharing one of a handful of tables with other guests, or with local residents, who drop by for morning coffee and chitchat. Around 3 p.m. on most days, the city's mayor and other Roaring Springs locals arrive in the dining room for a cup of java and an informal roundtable. By making arrangements in advance, guests can also enjoy a home-prepared lunch or dinner. The owner's backyard barbecue has turned out its share of smoked pork chops and brisket.

ESSENTIALS

Contact: P.O. Box 146, 201 Broadway, Roaring Springs, TX 79256; 806-348-7304, 806-348-7285; www.travelersinnbandb.com, edith_daniell@hotmail.com
Rooms: 7 rooms, three with private bath, remaining rooms share facilities down the hall, all guest rooms have sinks; claw-foot tub, walk-in shower, tub/shower combination; queen, full, twin beds.
Rates: $–$$, includes full breakfast.
Room amenities: hair dryer, iron and ironing board available upon request; free wi-fi.
Facilities: guest phone available, two TVs, DVD and VHS library; microwave, fridge, and sink available on second floor; lunch and dinner available from hotel kitchen with advance notice.
Smoking: in common areas.

Credit cards: V, MC, AE, D, DC.
Parking: free on street.
Accessibility: disabled access, one room on ground floor, no elevator.
Pets: not allowed.
Author's tips:—Upon request, hotel proprietors will build a fire in the hotel's fire pit for an evening of cowboy coffee and under-the-stars socializing with other guests.
National Register
    of Historic Places: no
Texas historical marker: no
Texas Heritage Trails Program: Texas Plains Trail Region, www.texasplainstrail.com
Visitor information: Motley County Chamber of Commerce, 828 Dundee St., Matador, TX 79244; 806-347-2968; www.motleycountychamber.org, motcocm@caprock-spur.com

As the only lodging in Roaring Springs (population 265) the hotel hosts a range of customers, from hunters after deer, turkey, quail, and feral hogs on area ranches to people conducting business in the area or visiting relatives. The hotel also welcomes family reunions and wedding parties, and its facilities allow guests to gather in a number of areas for socializing or entertainment. A Hammond organ, a Steinway and Sons piano, electronic keyboard, and karaoke machine await in the dining room for the musically inspired. For more low-key relaxing, the recliner-filled TV viewing areas are stocked with a video library. A kitchenette and table upstairs welcome guests to congregate over a snack.

The rooms have a neat, uncluttered feel and are furnished with a mixture of older furniture and some antiques. Walls are painted in light colors, and quilts adorn most beds. Each room has its own sink with separate hot and cold taps. Some are original to the hotel.

The Q, A, & P—called the "quit achin' and push" by locals—built a mission revival–style depot one block from the hotel, now a Recorded Texas Historic Landmark. The Roaring Springs Ranch Club three miles south of town includes the site of the springs, which has diminished from its roaring past but still gushes more than 800,000 gallons per day. Visitors must be guests of club members to enjoy the facilities, which include swimming in the spring-fed pool, playing golf on its nine-hole golf course, or fishing in its two lakes. Thacker Jewelry's manufacturing plant across the street from the hotel, known for its gold and diamond creations, offers free tours of its facilities and has a small store.

Hotel Turkey

Turkey ☙ 1927

The delicious, home-cooked breakfasts and laid-back country atmosphere make this hotel a good spot from which to pay homage to the King of Western Swing and plan hunting, hiking, or horseback riding trips.

During the annual Bob Wills Day celebration, lovers of western swing descend upon sleepy Turkey, population five hundred, swelling this prairie town to ten thousand. Grassy, unfenced backyards and business parking lots become RV camps overnight the last weekend in April. Regulars know better than to try to book a room at Hotel Turkey during the annual festival, which is held in honor of Wills, the King of Western Swing. By tradition the event's musicians call the 1927 railroad hotel home during the festival.

The Hotel Turkey was built by H. B. Jordan of Plainview to coincide with the extension of the Fort Worth and Denver South Plains railway to this ranching and farming town. Walking about three blocks from the depot—which is now gone—traveling salesmen, cotton brokers, ranchers, railroad workers, and prospective settlers found the Hotel Turkey and its dining room a welcome sight.

The hotel, which is of prairie school design, provided a sample room where drummers could display wares for locals to browse and place

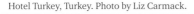

Hotel Turkey, Turkey. Photo by Liz Carmack.

orders. That room, just off the hotel's lobby, is now the hotel office and displays a few works of art by local painter Otho R. Stubbs.

The two-story, redbrick hotel is so packed with antiques and collectible accessories that visitors might feel as if they've walked into an antique store. Old black irons prop open doors, stacks of tattered hardback books tower on antique tables covered with crocheted scarves, and china and glass knickknacks adorn shelves and dressers.

Each of the hotel's fourteen rooms has an unmistakable theme, and most have a private bath. A guest who feels patriotic might like the old Navy uniforms, American flag, and WWII memorabilia in the All American Room. If cowboys are your thing, you might settle into the western motif of the Charles Goodnight Room, which is named for the famed Texas cattle drover and rancher. The two-room Gone with the Wind Suite, with its floral wallpaper and porcelain figurines of Rhett Butler, Scarlett O'Hara,

ESSENTIALS

Contact: P.O. Box 37, 3rd and Alexander, Turkey, TX 79261; 866-423-1151, 806-423-1151; www.turkeybb.com, hotelturkey@hotmail.com
Rooms: 14 rooms including one suite, most have private bath; claw-foot tubs, walk-in showers, tub/shower combinations; king, full, twin beds; 18 complete RV hookups also available.
Rates: $–$$, includes full breakfast.
Room amenities: TV; hair dryer, iron and ironing board available upon request; free wi-fi.
Facilities: house phone available in lobby; morning coffee served in dining room, group space for up to 40, group meals available if arranged in advance.
Smoking: outdoors only.
Credit cards: V, MC.
Parking: free on street.

Accessibility: some rooms are on ground floor.
Pets: yes, if well trained and in crate.
Author's tips:—Although hotel rooms are not available to the public during the Bob Wills Day festival, tent campers can stay at nearby Caprock Canyons State Park.—Tent campers can also rent one of the hotel's RV hookup spaces and have access to hotel bathroom facilities.
*National Register
    of Historic Places:* yes
Texas historical marker: yes
Texas Heritage Trails Program: Texas Plains Trail Region, www.texasplainstrail.com
Visitor information: City of Turkey, Texas; P.O. Box 415, Turkey, TX 79261; 806-432-1033

and the Tara plantation house, once hosted George W. Bush and his wife, Laura, while Bush was Texas governor.

Guests can relax on a brick patio or forget their cares in rocking chairs on the enclosed wraparound porch. The large, sunny lobby is filled with modern, overstuffed sofas and chairs and features a handy supply of books about the region's wildlife and history.

There are a few cracks in the plaster here and there, and the original pressed-tin ceilings in the lobby and dining room exhibit a few rusty spots. But the attention getters are the do-it-yourself decorating touches, including hand-painted stenciling and faux finishes on walls and doors, and winding silk vines on iron bedsteads and stair rails.

Guests are treated to a delicious cooked-to-order breakfast and may be joined by locals in the dining room. The fare includes a steaming cup of coffee, juice, a mound of homemade biscuits with jam and honey, bacon or sausage, hash browns, and eggs. As I buttered my second biscuit, I scanned the Norman Rockwell poster series lining one dining room wall and the dozens of photographs covering another. The photos are of Turkey residents, some of whom I ran into while sightseeing in town, and of past and present country music artists, autographs included. The legendary Bob Wills and his band members are of course featured in the collection.

In the 1920s the young Wills lived on his family's farm near Turkey. At age ten the budding fiddle player began to accompany his father at ranch dances around West Texas. Wills and his bands—the original Light Crust Doughboys and his Texas Playboys—played radio shows, recorded, and toured the country through the early 1960s. Turkey has dedicated a monument and a museum to the musician that are must-sees for visitors.

With a little planning, guests booking a stay at the hotel can coordinate their visit with the occasional live music performances held at the town's 1928 Gem Theater or the Church of Western Swing, a 100-seat no-smoking, no-alcohol facility in the town's 1927 Assembly of God church. Other activities include hunting on area leases and horseback riding, biking, and hiking at nearby Caprock Canyons State Park and Trailway. The 64-mile-long Rails to Trails path passes only a few blocks from the hotel.

Piney Woods

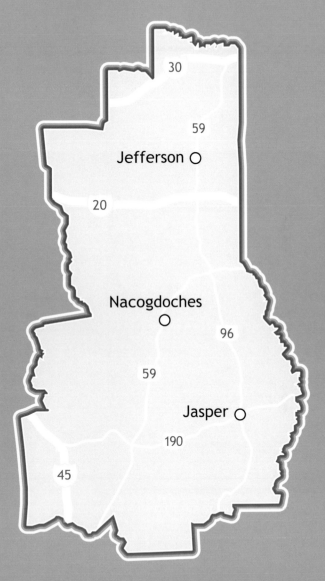

30

59

Jefferson ○

20

Nacogdoches
○

96

59

Jasper ○

190

45

Historic hotel locations in the
Piney Woods region.
Drawn by Jon Michael Grant

Belle-Jim Hotel

Jasper ⚜ 1910

Out-of-towners receive a delightful taste of East Texas small-town life while staying in this homey hotel and dining at its well-known restaurant on the Jasper County Courthouse square.

During a typical evening at the Belle-Jim Hotel, the clack of shuffled dominoes and laughter between old friends spill from a back parlor. Meanwhile, in the hotel dining room, a dozen Jasper Evening Lion's Club members discuss fund-raising plans over plates laden with chicken fried steak and coconut cream pie.

Hotel guests might easily get the feeling they're eavesdropping on Jasper's private affairs if they spend much time in the hotel's parlor and dining room, where many locals stop by to do business, enjoy a meal, and socialize. A crowd regularly gathers at breakfast and lunch to partake of southern favorites delivered hot

from the kitchen. Natives nod to hotel guests and greet neighbors by first names before discussing the latest Jasper Bulldogs' football game or a longtime resident's memorial service. Except for the 1970s and 1980s when it was a law office, this hotel and its dining room have served as a Jasper social hub and hostelry since 1910.

Mamie Patten, a widow with four children, had the two-story hotel built on the northeast corner of the Jasper County Courthouse square and named it after her two daughters. Mamie was a clever businesswoman and knew the art of promotion. On the second Tuesday of each January, she invited traveling salesmen and

Belle-Jim Hotel, Jasper. Photo by Liz Carmack.

ESSENTIALS

Contact: 160 N. Austin, Jasper, TX 75951; 409-384-6923; www.belle jim.com, belle-jim@sbcglobal.net

Rooms: 8 rooms, including 3 suites, all with private bath; tub/shower combination; king, queen, full beds.

Rates: $, includes full breakfast.

Room amenities: TV; iron and ironing board, hair dryer upon request.

Facilities: Belle-Jim Hotel Restaurant, 7 A.M. to 9:30 A.M. daily, 11 A.M. to 1:30 P.M. Mon.–Fri.; guest phone available in parlor.

Smoking: outdoors only.

Credit cards: V, MC, AE, D.

Parking: free on street.

Accessibility: with advance notice, a guest room is available on the ground floor.

Pets: yes, but guests must make arrangements in advance.

Author's tips:—Be sure to check out the antique pie safe, thought to be original to the hotel, now storing linens in a side dining room.—Don't leave Jasper without a stop in the P. N. Ashy store on Houston Street across from the courthouse. Mary Ashy, whose father opened the store in 1938, presides over stacks of shoes, work boots, and denim overalls piled practically to the rafters in this one-of-a-kind mercantile.

National Register of Historic Places: no

Texas historical marker: yes

Texas Heritage Trails Program: Texas Forest Trail Region, www.texasforesttrail.com.

Visitor information: Jasper/Lake Sam Rayburn Area Chamber of Commerce, 246 E. Milam, Jasper, TX 75951; 409-384-2762; www.jaspercoc.org, JasperCC@JasperCOC.org

their guests to a complimentary turkey dinner with all the trimmings, including her famous date cake. The salesmen would display their wares on long tables, take orders from merchants, and book their favorite room at the Belle-Jim for their upcoming visits.

After Mamie's death in 1936, daughter Jim continued to operate the hotel and regularly hosted traveling salesmen as well as officials with lumber companies operating in East Texas' forests and area farmers who had come to town to deliver their produce. The Belle-Jim has had famous guests, too. Jasper physician Joe Dickerson recalled to the current owners that shortly before WWII he saw generals George S. Patton, Dwight D. Eisenhower, and Walter Krueger at the Belle-Jim while the U.S. Army conducted maneuvers nearby.

For decades Jim ran the town's Western Union office adjacent to the hotel lobby, and before she died in 1974, it set a record as the longest-running family-operated Western Union business in the nation. The tiny room is now the office of owners Pat and David Stiles, the Belle-Jim's proprietors since 1992.

A sign that reads "Kindness, Pass it On" holds a prominent spot on the hotel's front desk, which is covered with stacks of guest receipts and mail, a well-stocked candy jar, and a bouquet of fresh daisies. Behind the desk hang the Stiles' family photos. Locally made jelly and note cards featuring illustrations of Jasper landmarks are for sale in the parquet-floored lobby. The room displays posters for an event at the Baptist church and the Jasper Bulldogs football schedule, evidence of this hotel's supportive role in the community.

Guests arriving are warmly welcomed into homey, lived-in surroundings that feature a hodgepodge of antiques and modern furniture with country-style decorating touches. The gray paint on the hotel's stairs has worn off under hundreds of footfalls, revealing the wood underneath. The stairs lead to a linoleum-floored hallway and eight wood-floored rooms, including three suites. Their doorways still sport the hinges where screen doors once hung. In my room, a vinyl wing chair was dressed up with a crocheted scarf. Grapevine and silk flower wreaths adorned the walls. A wooden trunk supported a potted ivy and a television. Soap was provided, but I was glad I had brought my own shampoo.

Visitors are nudged out of bed early by the smell of frying bacon and the calls of crows on the courthouse grounds. A full breakfast with choices that include homemade biscuits and gravy, pancakes, eggs, and hash browns is complimentary for guests. Daily lunch specials such as pork roast or grilled chicken complete with side dishes and dessert are listed on the front porch chalkboard in letters large enough to be read from a passing car.

Belle-Jim guests may be visiting family in the area, participating in a fishing tournament at Lake Sam Rayburn, or in town for an annual event such as Jasper's Azalea Trail and Festival held in March. The Belle-Jim also hosts people working temporarily in the area. Upon my stay, one room was occupied by a University of Texas at Galveston medical student in residency with a local physician, a common occurrence, according to my hosts.

The Belle-Jim's laid-back owners are used to accommodating guests' needs. They'll rise extra early to prepare breakfast for predawn hunting and fishing departures and fix box lunches for a day of hiking in the Angelina National Forest or birding in the Big Thicket Preserve. Visiting cyclists can bring their bicycles into their rooms, and hunters can do the same with their unloaded guns.

Swann Hotel Bed and Breakfast

Jasper ⚜ 1901

Guests are drawn to this turn-of-the-century hotel for the carefully decorated rooms, intimate atmosphere, and the toothsome dishes prepared by its proprietress.

The Swann Hotel's former proprietress, Eugenia Swann, and her mother before her were known as savvy businesswomen, excellent cooks, and gracious hostesses. "Miss Genie," as townspeople still refer to Eugenia, retired from her job as Jasper county clerk and began running the Swann when her mother, Mahala, became bedridden in the 1930s. Mahala had opened the hotel in this former Victorian home sometime around 1915, after her husband died and left her to provide for six daughters.

Under Mahala's hand, the Swann became well known for its southern hospitality and delicious food. Mahala's success allowed her to send each of her children to college. Eugenia assumed her mother's role as hotelier and chief cook with zeal, and ran the hotel and its restaurant until her death in 1972.

Eugenia's fluffy rolls, lemon pie, juicy fried chicken, and tart cabbage slaw were so outstanding that author Nida Marshall describes them in her history of Jasper, *The Jasper Journal.* Marshall says the weekly *Jasper News-Boy,* published continually since 1865, talked Eugenia into sharing her roll recipe with readers in the mid-1960s. No doubt many Jasper residents have a yellowed copy tucked into an old cookbook.

The Swann closed in the late

Swann Hotel Bed and Breakfast, Jasper. Photo by Liz Carmack.

1980s. The two-story, wood-frame building deteriorated until it was restored in the late 1990s. In 2000 Mary Silmon and her husband, Jerry, realized their dream of running a bed and breakfast inn when they purchased the renovated hotel. Mary continues the Swanns' legacy of serving delicious food. Guests tuck in to homemade biscuits, ham quiche, and honeyed fresh fruit served at individual tables in the hotel's dining room. Afternoon snacks are often fresh-baked cookies. Mary will prepare dinner for lodgers if they give her one day's notice. If you do so, be sure to request her delicious bread pudding. Simultaneously chunky and custardy,

the pudding is Mary's grandmother's recipe, and she serves it warm with either a caramel or rum sauce.

Overnight guests feel as if they are visiting a relative's antique-filled home. The hotel retains it original high ceilings, its dark wood floors in the parlor and in a few of the guest rooms, and carved woodwork around its doors and large windows. The hotel fireplace, with its ornate iron grillwork, and a baby grand piano are the focal points of the parlor. This space and the adjacent dining room provide a sunny and attractive space for local social club meetings, receptions, and other functions, such as bridal showers. Guests can relax outdoors in

ESSENTIALS

Contact: 250 N. Main, Jasper, TX 75951; 877-489-9717, 409-489-9010; www.hotelswann.com, swannhotel2005@yahoo.com
Rooms: 8 rooms, including 1 suite; 3 rooms share a bath, 5 have private bath; claw-foot tub, shower/tub combination; queen, full, and twin beds.
Rates: $$, includes full breakfast.
Room amenities: TV in two rooms; iron, ironing board, and hair dryer upon request; robe.
Facilities: lunch or dinner available if arranged at least one day ahead, coffee and snacks; group space for up to 50.
Smoking: outdoors only.
Credit cards: V, MC, AE, D.
Parking: free in hotel lot and on street.

Accessibility: disabled access, room on ground floor.
Pets: not allowed.
Author's tips:—Be sure to ask to see the owner's teapot and creamer collection displayed in the hotel kitchen.
National Register
of Historic Places: no
Texas historical marker: no
Texas Heritage Trails Program: Texas Forest Trail Region, www.texasforesttrail.com
Visitor information: Jasper/Lake Sam Rayburn Area Chamber of Commerce, 246 E. Milam, Jasper, TX 75951, 409-384-2762; www.jaspercoc.org, JasperCC@JasperCOC.org

white wicker furniture on the hotel's front porch or on its covered deck. A small sunroom off the parlor is stocked with board games and a TV.

The eight guest rooms, including one suite, are individually decorated and feature quilts, pastel-painted walls, porcelain figures, and plate collections. Three rooms share a bath down the hall. The rest have private facilities. The suite is on the ground floor, and the remaining rooms are off the second floor hallway, reached by a narrow staircase.

The Swann's lodgers can shop for jewelry, gifts, and antiques at the hotel's gift shop or walk to a handful of art galleries and specialty shops nearby. The hotel is one block off the Jasper County Courthouse square. The Jasper County Historical Commission, in the old county jail on the south side of the courthouse, has a list of state and nationally listed historic sites in and around Jasper, including a number of beautiful homes on Main Street.

Excelsior House

Jefferson 🏛 1858

Rescued and restored at the brink of demolition in 1961 by a preservation-minded garden club, the Excelsior House and its antebellum atmosphere welcome guests to one of the oldest hotels in Texas.

The community of Jefferson was so grateful to steamboat captain William Perry for keeping Big Cypress Bayou navigable that in 1846 it granted him land just a few blocks from the town's docks. Perry bought additional property and built a home for his family. He began to rent rooms to cotton merchants, planters, and other business associates, and word about his fine accommodations spread among those arriving at what was then Texas' largest inland port. Perry's hostelry today welcomes tourists and business travelers and has been in continuous operation since the captain first took in lodgers.

Perry was killed while walking home one night in 1868, and the hotel changed hands frequently over the next decade. In 1872 new owners added a classical revival–style brick addition west of the original wood building and leased the downstairs as commercial space and the upstairs rooms to traveling salesmen.

When the water level in Big Cypress Bayou dropped in 1873 after the U.S. Army Corps of Engineers removed a natural logjam on the Red River, the port closed and Jefferson's economy suffered a dramatic downturn. But the hotel continued to operate. Its patrons included numerous

Excelsior House, Jefferson. Photo by Jeff Carmack.

ESSENTIALS

Contact: 211 W. Austin, Jefferson, TX 75657; 800-490-7270, 903-665-2513; fax: 903-665-9389; theexelsiorhouse .com, jgoulds@aol.com

Rooms: 15 rooms, all with private bath; claw-foot bathtub with shower attachment, walk-in shower, tub/ shower combination; full, queen, and king beds.

Rates: $$

Room amenities: phone, TV, iron and ironing board; hair dryer available upon request.

Facilities: Excelsior House Restaurant; reservations recommended for hotel's Plantation Breakfast, 8 A.M. to 9:30 A.M. daily; morning coffee in lobby, group space for up to 100.

Smoking: outdoors.

Credit cards: V, MC, AE, D.

Parking: free on street.

Accessibility: rooms available on ground floor.

Pets: not allowed.

Author's tips:—The town's 1890 former federal courthouse and post office now houses the Jefferson Historical Museum, 223 Austin St., near the hotel.

National Register
 of Historic Places: yes

Texas historical marker: yes

Texas Heritage Trails Program: Texas Forest Trail Region, www.texasforesttrail.com

Visitor information: Marion County Chamber of Commerce, 118 N. Vale St., Jefferson, TX 75657; 800-GO-RE-LAX, 903-665-2672; www.jefferson-texas.com, visitjefferson@sbcglobal.net

travelers to East Texas who were escaping southern states ravaged by the Civil War.

In 1878 Catherine "Kate" Wood bought the hotel, which was then called the Commercial Hotel. She left it to her daughter, Amelia Wood Mc-Neeley, who operated it until 1920. Both were known for their pet dogs, and Amelia had a large birdcage built in front of the hotel for canaries. The hotel was sometimes called the Canary Hotel.

The hotel passed through a handful of owners during the next forty years and by 1961 was in great disre-

pair and near demolition. Its savior was Jefferson's Jessie Allen Wise Garden Club, which secured loans totaling $42,500 to purchase and restore it. Club members rolled up their sleeves and went to work in the hotel lobby (which was painted black), the ballroom, parlor, and the fifteen guest rooms. They scraped paint, ripped out the old rotted canary cage, polished fixtures, refinished furniture, and orchestrated plumbers, electricians, and carpenters to accomplish major repairs.

The hotel continued to take lodgers throughout the restoration so that it could maintain its claim of continuous operation since its 1858 opening. Fees collected from these guests and numerous fund-raisers and donations helped the club pay off the loans, hire a full-time hotel manager, and make it the successful business it is today. Now the hotel's whitewashed exterior walls and its ornate cast iron balustrade, which forms a long, covered entryway, convey the grace and charm of the Old South in Jefferson's well-preserved downtown historic district.

The two-story hotel is filled with an eclectic mixture of antiques and collectibles from private donations and previous owners, including Captain Perry. An antique Sèvres porcelain chandelier hangs in the hotel dining room. Five Oriental-style rugs cover the cypress plank floor of the large hotel ballroom, where the hotel daily serves its Plantation Breakfast of orange blossom muffins, sausage, eggs, and biscuits. The room is also used for receptions and other events.

Most of the eight guest rooms are named for famous guests, including the large and finely decorated Rutherford B. Hayes Presidential Room and the Lady Bird Johnson Room. All have private baths. Some feature claw-foot bathtubs and canopy beds. I stayed in the Victorian Parlor Room on the first floor, which was spacious, with a king-size bed and double doors that opened onto a comfortable covered sitting area in the hotel's landscaped courtyard. The courtyard, whose centerpiece is a fountain and fishpond, is a favorite spot for weddings.

The large lobby features the hotel's original registration desk, swivel register, and walnut secretary. A petit point titled "David Playing His Harp before King Saul" hangs on one wall. The work, made by former owner Amelia McNeely when she was a child, is said to comprise 275,000 stitches. Hotel memorabilia and past registers featuring signatures of famous guests fill a large glass case in the lobby—Ulysses S. Grant, who signed in 1883, and Lyndon Baines Johnson, a guest in 1969, are among them.

Members of the Jessie Allen Wise Garden Club offer free tours of the hotel each afternoon. Although the tour doesn't include information about ghost sightings at the Excelsior, the hotel has a reputation for being haunted. Guests and staff have reported seeing a woman in black, smelling perfume and cigar smoke in otherwise empty rooms, and hearing mysterious footsteps and conversations late at night on the hotel's unoccupied upper floor.

Visitors can also tour Jay Gould's private railroad car, which sits across the street from the Excelsior. Gould was a noted financier and owner of numerous railroad companies during the latter part of the nineteenth century. Touring Jefferson's historic district with its more than fifty historic structures, including Greek revival homes, is as easy as heading out the hotel's front door. Many downtown shops, museums, bookstores, and restaurants are in well-preserved nineteenth-century brick buildings.

Jefferson Hotel

Jefferson ⚓ circa 1851

Ghostly lodgers and an award-winning Italian restaurant,
which features the owners' Old World family recipes, are the
key attractions of this relic from East Texas' steamboat era.

Though details about the Jefferson Hotel's early days are sketchy, locals say it was built as a cotton warehouse by the A. G. Schluter family when steamboats brought a bus-tling trade to Jefferson. The building's current back door, which now opens onto a patio, was originally its front and faced the busy piers on Big Cypress Bayou. Here in the mid-nineteenth

Jefferson Hotel, Jefferson. Photo by Laura Lakey.

ESSENTIALS

Contact: 124 W. Austin, Jefferson, TX 75657; 866-33HOTEL, 903-665-2631; fax: 903-665-6222; www.historicjeffersonhotel.com, stay@historicjeffersonhotel.com

Rooms: 23 rooms and suites, all with private baths; claw-foot bathtubs with shower attachment, Jacuzzi, walk-in shower, tub/shower combination; king, queen, and full beds.

Rates: $$

Room amenities: phone, TV; hair dryer, iron and ironing board are available upon request.

Facilities: Lamache's Italian Restaurant and Bar, 11:30 A.M. to 2 P.M. Sat.–Sun.; 5 P.M. to 8 P.M., Wed., Thurs., Sun., 5 P.M. to 9 P.M. Fri. and Sat.; morning coffee available in lobby, group space for up to 100.

Smoking: outdoors.

Credit cards: MC, V, AE, D, DC.

Parking: free on the street.

Accessibility: ground floor rooms available.

Pets: yes, but guests must make arrangements in advance.

Author's tips:—Be prepared when staying in room 19 to see "Help Judy Murder" written on the steamy bathroom mirror after a hot shower. Housekeeping staff say years of cleaning won't remove the disturbing note.—Ask hotel about packages for special occasions. They can include champagne, flowers, and snacks.

National Register of Historic Places: no

Texas historical marker: no

Texas Heritage Trails Program: Texas Forest Trail Region, www.texasforesttrail.com

Visitor information: Marion County Chamber of Commerce, 118 N. Vale St., Jefferson, TX 75657; 888-GO-RELAX, 903-665-2672; www.jefferson-texas.com, visitjefferson@Fsbcglobal.net

century, tons of cotton and produce were loaded onto paddle wheel steamboats that delivered supplies and manufactured goods from Shreveport and New Orleans. Jefferson's era as the state's largest inland port ground to a halt after the U.S. Army Corps of Engineers' removed a natural logjam on the Red River in 1873. The resulting drop in the bayou's water level made it impassable to steamboat traffic.

The building was converted into a hotel in 1861. Around 1900 it became known as the Crystal Palace Hotel. Since that time it has also operated as the New Jefferson Hotel and the Hotel Jefferson. Commercial enterprises in the building have served thousands of Jefferson residents and visitors for more than a century—from cotton traders and Victorian lodgers in its early days to patrons of a bawdy house and customers of a butcher shop, Chinese laundry, roller skating rink, and boardinghouse.

The hotel has a reputation for being haunted by ghosts from its varied past. A notebook kept by the owner details in guests' handwriting numerous accounts of strange experiences. Visitors have sighted men and women in Victorian and early twentieth-century dress and have heard children laughing and running when no children were registered. Photographs taken inside and in front of the hotel display unexplained ghostlike images—wisps of white smoke and floating orbs. A photo taken by my husband in the hotel's deserted upstairs hallway captured a pink transparent orb floating in midair. Rooms 14 and 19 on the second floor are supposedly favorites for the hotel's unregistered guests; many paying visitors ask to stay in these rooms, hoping for an otherworldly experience. But a close encounter with the supernatural can happen anywhere in the building. Housekeeping staff report mussed bedspreads and children's handprints wrinkling pillow shams in rooms that have been freshly cleaned but not yet occupied.

The twenty-three guest rooms and suites all have private baths and are individually decorated with period decor. The Fox Run Suite features a gas-burning fireplace and antique claw-foot tub. The Honeymoon Suite has a canopy bed and large Jacuzzi tub.

The hotel's exterior includes a balcony with wrought iron railing. The sunny, spacious lobby has a large front desk and comfortable sitting area featuring antiques, marble-topped tables, and a crystal chandelier. Furnishings throughout the Jefferson are a mix of antiques and reproductions. Just off the lobby is Lamache's Italian Restaurant, where hotel owners Michael and Elise Lakey serve as chefs for the evening meal. Both lunch and dinner menus feature family recipes passed down from a maternal grandmother, who immigrated to America at the beginning of the twentieth century. The walls are lined with family photos and numerous Taste of Jefferson awards. In an odd coincidence, the owner has found evidence that an Italian restaurant occupied this same space in the 1870s.

Guests help themselves to coffee and tea in the lobby and can take away restaurant meals for in-room dining. The large dining room has been a center for community social occasions since the early 1900s, and Jefferson old-timers remember when diners in the 1940s could get a home-cooked meal served family style for less than a dollar.

The Jefferson is in the midst of the town's historic district. A number of two-story brick and stuccoed nineteenth-century warehouses, store buildings, and a bank line the bricked streets and are now filled with shops, restaurants, and offices. The town's annual Historical Pilgrimage in May includes a historic homes tour, plays, a quilt show, a parade, and crafts fair.

Fredonia Hotel

Nacogdoches ⚜ 1955

A monument to Nacogdoches' civic pride, this hotel is noted for its mid-twentieth-century architecture, its accommodations to suit many tastes, and its role as the community's "living room."

In 1952–53, more than 1,100 Nacodgoches residents agreed with community leaders that their town needed a first-class, modern hotel to serve business and leisure travelers. They bought Community Hotel stock at $50 a share and raised more than $500,000 toward the $1.3 million Fredonia Hotel project. The Fredonia became an instant success, an economic catalyst, and a focal point for the community's business and social activities. During its first year, the hotel hosted thirty-eight conferences and had an occupancy rate of 96 percent.

During the 1970s and early 1980s, absentee ownership and physical decline tarnished memories of the hotel's shining beginning, but the city's civic pride saved the Fredonia and ensured its rebirth. In the late 1980s, Nacogdoches leaders rallied, determined to renovate and reopen the shuttered landmark. Today the original salmon-pink terrazzo tile floor of the spacious, redecorated lobby again welcomes business and leisure travelers and local citizens as "Nacogdoches' living room."

Fewer stockholders now own a piece of this community hotel,

Fredonia Hotel, Nacogdoches. Photo courtesy Fredonia Hotel.

but some are descendents of the Fredonia's original boosters. Citizens' pride in the town's heritage is evident throughout Nacogdoches, from the plaques dotting the city center that describe buildings' histories and the lives of prominent citizens to the copies of eighteenth-century French maps of early Texas that include Nacogdoches and decorate the Fredonia's guest rooms.

The name *Fredonia*, selected through a hotel naming contest, is a nod to a chapter in the town's colorful history. The word is fashioned from *freedom* and was used by impresario Hayden Edwards, who in 1826 laid claim to land surrounding Nacogdoches and declared it the Fredonia Republic. For a short while, the white and red Fredonia flag featuring the words "Independence, Liberty, Justice" flew over the town. But in 1827 Mexican forces arrived to put a stop to this rebellion and forced Edwards, who had little local support, to retreat to Louisiana.

From the 1970s until it closed in

ESSENTIALS

Contact: 200 N. Fredonia St., Nacogdoches, TX 75961; 800-594-5323, 936-564-1234; fax: 936-564-1234; www.fredoniahotel.com

Rooms: 112 rooms and suites, all with private bath; tub/shower combinations; king and queen beds.

Rates: $$–$$$

Room amenities: phone, TV, coffee maker, hair dryer, iron and ironing board, free wi-fi, room service.

Facilities: Café Fredonia, 6:30 A.M. to 10 A.M. and 11 A.M. to 2 P.M. daily, 5:30 P.M. to 9 P.M. Mon.–Thurs. & Sat., 5:30 P.M. to 10 P.M. Friday; Nine Flags Bar, 4 P.M. to midnight Mon.–Fri., 4 P.M. to 1 A.M. Sat.; outdoor pool, group space for up to 1,000.

Smoking: in bar and on patio.

Credit cards: V, MC, AE, D, DC.

Parking: free in hotel lots.

Accessibility: disabled access, several rooms are on ground floor, elevator.

Pets: yes, $10 fee.

Author's tips:—Be sure to check out the huge catalpa tree growing up through the center of the hotel complex. The project was laid out around this tree.

National Register of Historic Places: yes, as part of Nacogdoches Downtown Historic District

Texas historical marker: no

Texas Heritage Trails Program: Texas Forest Trail Region, www.texasforesttrail.com

Visitor information: Nacogdoches Convention and Visitors Bureau, 200 E. Main St., Nacogdoches, TX 75961; 888-OLDEST-TOWN; www.visitnacogdoches.org, info@visitnacogdoches.org

1985, the hotel was known as the Sheraton Crest Inn, but it regained the name Fredonia after its renovation and reopening in 1989.

The building, designed by J. N. MacCammon and constructed by W. S. Bellows Construction Company of Houston, retains its distinctive, original mid-twentieth-century architectural style. Some original exterior details remain, such as the "Creole modern" wrought iron work of stylized acorns and oak leaves adorning the hotel entryway and patio. Long gone are the Fredonia's stylish 1950s furnishings and decor, featured in the June 1955 cover story of *Texas Hotel Review*.

The Fredonia is laid out in three distinct parts: the Tower, the Cabanas, and Oak Terrace. Each section has its own character and atmosphere. The Tower rooms, accessed via elevator from the elegant hotel lobby, have wide-ranging views of the leafy town and its many historic buildings. Cabana rooms, my favorite, offer parking directly outside the front door and have a back door within steps of a pool and lovely patio. Oak Terrace rooms, added in 1960, are in a separate building from the main hotel,

tucked away from most foot traffic and pool noise. They also have exterior corridor doors. All of the hotel's 108 rooms and suites have private baths and modern furnishings and decor.

In the hotel restaurant's sunny dining room, guests are likely to line up with county sheriff's deputies and local office workers for the well-known lunch buffet. The room's curved glass wall offers unobstructed views of the verdant patio and pool, a lovely accompaniment to a candlelight dinner. A convention center, a gift shop, and the hotel's original, wood-floored Banita Ballroom, named for a town creek, completes its facilities.

The redbrick streets of downtown Nacogdoches and the city's visitors' center on the Plaza Principal, where visitors can pick up a copy of the city's self-guided walking tour, are just a few blocks away. The tour highlights stops at historic homes, cemeteries, and a Caddo Indian mound. The town hosts numerous festivals throughout the year, including the Azalea Trail, the East Texas Cajun Cook-Off, the Americana Music Festival, and the Candlelight Tour of Homes.

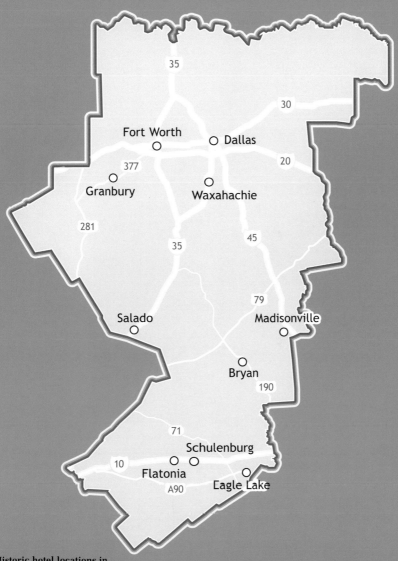

Prairies and Lakes

35

30

Fort Worth ○   ○ Dallas

377

20

Granbury ○

Waxahachie ○

281

35

45

79

Salado ○

Madisonville ○

Bryan ○

190

71

Schulenburg ○

10   ○ Flatonia

A90   ○ Eagle Lake

Historic hotel locations in
the Prairies and Lakes region.
Drawn by Jon Michael Grant.

LaSalle Hotel

Bryan ✿ 1928

A leader in downtown Bryan's revitalization, this hotel was built to rival modern hotels in Chicago and New York and at its completion was this city's tallest building.

Since its renovation and reopening in 2000, the LaSalle Hotel has bolstered efforts to save Bryan's historic buildings and rejuvenate the city's downtown. Now a number of the historic brick buildings along Bryan's wide Main Street, including the old Charles and Bryan hotels, have been renovated and are taking on new lives as office buildings and loft apartments. The three-story 1906 J. W. Howell building, across the

LaSalle Hotel, Bryan. Photo by Liz Carmack.

ESSENTIALS

Contact: 120 S. Main Street, Bryan, TX 77803; 866-822-2000, 979-822-2000; fax: 979-779-4343; www.lasalle-hotel.com

Rooms: 55 rooms and suites, all with private bath; shower/tub combinations, Jacuzzi-style claw-foot tub with shower attachment, walk-in shower; king, queen, and full beds.

Rates: $$–$$$, includes continental breakfast.

Room amenities: phone, TV, coffee maker, hair dryer, iron and ironing board, free wired Internet.

Facilities: LaSalle Café, 7 A.M. to 7 P.M. Mon.–Thurs., 7 A.M. to 9 P.M. Fri. and Sat., 8 A.M. to 1 P.M. Sun.; free wi-fi in lobby and café, group space for up to 75.

Smoking: designated rooms.

Credit cards: V, MC, AE, D, DC.

Parking: free on street.

Accessibility: disabled access, elevator.

Pets: not allowed.

Author's tips:—Be sure to let staff know whether you'd rather have a large bathroom or bedroom, or if you want a sitting area. A variety of room configurations are available.—This hotel sits between two railway lines, and although the trains don't rattle the windows, light sleepers might want to use earplugs, which are free from the front desk.

National Register
   of Historic Places: yes

Texas historical marker: yes

Texas Heritage Trails Program: Texas Brazos Trail Region, www.texasbrazostrail.com

Visitor information: Bryan-College Station Convention and Visitors Bureau, 715 University Dr. E, College Station, TX 77840; 800-777-8292, 979-260-9898; www.visitaggieland.com

plaza from the LaSalle Hotel, houses a restaurant, offices, and a ballroom/conference facility called the Brazos Cotton Exchange, in recognition of the space's original use.

Located in a rich agricultural area, Bryan was a key cotton shipping point in the early twentieth century and a main stop between Houston and Dallas on the Houston and Texas Central Railroad. The International and Great Northern Railroad also came through Bryan in the early twentieth century. The town also reaped the economic benefits, as it does today, from its proximity to Texas A&M University in nearby College Station. Texas A&M, established in 1876, is Texas' oldest public institution of higher education.

With Bryan's economic success, R. W. Howell, son of grocer J. W. Howell and a prominent city leader, envisioned a new hotel for the community with "all the modern convenience and devices of the hotels to be found in Chicago and New York City." R. W. hired Austin architect George Louis Walling to design the neoclassical revival–style LaSalle. At its grand opening in 1928, the seven-story, one-hundred-room, buff brick building was the tallest structure in town. The hotel's first floor featured a tailor shop, the LaSalle Café, and a barber shop. The hotel lobby still displays its original black, gray, and white terrazzo floor and green marble baseboards. Its second floor once consisted of a ballroom and meeting and dining rooms, all since turned into guest rooms.

In addition to being merchants, the Howell family was involved in banking, the Bryan Telephone Company, and medicine. They were also Bryan boosters. During the depression, R. W. spoke out against "foreign" chain stores from Chicago moving into the area and taking away community dollars for the benefit of Wall Street.

The hotel remained in the Howell family for more than thirty years. J. C. Jacques bought the LaSalle in 1959 and, with his son, ran it as a nursing home until a 1975 federal regulation required such facilities to have wider hallways and doors. The owner then turned the operation into a resident hotel with small apartments, which catered to the elderly. When demand for such housing decreased, the hotel closed in 1980 and fell into disrepair. A number of efforts to reopen the hotel went unrealized until late 1997, when a full-scale renovation was undertaken by a private developer with backing from the city. The hotel reopened in 2000.

Its reopening was an early step toward revitalizing downtown Bryan, which, in the late 1960s through the early 1980s, lost several merchants as they chose to locate nearer to College Station and followed Bryan's growth to the east. The city of Bryan stepped in to save the LaSalle in 2001 when it looked like the hotel might founder.

The LaSalle's fifty-five rooms and suites, which all have private baths featuring ceramic tile floors and gray and black granite vanities, are filled with antiques and antique reproductions collected by a former owner. The guest rooms are carpeted, and each has its own collection of art, a mixture of gold-framed botanical and floral prints and black-and-white photo portraits.

Many weekday guests at the LaSalle have dealings at the Brazos County Courthouse, at Texas A&M, or with the area's high-tech or other companies. Leisure travelers frequent the hotel on weekends. It's also a popular spot with locals to celebrate weddings and anniversaries. Lodgers can walk to a number of restaurants, antique stores, and live music venues in downtown Bryan. The Children's Museum of the Brazos Valley is a couple of blocks away. The town's 1903 classical revival–style Carnegie library sits across Main Street and now houses the Carnegie Center of Brazos Valley History. The George Bush Presidential Library and Museum is in College Station. Just east of Bryan, the Messina Hof Winery offers wine tasting, dining, and shopping.

Dallas ⚓ 1912

This elegant queen of Dallas hotels, built by the king of brewers, boasts a world-class art and antique collection, and its French Room restaurant is a feast for the eyes as well as the palate.

The Adolphus has survived almost a century of additions and extensive remodeling, economic booms and busts, and competition from newer accommodations to remain Dallas' bastion of elegance and European-style charm. In 1910 Adolphus Busch had a brewery in Dallas and owned the Oriental Hotel on the southeast corner of Commerce and Akard streets downtown. After a group of Dallas' leading businessmen approached Busch, he agreed to be the primary backer for the construction of a first-class hotel. Local investors purchased 10 percent of the hotel corporation's stock to build a new hotel catty-corner to the Oriental. Busch hired St. Louis architects Barnett, Haynes, and Barnett to design the nineteen-story, $1.8 million proj-

ect. For years, the Adolphus was the tallest building in downtown Dallas.

Today the neighboring glass and steel skyscrapers contrast with the impressive mansard roof of the beaux arts Adolphus and its elaborate French Renaissance and baroque details in bronze and granite. Although the Busch family expanded the hotel in 1918 and again in 1926, stretching it to an entire block, it is the original hotel building that has been called one of the city's most beautiful commercial structures.

Long ago its original ballroom and banqueting rooms were on the nineteenth floor. These facilities have since been moved to the mezzanine level and the nineteenth floor turned into guest rooms. Oddly enough, guests staying on this floor over the

The Adolphus, Dallas. Photo courtesy The Adolphus.

years have reported hearing loud big-band music. The hotel's drive-through entrance, the front desk, and its foyer occupy the area that once was its famous Century Room. During the 1930s, '40s, and '50s this was *the* place in Dallas to woo a girl, dance the fox-trot, and be entertained. Couples could twirl to bandleaders like Glenn Miller and their orchestras or choose among three floor shows daily. The Century Room's most popular act was the Ice Revue starring Olympic skater Dorothy Franey Langkop. She performed here for fourteen years.

Dallas investor Leo F. Corrigan purchased the hotel from Busch heirs in 1949. By the 1970s, the Adolphus was showing its age, and to compete with newer Dallas hotels the landmark needed rejuvenation. The investment came from new corporate owners, who in the early 1980s spent $65 million on the project. A public auction cleaned out almost all the hotel's fixtures and furnishings before the eighteen-month renovation began. Saved were the dark walnut paneling throughout the Lobby Living Room and a large brass chandelier, which now hangs over the escalator between the front desk foyer and the lobby. This shiny crown is ringed with eagles—recognizable from the Anheuser-Busch beer logo—and hop vines.

ESSENTIALS

Contact: 1321 Commerce Street, Dallas, TX 75202; 800-221-9083, 214-742-8200; fax: 214-651-3588; www.hoteladolphus .com, ddavis@adolphus.com

Rooms: 422 rooms and suites, all with private bath; tub/shower combinations and walk-in showers; king, queen beds.

Rates: $$$–$$$$

Room amenities: phone, TV, coffee maker, hair dryer, iron and ironing board, free wi-fi, robe, room service.

Facilities: French Room, 6 P.M. to 10 P.M. Tues.–Sat.; the Bistro, 6:30 A.M. to 10 P.M. daily; Walt Garrison Rodeo Bar and Grill, 11 A.M. to 9 P.M. Mon.–Fri.; Bistro Bar, 6:30 a.m. to 10 P.M. daily; fitness center, group space for up to 750, complimentary car service within downtown.

Smoking: outdoors only.

Credit cards: V, MC, AE, D, DC.

Parking: valet only, $20.

Accessibility: disabled access, elevator.

Pets: not allowed.

Author's tips:—A three-course traditional afternoon tea is served in the Lobby Living Room from 3 P.M. to 4:45 P.M. Thurs.–Sun., Sept.–June. The hotel's seasonal decorations make afternoon tea during the holidays extra special. Reservations are required; dining@adolphus.com, 214-742-8200

National Register of Historic Places: yes

Texas historical marker: yes

Texas Heritage Trails Program: Texas Lakes Trail Region, www.texaslakestrail.com

Visitor information: Dallas Convention and Visitors Bureau, 325 North St. Paul Street, Suite 700, Dallas, TX 75201; 800-232-5527, 214-571-1300; www.visitdallas.com

The Adolphus has one of the country's most impressive hotel collections of art and antiques. Camera-toting tourists and curious conventioneers wander through the Lobby Living Room ogling the Napoleon II oval mirror and ornately carved 1893 Steinway piano once owned by the Guggenheim family. A pair of late seventeenth-century Flemish tapestries hang opposite one another in the hotel's atrium entryway. This collection, combined with the antique furnishings, subdued lighting, and fresh arrangements of roses and daylilies give the hotel's Lobby Living Room a cultured, intimate flavor. It is a refined yet comfortable place to enjoy an afternoon pot of tea with the ladies or an early evening glass of wine with colleagues.

It's not unusual to see women in backless evening gowns and men in suits on their way to the adjacent French Room. This restaurant's lauded classic French cuisine is matched by the room's opulent rococo artistry. Rosy-cheeked cherubs stream pink ribbons across a vaulted ceiling bordered by gold ornamental plaster. Light from crystal chandeliers hand-blown in Murano, Italy, and flickering tapers on linen-topped tables reflects off crystal, silver, and china designed especially for the room.

The Adolphus' elegant atmosphere lends itself to more formal dress. Men will be most comfortable wearing jackets and collared shirts and women at least slacks or skirts at most of the hotel's restaurants and in its Lobby Living Room during afternoon tea and in the evening. Patrons who don't pack accordingly shouldn't panic. I found a few glittery gowns hanging amid the usual sundries of candy bars and cigarettes in the hotel gift shop, and the original Neiman Marcus department store is down the street. If you need assistance finding the right outfit or have other special requests, ask the concierge for help. The Adolphus' concierges are members of the prestigious Les Clefs d'Or, which says its members "will accommodate every guest request so long as it is morally, legally, and humanly possible."

In 2005 the Adolphus renovated its 422 guest rooms and suites. The carpeted accommodations all have private baths. They feature modern Queen Anne–style furnishings. Beds linens are fine enough for a well-appointed home, and the hotel hand presses its 300-thread count cotton sheets. Each room has a desk and may have a separate sitting area. Baths feature tan marble and gold-tone fixtures. Suites are available with a terrace, one or two bedrooms, a separate sitting area, or a full kitchen.

A mixture of business and leisure travelers stay at the Adolphus, which is operated by Noble House Hotels and Resorts. The list of famous guests who have registered at the hotel is pages long and ranges from Her Majesty Queen Elizabeth II, Rudolph Valentino, and President Franklin D. Roosevelt to Dizzy Gillespie, Tom Wolfe, and Sean Penn. Notes of appreciation from celebrity visitors fill the beveled glass cabinets at the eastern end of the Lobby Living Room.

The Adolphus is a short walk from Dallas' West End Historic District and its many shops, restaurants, and bars.

Hotel Indigo

Dallas ⚜ 1925

Bright colors, hardwood floors, and spa-inspired bathrooms in this hotel aim to comfort frequent business travelers in the first high-rise hotel building constructed by international hotelier Conrad Hilton.

Conrad Hilton retained the Dallas architectural firm Lang and Witchell to design this $1.3 million beaux arts style–hotel on the east side of Dallas' downtown. It was the first hotel built by the famous hotelier, the first structure to bear Hilton's name, and at its opening in 1925, was the tallest building on the east end of Main Street. In its latest incarnation, it's switched from a run-of-the-mill Holiday Inn into boutique quarters within the InterContinental Hotels Group. Hotel Indigo caters to business travelers and offers what they call a colorful and comforting alternative to the usual "dull beige business hotel."

When the Dallas Hilton opened in 1925, it had 325 moderately priced rooms in a market that offered primarily a choice between aging hotels and luxury properties. Business travelers were key customers to the hotel then, too, which provided the traveling salesman a combination sample/guest room with a foldaway Murphy bed to make room for displaying merchandise to customers. Hilton's offices were in the mezzanine of the fourteen-story hotel.

Hilton's autobiography, *Be My Guest,* says that with the ground-breaking of the Dallas Hilton he left the older, "dowager" circuit of hotels

Hotel Indigo, Dallas. Photo by Liz Carmack.

ESSENTIALS

Contact: 1933 Main Street, Dallas, TX 75201; 800-231-4235, 214-741-7700; fax: 214-760-9755; www.hotelindigo.com

Rooms: 170 rooms and suites, all with private bath; walk-in shower; king, queen, and full beds.

Rates: $$–$$$

Room amenities: phone, TV, coffee maker, hair dryer, iron and ironing board, free wi-fi, room service.

Facilities: Golden Bean Restaurant & Bar, 7:00 A.M. to 2 P.M. and 5 P.M. to 10 P.M. daily, business center, fitness center, complimentary car service within 3 miles, group space for up to 120.

Smoking: outdoors only.

Credit cards: V, MC, AE, D, DC.

Parking: self-park in public garage across street; valet $18.

Accessibility: disabled access, elevator.

Pets: yes, $75 fee.

Author's tips:—Campisi's and the Iron Cactus are dining choices a few blocks away. Have the hotel's complimentary car service drop you off at Dallas' West End Historic District, which features dozens of restaurants, bars, and shops in historic buildings.

National Register of Historic Places: yes

Texas historical marker: yes

Texas Heritage Trails Program: Texas Lakes Trail Region, www.texaslakestrail.com

Visitor information: Dallas Convention and Visitors Bureau, 325 North St. Paul Street, Suite 700; 800-232-5527, 214-571-1300; www.visitdallas.com

---

he had been operating and turned a business corner. His new company slogan was Minimax: "minimum charge for maximum service." Hilton Hotels Corporation now operates a chain of more than two thousand hotels in more than eighty countries.

After Hilton relinquished his operating lease on the hotel in 1938, it passed through numerous hands and had a multitude of names, including the Aristocrat, the Plaza, and the White-Plaza, a name it bore for thirty-five years. In its most recent redo, the rooms and public spaces have hardwood floors with area rugs and paint and fabrics in shades of bright blue, yellow, and white. Headboards and bedside tables are whitewashed wood. Furniture includes overstuffed chairs, ottomans, and love seats with slipcovers. Bathrooms have a spa touch, with glass-enclosed shower stalls, oversized showerheads, and teak tables for toiletries.

Large photographic murals of nature scenes—irises, frost-covered leaves—cover one wall in each guest room and change seasonally in the lobby, as do bowls filled with complimentary candy or fruit. Guests even get a dose of aromatherapy in public spaces. The smell of spiced apples wafting through the lobby in October becomes pine in December and changes appropriately throughout the seasons. Catering to business travelers in a hurry, the hotel's informal restaurant, bar, and coffee shop are combined and provide counter service.

Across the street is the 1921 Majestic Theater, Dallas' last standing vaudeville theater and movie house from the 1920s. Restored, it now hosts local and touring theater, dance, music, and comedy.

Hotel Lawrence

Dallas ⚜ 1925

This last of Dallas' railroad hotels near Union Station sets an intimate mood for guests with warm tones and contemporary decor blocks from Dealey Plaza, Dallas' West End, and other popular attractions.

Hotel Lawrence is the last operating hotel of many that were built across from Dallas' Union Station to serve passengers riding railways such as the Missouri, Kansas and Texas, and the Gulf, Colorado, and Santa Fe. Originally named the Scott Hotel, it was opened in 1925 by hotelier George C. Scott, who also operated hotels in Waco and Houston at the time. The Scott opened with 160 rooms. Each had a private bath. The Dallas Chamber of Commerce announced that the new hotel was "elaborately furnished throughout with velvet carpets and mahogany furniture." It became the Hotel Lawrence in the late 1930s. By 1975 this area of downtown and the hotel had deteriorated so much that Dallas

Hotel Lawrence, Dallas. Photo by Liz Carmack.

ESSENTIALS

Contact: 302 S. Houston, Dallas, TX, 75202; 877-396-0334, 214-761-9090; fax: 214-761-0740; www.hotel lawrencedallas.com, info@hotellawrencedallas.com

Rooms: 118 rooms and suites, all with private bath; tub/shower combination; queen beds.

Rates: $$–$$$, includes continental breakfast.

Room amenities: phone, TV, coffee maker, hair dryer, iron and ironing board, free wired Internet and wi-fi.

Facilities: Founder's Grill, 6 A.M. to 10 P.M. daily; Founder's Bar, 2 P.M. to 10 P.M.; fitness center, business center, complimentary car service up to 3 miles, group space for up to 30. Smoking: designated rooms.

Credit cards: V, MC, AE, D, DC, JCB.

Parking: valet only, $15.

Accessibility: disabled access, elevator.

Pets: yes, under 30 lbs., $25 fee;

treats at check-in and dog walkers available.

Author's tips:—Save a few dollars by leaving your bags with the hotel and then parking for $5 a day (fee is $5 each time you reenter) at Union Station across the street.—It's easy to access the hotel from Interstate 35 East (also called Stemmons Freeway), but be prepared to navigate downtown Dallas' one-way streets. It's best to approach the hotel on Jackson, which is westbound and one-way.

National Register of Historic Places: no

Texas historical marker: no

Texas Heritage Trails Program: Texas Lakes Trail Region, www.texaslakestrail.com

Visitor information: Dallas Convention and Visitors Bureau, 325 North St. Paul Street, Suite 700, Dallas, TX 75201; 800-232-5527, 214-571-1300; www.visitdallas.com

County considered buying the building to turn it into a minimum-security jail. Guests at that time included elderly staff who had worked at the hotel since opening day and were permanent residents who paid little for their rooms.

In 1980 when downtown Dallas experienced a resurgence of economic development, new owners totally renovated the property and reopened the hotel. It changed hands a number of times over the following

two decades and was known as both the Bradford and the Paramount. The building was rechristened Hotel Lawrence during its latest renovation, which took place in 2000 to the tune of $4 million.

The hotel's lobby once had terrazzo tile floor and marble wainscoting. But these and other significant original interior details were lost during the hotel's many renovations. Today the dark, wood-paneled lobby space has an art deco feel. Faux animal and snakeskin fabrics cover the sleek sofas and chairs. Light from small table lamps with crème and black shades and cream-frosted glass sconces set a subdued, intimate mood. A metal starburst sculpture on the ceiling radiates over the main sitting area.

The 118 guest rooms and suites all have contemporary furnishings, also with an art deco touch, in subdued green and gold tones. All have private baths. The bright white bathrooms have tub-shower combinations that feature two showerheads. One is long, tubelike, and horizontal and the other round and flat. Together they supply an avalanche of water. Stylized waves, crescent moons, and other nature-inspired images decorate the brown, blue, and yellow tiles trimming bathroom walls.

The Lawrence markets itself as an affordable "European boutique-style" hotel because of its moderate prices, its decor, and its size, which is smaller than some of its nationally known Dallas competitors (such as the 1,100-room Dallas Hyatt across the street). It also serves complimentary cookies and milk in the lobby every evening, provides designer toiletries and CD players in guest rooms, and has a CD lending library. But don't expect a concierge or the highly personalized service found at other, more expensive boutique hotels.

Hotel Lawrence welcomes pets of 30 pounds or smaller for a $25 fee. Upon arrival, four-legged guests receive a treat and a toy. Their owners receive a list of Dallas' pet-friendly restaurants, stores, and dog parks.

I breakfasted on complimentary yogurt and cereal during my morning at the Lawrence and found a table next to Mary Kay representatives attending the Texas beauty products company's annual convention. The dining room has an unobstructed view of the former Texas School Book Depository and Dealey Plaza three blocks away. Pres. John F. Kennedy was assassinated in the plaza while riding in his motorcade on Nov. 22, 1963. The hotel offers a JFK package, which includes a room for two and two tickets to the Sixth Floor Museum, which documents the event and examines Kennedy's life and legacy. The previous evening I walked a few blocks to the city's West End Historic District, which features restaurants, shops, and other attractions. Union Station, across the street, is now part of a complex that includes the Dallas Convention Center and Reunion Arena. Amtrak's Texas Eagle passenger service stops at the station, as does Dallas' light-rail, commuter rail, and buses.

Stoneleigh Hotel and Spa
Dallas 🌳 1923

*Originally a full-service apartment hotel, this hostelry features
a bar and restaurant that have long been patronized by
national celebrities, local politicians, and recently divorced
Dallas men, who appreciate the low-key átmosphere and staff
respect for privacy.*

When the $1.1 million Stoneleigh
Court Apartment Hotel opened
in 1923, the ultramodern accommodations fit nicely with its location, a
leafy, upscale neighborhood of stately
homes on the north edge of Dallas.
Almost a century later, the Uptown
neighborhood is now in the center
of a much larger metropolis and has
more than a hundred art galleries,
designer clothing boutiques, and antiques shops.

By late 2007 the Stoneleigh is ex-
pected to have completed a multimillion-dollar renovation to keep pace
with its tony surroundings. During
the writing of this book, interior designers were plotting a total revamp
of the public spaces and guest rooms
using new art deco-inspired furnishings, carpets, and tile. Likewise,
plans were being laid to enhance the
hotel's services to include a full-time
concierge, 24-hour room service, and
on-site spa.

When the Efficiency Apartment Corporation first opened
the Stoneleigh, designed by local
architect F. J. Woerner, the facility
attracted tenants with its innovative
features. As an apartment hotel it offered long-term leases with the amenities of a hotel. Apartments were as
large as five rooms to accommodate

Stoneleigh Hotel and Spa, Dallas. Photo by Liz Carmack.

ESSENTIALS

Contact: 2927 Maple Avenue, Dallas, TX 75201; 800-678-8946, 214-871-7111; fax: 214-871-1145; www.stoneleighhotel.com, info@stoneleighhotel.com

Rooms: 153 rooms and suites, all with private bath; shower/tub combinations; queen, king beds; some suites have full kitchens.

Rates: to be announced

Amenities: phone, TV, coffee maker, hair dryer, iron and ironing board, room service, robes, wi-fi.

Facilities: restaurant and bar open daily; spa, fitness center, car service within five miles, group space for up to 350.

Smoking: outside only.

Credit cards: V, MC, AE, D, DC.

Parking: valet only.

Accessibility: disabled access, elevator.

Pets: yes, $50 fee.

Author's tips:—Visit www.uptown dallas.net for a map and details about this neighborhood's events and attractions.—Enjoy a relaxed meal or happy hour at the Stoneleigh P, 2926 Maple Ave., across the street from the hotel. This restaurant and bar has been in this WWI–era drugstore, complete with original fixtures and soda counter, for more than 25 years.

National Register
    of Historic Places: no

Texas historical marker: no

Texas Heritage Trails Program: Texas Lakes Trail Region, www.texaslakestrail.com

Visitor information: Dallas Convention and Visitors Bureau, 325 North St. Paul Street, Suite 700, Dallas, TX 75201; 800-232-5527, 214-571-1300; www.visitdallas.com

---

families. One- and two-room apartments were marketed to bachelors. Furnishings came from the Sanger Brothers' department store in Dallas. Residents enjoyed maid and janitorial service, and the rooms were fully stocked with linens, kitchen appliances, cookware, china, silverware, and electric irons. Murphy beds, which had recently become popular, folded into wall closets to save space, and chilled air and water flowed to each room. The basement housed a grocery store. Residents could socialize in the ladies' parlor or men's smoking room and visit the hotel barber and beautician. Guests attending a function at the hotel ballroom or dining atop the hotel's eleventh floor could take in views of the attractive surroundings.

The Stoneleigh, like many businesses, struggled through the Depression. It is thought that by at least the 1930s the facility began to accept transient lodgers. In 1938 then-owner Harry E. Stewart turned a portion of the hotel's eleventh floor into a 7,500-

square-foot penthouse for his family. The luxurious apartment had imported 500-year-old oak paneling from the English Charterhouse School, ornamental plaster ceilings, and secret passageways with sliding doors.

For more than four years in the 1980s, Isaac Tigrett, cofounder of the Hard Rock Café chain, called this penthouse home. During his residency, hotel visitors and staff would occasionally bump into Tigrett's famous houseguests, such as Paul Simon and Joe Walsh. During my visit, these rooms and rooftop patio were part of the hotel's meeting and banquet space—a favorite spot for Dallas weddings. Hotel management planned to lavishly restore the space for private and corporate events. If the well-worn oak paneling in the main salon of these rooms could talk, it might report details of the illicit poker games supposedly staged here in the 1930s and the celebrity partying of the 1980s. The eleventh floor of the Stoneleigh has also played a part in Dallas' media history. Radio station KSKY broadcast from here from the 1940s to the 1980s.

The Stoneleigh has had numerous owners, including Dallas' Corrigan family, who operated the hotel for half the twentieth century and into the 1990s.

A feature writer in the 1970s christened the Stoneleigh the "Heartbreak Hotel" in an article for *D Magazine,* a nickname that stuck. Recently separated or divorced Dallas men have been known to call the hotel home

for months at a time and contribute to the interesting mix of locals and guests that patronized its Lion's Den bar. The lounge took its name from the two stone lions outside the hotel's east entrance.

Veteran hotel staff have been privy to numerous brokered business deals and political planning sessions as they unobtrusively serve drinks or meals in the restaurant. Staff discretion and the Stoneleigh's low-key atmosphere have kept the hostelry a favorite of those seeking privacy. The hotel's long list of famous guests includes Elvis Presley, Judy Garland, Oliver Stone, Britney Spears, and the Fab 5 from the "Queer Eye for the Straight Guy" television show.

Despite the major changes at the Stoneleigh, plans included retaining the original four black, white, and rust colored marble columns in the lobby and the parquet floor in the first floor hallways. The 153 guest rooms, all with private bath, have varied sizes and configurations—a legacy of the Stoneleigh's former life as an apartment hotel.

Those doing business with one of the nearby law or architectural firms choose the hotel for its convenience, and tourists like the hotel's Uptown neighborhood location and its easy access via the McKinney Avenue Trolley to the city's West Village and the Arts District. Reverchon Park and the Katy Hike and Bike Trail are only blocks away.

Warwick Melrose Hotel

Dallas ♨ 1924

The mostly corporate clients who frequent this former apartment hotel in Dallas' upscale Oak Lawn neighborhood return for its well-appointed rooms, understated luxury, and personalized service.

The faux suede coverlet at the foot of the king-size bed, the live potted plants, and the terry robe and cushy rug in the spacious bathroom make a room at the Warwick Melrose feel like a well-appointed apartment. In fact, when this hotel opened in 1924 as the Melrose it was an apartment hotel. Hundreds of apartment-dwellers enjoyed the conveniences of a pharmacy, beauty shop, and grocery store on the premises. Residents could order a roast or a bottle of Scotch through room service. They could schedule a catered bridge party in an air-conditioned parlor and have

their car's gas tank topped off by the valet.

Hotel financiers Hamilton Investment Company and S. W. Strauss Company chose noted Dallas architect C. D. Hill to design the eight-story brick building, at a cost of $2 million. The hotel is situated in the city's upscale Oak Lawn neighborhood, originally a farm owned by Civil War veteran Col. George Mellersh. He named his property Oak Lawn in recognition of the oaks found here.

From its start, the Melrose also welcomed transient guests. The Dallas Chamber of Commerce in a 1924

Warwick Melrose Hotel, Dallas. Photo courtesy Warwick Melrose Hotel.

publication bragged about Dallas' growing number of hotel rooms and wrote that the Melrose and other apartment hotels were available to house conventioneers and visitors to the state fair.

After a number of successful decades, the Melrose hit rough times. Even with new owners and a major renovation in the early 1980s, it couldn't turn a profit and went into foreclosure. In 1999 new investors undertook their own renovation. The hotel has since held its own with a well-appointed, refined atmosphere and high level of service that hotel staff call "comfortable luxury." Today repeat business from well-heeled corporate clients is the Warwick Melrose's bread and butter. On one weekday afternoon I watched three men in business suits gather around a laptop. They chatted in French beneath the lobby's hand-painted, coffered ceil-

ESSENTIALS

Contact: 3015 Oak Lawn Ave., Dallas, TX 75219; 800-521-7172, 214-521-5151; fax: 214-521-2470; www.warwickmelrosedallas.com, res.dallas@warwickhotels.com
Rooms: 184 rooms and suites, all with private bath; tub/shower combination; king and full beds.
Rates: $$$–$$$$
Room amenities: phone, TV, coffee maker, hair dryer, iron and ironing board, wired Internet for a fee, robe, room service.
Facilities: The Landmark Restaurant, 6:30 A.M. to 2 P.M. daily and 6 P.M. to 10 P.M. Mon.–Sat.; Library Bar, 2 P.M. to midnight Sun.–Thurs.; 2 P.M. to 1 A.M. Fri. & Sat.; fitness center, business center, group space for up to 250, complimentary car service within 3 miles; free wi-fi in lobby.
Smoking: designated rooms, outdoors.
Credit Cards: V, MC, AE, D, DC.

Parking: valet only, $18.
Accessibility: disabled access, elevator.
Pets: allowed with advanced notice, no fee; complimentary pet bowls, beds, and treats.
Author's tips:—Resist the temptation to pull into the hotel's circular front drive. The main entrance is in the back.—Local favorites Eatzi's Market and Bakery, 3403 Oak Lawn Blvd., and Lucky's Cafe, 3531 Oak Lawn Blvd., are a few blocks away.
National Register of Historic Places: no
Texas historical marker: no
Texas Heritage Trails Program: Texas Lakes Trail Region, www.texaslakestrail.com
Visitor information: Dallas Convention and Visitors Bureau, 325 North St. Paul Street, Suite 700, Dallas, TX 75201; 800-232-5527, 214-571-1300; www.visitdallas.com

ing. Meanwhile, the front desk staff greeted a chicly attired businesswoman by name as she crossed the antique floor of brown marble and inlaid wood. A valet soon delivered her car from the hotel parking lot.

Patrons for whom money is no object (read: expense account) and who like to depart Dallas in style can have the hotel arrange a town car to take them to the airport. And forget airline food—the hotel chef can prepare a roast turkey and apple smoked bacon sandwich or a salad of baby greens, portobello mushrooms, and goat cheese for a brown bag lunch.

Dallas' social set often picks the Warwick Melrose to host events, whether it's a board meeting of the Dallas Symphony or a thank-you dinner thrown for top donors to the city's ballet. And residents from the Oak Lawn and Highland Park neighborhoods can often be seen having a drink or light supper in the dark, clubby Library Bar. After 10 P.M. on weekends the lobby fills with hopefuls waiting to snag a seat in this wood-paneled watering hole, which features live jazz and lounge music. The hotel's award-winning Landmark Restaurant also attracts locals and

guests alike, especially to its Sunday champagne brunch, which requires reservations.

Each of the Warwick Melrose's 184 guest rooms and suites features modern furniture and private baths with European marble. Crème painted walls are a classic backdrop for the rich fabrics in gold, blues, browns, and wine red used throughout the carpeted quarters. Rooms are oversized, and each has a slightly different configuration. Each comes with a sitting area and writing desk; suites may have small hallways, foyers, separate bedrooms, or a wet bar.

The hotel is a favorite spot for wedding parties and hosts more than seventy a year. Many couples marry across the street in the Oak Lawn Methodist Church, also designed by C. D. Hill, before celebrating at the hotel.

The Oak Lawn neighborhood was one of Dallas' first suburbs and is just a few minutes north of downtown. A short drive away, free parking is available at the pedestrian-friendly West Village, home to residential lofts, restaurants, clothing stores, boutiques, and the Magnolia, a theater featuring art and independent films.

Farris Hotel
Eagle Lake ⚓ 1912

Hunters pack this former railroad hotel and its bar during the goose and duck hunting season, and its restaurant is well-known for steak and seafood dinners and Sunday champagne brunch.

As Eagle Lake has evolved from a commercial center with three rail lines in the early twentieth century to its current fame as the self-proclaimed goose capital of the world, the Farris Hotel has adapted to cater to its changing clientele. When W. A. Dallas, an official with the San Antonio–Aransas Pass Railroad, built the hotel, it was the only brick building and the only hostelry in town that offered running water in each room and flush toilets. Drummers were its primary customers, and the hotel dedicated a room off its lobby to showcase the wares of these traveling salesmen. Today this "drummer's room" is the Cooked Goose Saloon, a favorite watering hole for hunters who flock to Eagle Lake from mid-September to February.

Guns aren't allowed in the bar, but they're welcome in the hotel unloaded, as are crated hunting dogs. The Farris innkeepers further cater to early-rising guests by providing a light breakfast and sending them off with thermoses brimming with coffee or cocoa. Up to three meals a day are available through special meal-lodging packages. Hunters can also use the hotel's gun-cleaning facilities after a day in the area's rice fields and wetlands stalking Canada, snow, and

Farris Hotel, Eagle Lake. Photo by Liz Carmack.

speckled belly geese or teal, mallard, and pintail ducks.

The Good Hotel stood on this site from 1857, initially serving those traveling to town by stagecoach or horse and later by rail. W. A. Dallas purchased the hotel and razed it to make way for his new hostelry, the Dallas Hotel. A. E. Barnes designed the building, which was built by O. J. Howard. In the late 1920s new owners changed the name to the Hotel Ramsey. A decade later, the Depression and decline of rail travel forced the hotel's restaurant to close. The downstairs became apartments, while transient guests continued to lodge upstairs. Through the next few decades the hotel changed hands and suffered hard times. By the early 1970s the plaster was crumbling, and the plumbing was disintegrating.

ESSENTIALS

Contact: 201 N. McCarty, Eagle Lake, TX 77434; 888-327-7471, 979-234-6500; fax: 979-234-6525; www.farrishotel.com, farrishotel@msn.com

Rooms: 16 rooms in original hotel, all with sinks, 2 with private bath, 4 with semiprivate bath, 10 rooms share separate women's and men's showers and toilets; claw-foot tub with shower attachment, walk-in shower; twin and full beds; 2 suites in Bentley House annex, with private baths.

Rates: $

Room amenities: coffee maker, free wi-fi; hair dryer, iron and ironing board available upon request.

Facilities: 1912 at the Farris Hotel restaurant, 5 P.M. to 9 P.M. Thurs.–Sat., 10 A.M. to 2 P.M. Sun.; Cooked Goose Saloon, 5 P.M. to midnight Thurs.–Fri., 5 P.M. to 1 A.M. Sat.; house phones and TV in great room, group space for up to 150.

Smoking: in great room, saloon.

Credit cards: V, MC, AE, D.

Parking: free in hotel lot.

Accessibility: ramp available for access to restaurant dining rooms only.

Pets: yes, crated dogs; no fee or deposit.

Author's tips:—Hotel staff can help guests find local hunting guides and outfitters.—Light sleepers might want to bring earplugs, or use those supplied by the hotel, for the nighttime trains and should know the saloon can become boisterous on weekend nights during hunting season. Those wanting more privacy and quiet should lodge in the Bentley House annex.

National Register of Historic Places: no

Texas historical marker: yes

Texas Heritage Trails Program: Texas Independence Trail Region, www.texasindependencetrail.com

Visitor information: Eagle Lake Chamber of Commerce, 303 East Main St., Eagle Lake, TX 77434; 979-234-2780; visiteaglelake.com, chamber@ecl.net

History buffs William and Helyn Farris bought the hotel, renamed it, and made extensive renovations, including restoring the original public rooms downstairs and moving the staircase to its original position. The stairs today have a black wrought iron rail the Farrises salvaged from a home in Houston and installed during their renovations. A few antique gaslight fixtures that they found in a Kentucky home and converted to electric still hang on the first floor.

Two dining rooms and two parlors open onto the hotel's central lobby, which has a tan painted concrete floor. The large main dining area is decorated in a western theme and features extensive original millwork—including a plate rail that extends across all four walls. The hotel's Pink Parlor and Red Parlor just off the lobby are named for good reason, and the Green Room displays old photos of Eagle Lake and the hotel. The dining rooms and parlors fill with diners when patrons pack the Farris to enjoy its restaurant's steak and seafood dinners and Sunday champagne brunch.

Most of the hotel's original furniture is gone, although some rooms still have the early oak mission-style rockers. The sunny, carpeted rooms are now furnished with a mixture of antiques and vintage pieces. Rooms are simply decorated, with lace curtains, cotton bedspreads, and prints of nature and hunting scenes. Most of the sixteen rooms have twin beds. All rooms have sinks, some of them original. Two rooms have private baths. The others share separate men's and women's bathroom facilities or share a semiprivate bath. The hotel also rents two suites with private baths in the adjacent historic Bentley House.

All rooms in the original hotel are upstairs and open onto a central "great room," which has modest decor and is arranged and outfitted so guests can socialize and entertain themselves. At one end are sofas with a large-screen TV, DVD player, and a selection of DVDs. Poker tables sit stocked with cards and chips. The large cupola and a skylight provide natural lighting for the mostly windowless room. Guests can also relax on the second floor veranda or on a covered brick patio.

Since its opening, the Farris has been favored by locals for bridge parties, banquets, business meetings, and receptions. Overnight guests are not only hunters; during the off-season the hotel hosts a number of family and school reunions, and religious retreats. The hotel also offers meal-lodging "getaway" packages for those just seeking a quiet escape.

Bird-watchers are drawn to Eagle Lake year-round. The Prairie Edge Museum, whose exhibits include information on prairie plant and animal life and area pioneers, is only a few blocks from the hotel.

Olle Hotel

Flatonia ※ circa 1881

The airy, comfortable rooms of this intimate hotel make a good base for antique hunting and touring in Fayette County and are a convenient layover for travelers of Interstate 10 between Houston and San Antonio.

The Olle family name is an old and well-respected one in Flatonia, a small community of German-Czech heritage in the rolling Fayette County countryside. Otto Olle was already well known for managing Flatonia's Buckhorn Saloon and the Otto Café when in 1926 he and his wife, Agnes, purchased this two-story brick building. It had been a boardinghouse since the early 1880s. When Otto died in 1938, Agnes continued to operate the hotel and its restaurant until she passed away in 1967. The Olles' early lodgers included drummers who came to town hawking their wares to

businesses such as the local hardware store, saloon, grocery, and lumber-yard. Old-timers remember the hotel as a well-run establishment, and Agnes had a reputation as being kind and generous to her guests and the community.

She made the guest room quilts by hand, and the metal loops that once held her quilt frame remain embedded in the ceiling of room 1, where she lived. When Agnes had a spare minute to herself, she would lower the quilt on its frame from the ceiling and start stitching. Although most of those quilts are long gone, guests

Olle Hotel, Flatonia. Photo by Liz Carmack.

can still see one, as well as a sample
of Agnes' crochet work, by asking
the hotel's new proprietor, Kathryn
Geesaman.

Geesaman reopened the hotel in
2005 under the Olle family name,
which pleased many locals. It had
been closed since Agnes Olle's death
except for a short stint as a bed and
breakfast decorated in Victorian style.
It took six months to rid the rooms
of bold, busy wallpapers and heavy
drapes. The Olle now has a restful

interior design that is best described
as Pottery Barn meets the Round Top
Antiques Fair. Geesaman selected
antique furniture and chandeliers
found at the nearby fair, which is
held twice yearly, and thoughtfully
mixed them with new ceiling fans,
white iron beds, and new leather and
wood chairs. Few knick-knacks adorn
surfaces, and the mostly Texas and
western-themed art is used sparingly
on the hotel's crème and putty-col-
ored walls. Oriental-style and sisal

ESSENTIALS

Contact: 218 S. Market Ave., Flatonia, TX 78941; 361-772-0310; fax:
361-865-9269; ollehotel.com, info@
ollehotel.com
Rooms: 10 rooms, all with private
bath; tubs with hand shower attachment, walk-in showers; queen and
full beds.
Rates: $$, includes full breakfast.
Room amenities: TVs with head-
phones and DVD players, DVD library
available; hair dryers; iron and iron-
ing board available upon request; free
wi-fi.
Facilities: house phone for guests,
group space for up to 20.
Smoking: outdoors only.
Credit cards: V, MC.
Parking: free on street.
Accessibility: some rooms are on first
floor.
Pets: not allowed.

Author's tips:—Flatonia is a popular
spot for train watchers, and nighttime
trains might bother light sleepers
without earplugs.—The town has pre-
served one of Texas' longest standing,
manually operated railroad switching
towers. Contact the Flatonia Chamber
of Commerce for tours.
National Register
   of Historic Places: no
Texas historical marker: no
Texas Heritage Trails Program:
Texas Independence Trail Region,
www.texasindependencetrail.com
Visitor information: Flatonia Cham-
ber of Commerce, 208 East N. Main,
P.O. Box 610, Flatonia, TX 78941;
361-865-3920; www.destination
flatonia.com

rugs set off the polished hardwood floors. Glass-topped wrought iron tables, handcrafted by an area artist, complete the uncluttered look.

All ten airy guest rooms have private baths. Five rooms are on the first floor, off the main hallway, where Geesaman spreads a complimentary breakfast buffet. Guests eat in the adjacent small dining room on a half-dozen tables dressed with bouquets of fresh flowers on white linen.

Geesaman thoroughly researched the Olle Hotel history and collected materials into a notebook she leaves in the small lobby to share with guests. I paged through the photos and handwritten accounts one evening and then kicked back in a rocking chair on the quiet front porch, just as the drummers and other lodgers used to after dinner decades ago. Room and board back then cost $1 a day or $2 a day with private bath.

Today's visitors are a mix of business travelers, vacationers, and those in the area for a wedding or reunion. Geesaman is an affable hostess and enjoys sharing tips about where to eat and what to see and do in the area. Attractions include the numerous antique stores in Flatonia and nearby towns, the painted churches of Fayette County, and a number of locally sponsored events, including church festivals, dances, and fiddling contests.

Courtyard Fort Worth Downtown/ Blackstone Hotel

Fort Worth ⚖ **1929**

Fort Worth's first art deco skyscraper and the site of much history making, this hotel remains a landmark in the city's skyline.

The Blackstone Hotel was Fort Worth's first art deco skyscraper when it opened in 1929, towering twenty-two floors and 268 feet above the city's growing downtown commercial district. Today its stepped-back ziggurat design, which creates terraces on its upper floors, and its exterior ornamentation, which includes stylized griffins, dolphins, pineapples, and panther heads, remain the building's outstanding features. Inside, its

Courtyard Fort Worth Downtown/Blackstone Hotel, Fort Worth. Photo courtesy Courtyard/Blackstone Hotel.

ESSENTIALS

Contact: 601 Main Street, Fort Worth, TX 76102; 800-249-0800, 817-885-8700; fax: 817-885-8303; www.Courtyard.com/dfwms

Rooms: 203 rooms and suites, all with private bath; tub/shower combination; king, queen, and full beds.

Rates: $$–$$$

Room amenities: phone, TV, coffee maker, hair dryer, iron and ironing board, free wired Internet, wi-fi for a fee.

Facilities: Corner Bakery, 6 A.M. to 7 P.M. Mon.–Fri., 7 A.M. to 3 P.M. Sat.–Sun.; lobby bar, 5 P.M. to 11 P.M. Mon.–Sat.; outdoor heated pool, indoor whirlpool, fitness center; group space for up to 50.

Smoking: outside only.

Credit cards: V, MC, AE, D, DC.

Parking: valet only, $10.

Accessibility: disabled access, elevator.

Pets: allowed, $75 fee.

Author's tips:—Room numbers 1606, 1608, 1611, and 1612 have terraces and patio furniture. Guests can specifically request these when making reservations directly through the hotel.

National Register of Historic Places: yes

Texas historical marker: yes

Texas Heritage Trails Program: Texas Lakes Trail Region, www.texaslakestrail.com

Visitor information: Fort Worth Convention and Visitors Bureau, 415 Throckmorton, Fort Worth, TX 76102; 800-433-5747, 817-336-8791; www.fortworth.com

interior is unmistakably a modern Courtyard Marriott.

Fort Worth cattleman C. A. (Gus) O'Keefe built the Blackstone, choosing the name after he had visited the Blackstone Hotel in Chicago. He hired prominent St. Louis architects Mauran, Russell, and Crowell for its design. Fort Worth architect Elmer G. Withers supervised the work of local construction company Bellows and Maclay. Upon its opening, this was a luxury hotel with 300 guest rooms, each with a private bath and shower, ceiling fan, and closet. A twelve-piece orchestra led by conductor Herman Waldman, who had recently performed at The Adolphus in Dallas, serenaded dancers in its lavish Venetian Ballroom, now gone. A menu from the 1940s lists broiled Gulf trout and French fried potatoes for $1.50. A glass of Blue Ribbon beer was 30 cents.

The Blackstone has hosted famous guests including Will Rogers, Clark Gable, Al Jolson, Gene Autry, Herbert Hoover, and Richard Nixon. Here Bob Wills cut the first recording of "San Antonio Rose" and performed with the Light Crust Doughboys in the early 1930s—in the twenty-second-floor studios of WBAP, Fort Worth's first radio station. In 1948 the state's

Democratic Executive Committee gathered in the ballroom to debate whether it should ratify Lyndon Baines Johnson's 87-vote victory over former Governor Coke Stevenson in the Democratic primary for U.S. Senate. Stevenson lost, 28 to 29.

In 1982 the hotel was sold at a foreclosure auction on the Tarrant County courthouse steps, and a handful of permanent residents—elderly people, college students, and hotel workers—were given the boot. The hotel sat empty, deteriorating and in danger of demolition until 1997 when Historic Restoration of New Orleans bought and completely renovated it. Property and income tax credits aided the effort.

The Blackstone reopened in 1999 as a Courtyard Marriott with 203 colorfully decorated rooms and suites, all with private bath. Rooms have bright multicolored carpets, modern upholstered furnishings, and prints of colorful abstract art. Four terrace suites provide views of downtown from the sixteenth floor, just as they did in 1929. The Presidential Suite has a private stairway leading to another of the original balconies on the fourteenth floor. Interior hints from the hotel's past remain in nine rooms on the second floor, which have their original French doors, facing Main and Fifth streets; some have the molded plaster crests that were once in the hotel's lobby.

Lodgers are primarily business travelers, conventioneers, and tourists. The Blackstone is close to Sundance Square, which offers restaurants, nightclubs, and live performance and movie theaters. The Sid Richardson Collection of Western Art is just up the street and features art by Frederic Remington and Charles M. Russell. More art can be found in the city's Cultural District west of downtown, home to the Kimbell Art Museum, Amon Carter Museum, and the Modern Art Museum of Fort Worth, as well as the Fort Worth Museum of Science and History.

Hilton Fort Worth

Fort Worth ⚜ 1921

Pres. John F. Kennedy was an overnight guest here before his
tragic visit to Dallas on Nov. 22, 1963. This hotel began as a
dream to help transform Fort Worth's rough and tumble image.

In 1919 Fort Worth's leading businessmen felt the city needed a top-notch hotel to support the area's thriving oil business and to help turn Fort Worth from a rowdy cow town into a modern commercial and cultural center. Visionaries behind the project were Amon G. Carter, William Monnig, W. K. Stripling, W. C. Stonestreet, Van Zandt Jarvis, and O. K. Shannon. Together they supplied $1.2 million, formed the Citizens Hotel Company, and sold another $1.8 million in stock to Fort Worth citizens to build Hotel Texas. The fourteen-story hotel with its 500 rooms, restaurants, barbershop, and magnificent rooftop

Crystal Ballroom (where Rudolph Valentino and his wife once tangoed) opened with great ceremony. The multipage souvenir program from the Dec. 3, 1921, celebration praised the accommodation and called it the "Downtown Home of All Fort Worth." The redbrick building, the tallest in Fort Worth at the time, was designed by architects Sanguinet and Staats of Fort Worth and Mauran, Russell, and Crowell of St. Louis. It exhibits Chicago school, Renaissance, and Georgian architectural styles.

The exterior remains largely as it was. Its original terra-cotta trim incorporates classical triglyphs, medal-

Hilton Fort Worth, Fort Worth. Photo by Liz Carmack.

ESSENTIALS

Contact: 815 Main Street, Fort Worth, TX 76102; 800-HILTONS, 817-870-2100; fax: 817-882-1300; www.fortworthhilton.com

Rooms: 294 rooms and suites, all with private bath; tub/shower combinations; king and full beds; three-room Presidential Suite is 2,600 square feet and has a Jacuzzi tub.

Rates: $$–$$$$

Amenities: phone, TV, coffee maker, hair dryer, iron and ironing board, room service, wi-fi and wired Internet for a fee.

Facilities: Café Texas, 6 A.M. to 10 P.M. daily; Skylight Court Lounge, 4 P.M. to 1 A.M. daily; fitness center, group space for up to 1,000.

Smoking: designated rooms, bar.

Credit cards: V, MC, AE, D.

Parking: valet, $14.

Accessibility: disabled access, elevator.

Pets: not allowed.

Author's tips:–Angelo's Barbeque, 2533 White Settlement, is a short drive from the hotel and a favorite with locals.–The free Main Street Fort Worth Arts Festival, www.msfwaf.org, is held each April just outside the hotel. The four-day festival features juried art, food, and live entertainment.

National Register of Historic Places: yes

Texas historical marker: yes

Texas Heritage Trail Program: Texas Lakes Trail, www.texaslakestrail.com

Visitor information: Fort Worth Convention and Visitors Bureau, 415 Throckmorton, Fort Worth, TX 76102; 800-433-5747, 817-336-8791; www.fortworth.com

lions, and images of Texas longhorn steer draped with yucca garlands. But numerous renovations have significantly changed the interior. The brass mailbox near the front desk is the only recognizable feature from the hotel's early days.

Since its 2006 metamorphosis into a Hilton, the hotel's historic past is now more prominently incorporated into the hotel's printed materials and is on display in guest rooms and public areas. In the hotel's second-floor mezzanine, ten black-and-white photographs document the Nov. 21–22, 1963, stay of Pres. John F. Kennedy

and his wife, Jacqueline. In one photo Kennedy is seen delivering an early morning speech outside the hotel's Eighth Street entrance to a crowd of nearly eight thousand before his departure for Dallas, where he was shot while riding in his motorcade. The Hotel Texas marquee, seen over the shoulders of JFK, Gov. John Connally, U.S. Rep. Jim Wright, and Vice Pres. Lyndon B. Johnson, reads, "Welcome to Fort Worth, Where the West Begins." That marquee is gone, and the entrance has been modified with the addition of an automatic door and a portico, but visitors will recognize the building's tall arched, multipaned lobby windows, unchanged since the 1963 photo.

Before the hotel became a Hilton, these photos, tucked away in a corner of the mezzanine, were the only reference to the president's untimely visit. Many guests never knew of the hotel's JFK connection. But today a second group of photos and a reproduction of the *Fort Worth Star Telegram*'s front-page coverage of the president's stay are also displayed in the room. In addition, large photos of JFK dominate the elevator foyer on each floor. Guest room bathrooms feature an artist's rendering of Hotel Texas labeled with a prosaic reference to its place in history, which ends "the President's motorcade departed, taking with it the final moments of a more innocent America."

Prior to the first couple's brief stay, Amon G. Carter's daughter, Ruth, collected prized pieces by artists such as Raoul Dufy, Pablo Picasso, and Claude Monet from prominent Fort Worth residents and the Amon G. Carter Museum and placed them in the presidential suite for the couple's enjoyment. The president and first lady called to thank her before their departure for Dallas.

Today the Kennedys' suite has been broken up into multiple guest rooms. The new 2,600-square-foot Presidential Suite features a color scheme used in the Kennedy White House and includes two and one-half baths, a wet bar, and Jacuzzi tub.

The hotel's guest rooms were renovated during its transformation into a Hilton in 2006. All 295 rooms and suites have private baths with new cherry furnishings. The modern decor features shades of brown, taupe, and gold. The Hilton's trademark "Serenity Bed" is made extra comfy by a generous supply of down-filled pillows. The carpet and furnishings throughout the hotel's public spaces were also replaced. At the lobby's center a small waterfall prominently features two horse statues and an etched glass backdrop. A two-story atrium links the lobby to the hotel's extensive conference facilities.

The Hilton sits across the street from the Fort Worth Convention Center, which makes it a popular choice for conventioneers. The hotel also caters to business travelers and tourists. Within walking distance from the hotel are downtown Fort Worth's Sundance Square and several restaurants, shops, bars, galleries, and theaters, including the Nancy Lee and Perry R. Bass Performance Hall. Short drives away are the Fort Worth Stockyards, the city's Cultural District, the Fort Worth Zoo, and the Texas Motor Speedway.

Hotel Texas

Fort Worth ⚜ 1939

A convenient choice for visitors to the historic Fort Worth Stockyards, this hotel has free curbside parking and is only a short walk to restaurants, saloons, and historic attractions.

The Exchange Hotel opened in 1939 just west of the Fort Worth Stockyards and was run by Leo H. Koestler. The two-story light yellow brick building remained in the hands of the Koestler family for several decades. The moderne-style hotel sits within the Fort Worth Stockyards Historic District. Now under new ownership and called Hotel Texas, the hotel was renovated in 1995.

The decor in its 19 guest rooms leans toward country/cowboy with well-worn contemporary wooden dressers, nightstands, and writing tables. Many of the rooms have black iron canopy beds, and the hotel is carpeted throughout. Each of the rooms, on the first and second floors, has a small private bath with a walk-in shower. Each sink and small vanity is inset into the guest room wall with a shelf above for a TV. The guest room dubbed Honeymoon Suite has the only large bathroom in the hotel and features a huge Jacuzzi tub and shower.

Groups of friends like to book the Bob Wills Suite on the second floor, which is actually four separate guest rooms, each with its own private bath. Room doors face one another. Curtained double doors at that end of

Hotel Texas, Fort Worth. Photo by Liz Carmack.

ESSENTIALS

Contact: 2415 Ellis Avenue, Fort Worth, TX 76164; 800-866-6660, 817-624-2224; fax: 817-624-7177; www.hoteltexasdfw.com

Rooms: 19 rooms and suites, all with private bath; walk-in shower, Jacuzzi tub; king, queen, full, twin beds.

Rates: $$, includes continental breakfast.

Room amenities: phone, TV, hair dryer; iron and ironing board available upon request.

Smoking: designated rooms.

Credit cards: V, MC, AE, D, DC.

Parking: free on street.

Accessibility: short flight of stairs to first-floor rooms, no elevator.

Pets: not allowed.

Author's tips:—Two buildings on the same block were also once hotels: the brick Llano Hotel (circa 1924), at 2400 Ellis Avenue, and the sandstone Myrtle Robbins Boarding House (circa 1936), at 2401 Ellis Avenue.

National Register of Historic Places: no

Texas historical marker: no

Texas Heritage Trails Program: Texas Lakes Trail Region, www.texaslakestrail.com

Visitor information: Fort Worth Convention and Visitors Bureau, 415 Throckmorton, Fort Worth, TX 76102; 800-433-5747, 817-336-8791; www.fortworth.com

the hallway can be closed to partition the area from the rest of the hotel.

Framed posters of stockyards events, a velvet painting of a matador, and autographed photographs of touring musicians line the hotel's long corridors. Guests help themselves to a minimal continental breakfast in the hotel's small, living room–like lobby.

There is no hotel parking lot, but the free parallel parking around the hotel is a boon, since free parking is hard to find closer to the stockyards and its many attractions. These include Billy Bob's Texas, billed as the world's largest honky-tonk, the Cowtown Museum, and shopping and dining at Stockyards Station.

Miss Molly's Hotel
Fort Worth 🐎 1910

This small hotel, supposedly haunted, gets high marks from partying couples who want a convenient refuge after a night of saloon-hopping and two-stepping in the Fort Worth Stockyards.

Amelia Elsner, the first owner of this hotel, supposedly demanded that her guests prove they were married before she would rent them a room. The story, told by an Elsner relative, is likely true, given that the Fort Worth Stockyards at the time had its share of saloons, bordellos, and vice. Elsner operated this small, second-floor hotel through the 1920s and early '30s, at one point calling it the Palace Rooms, according to old Fort Worth telephone directories. But legend has it that the hotel's reputation changed in the early 1930s when an individual running the café on the first floor turned the hotel into a bordello that hosted high-stakes poker games for stockyards patrons. It is not known how long the bordello was in business, but directory records show that in 1943 Walker Andrews ran the Gaiety Hotel here.

This intimate inn is located inside the Fort Worth Stockyards National Historic District. A huge center of livestock trading, packing, and shipping during the first half of the twentieth century, the stockyards district now draws tourists from around the world with its western color, history, and live entertainment. Stockyards nightlife can be pretty raucous, and Miss Molly's is in the midst of the

Miss Molly's Hotel, Fort Worth. Photo by Liz Carmack.

ESSENTIALS

Contact: 109 1/2 W. Exchange Avenue, Fort Worth, TX 76164; 817-626-1522; fax: 817-626-2589; www.missmollyshotel.com

Rooms: 7 rooms share three bathrooms down the hall; Miss Josie's Suite has private bath; claw-foot tub with shower, walk-in shower; queen and full beds.

Rates: $$–$$$, includes full breakfast on weekends.

Room amenities: hair dryer, iron and ironing board available on request, robe.

Facilities: phone for guest use.

Smoking: outdoors only.

Credit cards: cash or check only.

Parking: free on street.

Accessibility: steep stairway to lobby, all rooms on second floor.

Pets: not allowed.

Author's tips:—Children 12 and older are welcome.—Those seeking quiet and a lot of privacy might not appreciate the intimate atmosphere and proximity to other guests.—The Star Café below the hotel offers tasty, reasonably priced lunches and dinners.

National Register of Historic Places: no

Texas historical marker: no

Texas Heritage Trails Program: Texas Lakes Trail Region, www.texaslakestrail.com

Visitor information: Fort Worth Convention and Visitors Bureau, 415 Throckmorton, Fort Worth, TX 76102; 800-433-5747, 817-336-8791; www.fortworth.com

action. Weekend lodgers who want to party instead of retire early will enjoy the hotel's location. Eight saloons are within a block of the hotel, and more are nearby. During weekends the sidewalks are crowded with cowboy-booted revelers. Live country and western music spills out of spots like the White Elephant Saloon, the Stockyards Saloon, and Pearl's Dancehall. A ten-minute walk away, the super-sized honky-tonk Billy Bob's Texas hosts national stars like Willie Nelson, Glenn Campbell, and Robert Earl Keen.

Miss Molly's front door is just east of the Star Cafe entrance and opens to a steep, wide staircase that leads to its tiny parlor. A handful of floor and table lamps and a ceiling light behind a large pink, green, and yellow stained glass–panel illuminate the living area.

Tiffany Hicks, former Miss Molly's owner, readily shared bordello and ghost tales, such as the story of a maid who regularly found loose change in rooms that hadn't been occupied. The nervous woman eventually threw up her hands, said "it just ain't right," and quit. A coffee table in the parlor is piled high with newspaper clippings featuring the hotel and a report from the North Texas Paranormal Research Society about the paranormal activity detected in its rooms. After all this talk of ghosts, I got a distinctly eerie feeling sitting alone in the dimly lit parlor one weekday morning as the hotel's only guest. But I can see how the atmosphere would be much different on a busy Saturday night.

Furnishings are mostly antiques, and the decor is undeniably western. Collectible adornments include old woodstoves, spurs, tack, and old photos of trick horseback riders and cowgirls. Throw rugs cover the well-worn wood floors throughout. Each of the seven guest rooms and one suite opens onto the central parlor and has a slightly different theme, from rustic ranching/cowboy to plush, turn-of-the-century bawdy. Colorful handmade quilts, softened with many washings, and satin comforters in deep reds cover the beds. Miss Josie's Suite has a silk-draped ceiling and a private bath with a claw-foot tub and brass shower attachment. The other rooms share three bathrooms.

Partying couples favor the hotel on weekends, and Miss Molly's has been known to host a few bachelorette parties. It is also often home to business travelers and foreign tourists who want a taste of the Old West. Attractions within a few blocks of the hotel include not only saloons and dance halls, but the Texas Cowboy Hall of Fame, the Livestock Exchange Building, the Cowtown Coliseum, and gift shops.

Stockyards Hotel

Fort Worth ⚖ 1907

An atmosphere that hearkens back to Fort Worth's rugged cowtown past but has been made comfortable by modern appointments awaits guests at this century-old hostelry.

The Stockyards Hotel has a prime location in the historic Fort Worth Stockyards and rooms with authentic western decor, art, and artifacts, making it popular with those seeking a taste of the old West in a setting filled with modern appointments. Guests hang out inside the hotel lobby or on a saddle-topped bar stool in its adjacent saloon, named for legendary Texas bronc-busting champion Booger Red, to soak up the atmosphere and people watch.

The hotel's roots lie in an era when the Fort Worth Stockyards was the key livestock market of the southwest, helping to transform Fort Worth from a small frontier town into a major metropolis. The historic arched stockyards entrance sits adjacent to the hotel's three-story, yellow-orange brick building; both are part of the Fort Worth Stockyards Historic District.

Local businessman and civic leader Col. Thomas M. Thannisch constructed this building, then known as the largest individually owned commercial structure on Exchange Street, in two phases. The eastern portion was designed by Thannisch and built by C. E. Brown. It opened in 1907. Local architectural firm Field and Clarkson designed a 1913 addition to the west that melded so well with the original structure that they appear to

Stockyards Hotel, Fort Worth. Photo by Liz Carmack.

ESSENTIALS

Contact: 109 E. Exchange Ave. Fort Worth, TX 76164; 800-423-8471, 817-625-6427; fax: 817-624-2571; www.stockyardshotel.com

Rooms: 52 rooms and suites, all with private bath; claw-foot tub with hand shower attachment, tub/shower combination; king, queen, full beds.

Rates: $$–$$$$

Room amenities: phone, TV, coffee maker, hair dryer, iron and ironing board, free wi-fi, room service.

Facilities: H3 Ranch, 11 A.M. to 10 P.M. Mon.–Thurs., 11 A.M. to 11 P.M. Fri., 9 A.M. to 11 P.M. Sat., 9 A.M. to 10 P.M. Sun.; Booger Red's Saloon, 11 A.M. to 10 P.M. Mon.–Thurs., 11 A.M. to 12 A.M. Fri. and Sat., noon to 10 P.M. Sun.; group space for up to 120.

Smoking: allowed in all guest rooms, saloon.

Credit cards: V, MC, AE, D, DC.

Parking: valet only, $8.

Accessibility: elevator.

Pets: allowed, $50 fee.

Author's tips:—Guest staying in rooms overlooking Main Street should expect traffic noise.—Stockyards landmark the White Elephant Saloon, 106 E. Exchange, is across from the hotel. The bar is known for hosting Texas musicians seven nights a week and has a huge collection of cowboy hats (and elephants, of course).

National Register of Historic Places: yes, part of Fort Worth Stockyards Historic District.

Texas historical marker: no

Texas Heritage Trails Program: Texas Lakes Trail Region, www.texaslakestrail.com

Visitor information: Fort Worth Convention and Visitors Bureau, 415 Throckmorton, Fort Worth, TX 76102; 800-433-5747, 817-336-8791; www.fortworth.com

---

be one building of chevron style. It's known as the Thannish Block. During its early days, the ground floor housed many businesses, including physicians' offices, a barbershop, the Club Bar, a restaurant, and real estate and brokerage firms. Lodging was upstairs. Overnight guests were cattlemen and their families, cowboys, rail passengers, and employees of the stockyards and its associated meatpacking and rail shipping operations.

After several decades of success, changes in transportation and the decentralization of livestock markets caused the stockyards' prominence to diminish. The hotel, which had been operated as the Stock Yards Hotel, the Club Hotel, the Chandler Hotel, Planters Hotel, and the Right Hotel, badly deteriorated and became a flophouse in the 1970s. It was closed by the city health department in 1981. Two Texas businessmen with a vision rescued the building and restored it in the 1980s, paying exacting attention to original hotel details. For instance, the design of the new handrail on the hotel's wide main stairway was based on the original rail. And new room doors were made to match original doors.

This hotel's heritage is expressed through its old West decor. Deep burgundy suede covers the walls in the large, sunny lobby. The room is filled with leather sofas, potted ferns, hand-carved cowhide chairs, and bronzes of American Indians and buffalo. While I was soaking up the atmosphere one afternoon, in walked a man in a cowboy hat and boots, tourists toting cameras, businessmen with their briefcases, and actor John Leguizamo with his entourage.

The hotel's Texas-sized elevator is big enough to host a small party and still has the brass mechanism once used by its operator to shuttle guests between floors. Mounted longhorn heads preside over the longhorn-themed carpet on the stairway and in the halls.

The Stockyards' fifty-two rooms and suites, all of which have private baths, are decorated in themes the hotel calls Victorian, mountain man, cowboy, and Native American. They are furnished mostly with hand-crafted furniture and period repro-ductions. Western-style adornments include spur-and-horseshoe sconces, photos of oil rigs and longhorn herds, and wormwood shutters that, when closed, appear to be riddled with bullet holes. Guests can choose from numerous suites, including the Bonnie and Clyde, which displays Bonnie's pistol and letters, and the Butch Cassidy, a colorful room of rough-hewn pine furniture. The two-room, $425-a-night Celebrity Suite has been a favorite of guests such as Willie Nelson, Tanya Tucker, George Strait, and Chuck Norris. It includes a private deck with outdoor hot tub, a lavish bathroom with Jacuzzi tub, a fireplace, and a state-of-the-art stereo system. Celebrities have asked hotel staff more than once to fill the Jacuzzi tub with champagne. They've obliged on occasion.

The hotel is in the midst of the Fort Worth Stockyards Historic District and its many museums, restaurants, bars, and shops.

Couples pamper themselves in this small hotel's spacious, individually decorated rooms on Granbury's historic and tourist-friendly courthouse square.

As a Granbury teenager in the 1930s and early 1940s, Mary Kate Durham would walk from school to the Nutt House dining room each day for lunch. Durham's family operated a dairy, and her father traded milk to the hotel restaurant for her meals. She remembers the family-style dining at one long table, sharing mounding platters of delicious roast pork, fried chicken, mashed potatoes, and cornbread. Traveling salesmen staying at the hotel would regularly schedule their routes so they could be in Granbury on the day the restaurant served their favorite dish.

This building on the Hood County Courthouse square initially housed the mercantile business of town pioneers Jesse and Jacob Nutt, both of whom were blind, and their sighted brother David. The Nutts constructed the two-story native limestone building in 1893 to expand their business, which had been operating in a log cabin on this same site. David and his wife were already accommodating mercantile customers overnight at their plantation-style home down the street. But in 1911 they decided to remodel the mercantile to add a parlor and twenty guest rooms upstairs. The hotel became known as, no pun intended, the Nutt House.

Today's Nutt House guests relax in much more spacious quarters than its

Nutt House Historic Hotel, Granbury. Photo by Liz Carmack.

former lodgers were accustomed to. The seven guest rooms are twice their original size. The large private bath in each room features a super-sized tub, a shower, and small luxuries such as bottles of bubble bath and robes. The hotel's guest rooms attract vacationing clientele, mostly couples on romantic getaways from Dallas-Fort Worth who are drawn to tourist-friendly Granbury.

Owners brought in an interior designer in 2002 to help create this upscale-antique atmosphere. Antiques, collectibles, and fabrics have been thoughtfully arranged to give each room its own personality. In one the carved top of an antique dresser is hung upside down, above five old hand mirrors hung in a row. In another, a leather-strapped trunk serves as a de facto suitcase rack, and a beautiful antique buffet displays a vase of iridescent feathers alongside a stack of old hardbacks.

The pillow-mounded beds have luxurious, handmade duvet covers and pillow shams in rich fabrics. The furniture, mostly antique, has been expertly refinished and reupholstered, and some pieces whitewashed and given a distressed look. Color schemes in each room range from dark and earthy to warm and cheery. Wooden shutters cover the windows, and the floors are carpeted. All rooms

ESSENTIALS

Contact: 119 E. Bridge, Granbury, TX 76048; 888-678-0813, 817-279-1207; fax: 817-579-8043; www.nutt-hotel.com, stay@granbury-lodging.com

Rooms: 7 rooms, all with private bath; walk-in showers, large tubs, tub/shower combination; king and queen beds.

Rates: $$–$$$

Room amenities: TV, coffee maker, iron and ironing board, hair dryer, robe, free wi fi.

Facilities: Texas Nutt House Restaurant, in-house massages, complimentary Blue Bell ice cream.

Smoking: outdoors only.

Credit cards: V, MC, AE, D.

Parking: free on street and in lot across from hotel.

Accessibility: all rooms on second floor reached by stairs only.

Pets: not allowed.

Author's tips:—The hotel discourages bringing children.—Sample the fruits of D'Vine Wine of Texas, 107 E. Bridge St., and order custom labeled bottles of your favorite varietals.

National Register of Historic Places: yes, part of Hood County Courthouse Historic District.

Texas historical marker: yes

Texas Heritage Trails Program: Texas Lakes Trail, www.texaslakestrail.com

Visitor information: Granbury Convention and Visitors Bureau, 116 W. Bridge St., Granbury, TX 76048; 800-950-2212, 817-573-5548; www.granburytx.com, gcvb@granburytx.com

still have their original high bead-board ceilings. All guest room doors have their original transoms. The original screen doors (rescreened) were left on room doors that are no longer used. All rooms open onto one of two hallways or a small, antique-filled parlor where a handful of sitting areas are overseen by mounted steer and deer heads. The hotel's restaurant serves lunch, dinner, and Sunday brunch.

This building was the first of the historic limestone and brick structures along Granbury's turn-of-the-century courthouse square to be restored in the early 1970s. Mary Lou Watkins, granddaughter of David

Nutt, kicked off the town's preservation efforts by reopening its then-closed restaurant and selling antiques in the upstairs rooms. She is credited with leading the transformation of Granbury's downtown into a tourist mecca. The square is now a national historic district.

Restaurants, a coffee house, and shops ring the town square, although many have limited hours during the early part of the week. Granbury Live and the historic Granbury Opera House provide regular musical entertainment. Lake Granbury, formed when the Brazos was dammed in 1969, is a favorite for fishing and cruising on the Granbury Riverboat.

The Woodbine Hotel

Madisonville ⚓ 1904

This hotel, known for its fine-dining restaurant, Victorian decor, and relaxed atmosphere, is headquarters for the annual Texas Mushroom Festival in Madisonville.

This three-story, 7,500-square-foot hotel, distinguished by its turrets and fish-scale shingles, is one of the most impressive historic structures in Madison County. Called the Shapira Hotel when it opened in 1904, it initially catered to lodgers with interests in the county's cotton, cattle, or oil businesses, many of whom arrived on the International-Great Northern Railroad. Townsfolk also frequented the hotel, as they do today, to dine in its restaurant or attend social gatherings.

After Russian immigrants Jacob and Sarah Shapira's first boarding-house in Madisonville was destroyed by fire, this hotel became its replacement. The fire was at least the second tragedy within a year for Sarah. Her husband, Jacob, died the same year, a few weeks after stepping on a nail. His death came just a few days after the wedding of their eldest daughter.

The family sold the hotel in 1928. It operated as the Wills Hotel until 1978, when new owners undertook a lengthy renovation and changed its name to the Woodbine, after the woodbine sandstone found in this area. Though the narrative about the hotel in the National Register of Historic Places doesn't mention this, some locals say the large hotel, built of yellow pine with cedar shingles, is the product of two kit houses, one Eastlake Style, the other Queen Anne, connected with a forty-foot gallery.

The Woodbine Hotel, Madisonville. Photo by Liz Carmack.

ESSENTIALS

Contact: 209 N. Madison, Madison-ville, TX 77864; 888-966-3246, 936-348-3333; fax: 936-348-6268; www
.woodbinehotel.com, woodbine@
woodbinehotel.com

Rooms: 8 rooms including 1 suite, all with private bath; whirlpool baths, tub/shower combination, walk-in showers; king and queen beds.

Rates: $–$$, includes full breakfast.

Room amenities: phone, TV, iron and ironing board available upon request, free wi-fi.

Facilities: Woodbine Restaurant and Bar, 7 A.M. to 9:30 A.M. Tues.–Fri., 8 A.M. to 9:30 A.M. Sat. and Sun. (breakfast for guests only); 11 A.M. to 2 P.M. Tues. through Fri. ; 6 P.M. to 9 P.M. Tues. through Sat., 11 A.M. to 2 P.M. Sunday brunch; morning coffee for guests available in kitchen; group space for up to 100.

Smoking: outdoors only.

Credit cards: V, MC, AE, D.

Parking: free in hotel lots.

Accessibility: all rooms on second floor and reached by stairs only.

Pets: not allowed.

Author's tips:—The hotel welcomes children 13 and older.

*National Register
of Historic Places:* yes

Texas historical marker: yes

Texas Heritage Trails Program: Texas Brazos Trail Region, www.texas
brazostrail.com

Visitor information: City of Madison-ville, 210 W. Cottonwood, Madison-ville, TX 77864; 936-348-2748; www.ci.madisonville.tx.us

All eight of the hotel's guest rooms are on the second floor and have entrances off the large second floor parlor or off the wide balcony along the U-shaped back of the hotel. The third floor is off-limits to guests and is supposedly inhabited by the ghosts of Jacob and Sarah Shapira.

Lace curtains hang on the hotel's more than ninety tall, double-hung windows. Antiques fill much of the wallpapered guest rooms and common areas, where Oriental-style rugs cover the dark pine floors. Additional decorating touches include crocheted table scarves, porcelain wash pitchers and bowls, and the owner's extensive collection of copper serving pieces. Original ornate lattice work and carved corner blocks accentuate interior doorways and the small bay rooms formed by the turrets on the buildings' northern and southern wings. These sunny sitting areas enhance two of the hotel's more spacious guest rooms.

The hotel's lobby opens onto two dining rooms at one end and a bar at the other, which features the phone booth that once housed the town's sole telephone. The Woodbine's restaurant, Madisonville's only fine-dining establishment, is well known in the area. Hotel guests enjoy complimentary cooked-to-order breakfasts alongside locals who drop in for the crispy Woodbine Waffle topped with pecans grown at nearby Rattlesnake Ranch. At lunch and dinner, the chef turns out favorites including prime rib, pan-sautéed fresh tilapia, and homemade soup. The Madisonville Monterey Portabello Mushroom Burger's main ingredient is from the city's Monterey Mushroom Farm.

The hotel's overnight patrons include many business travelers—including those in the oil and gas business—who make this their home for a few days or weeks. Tourists also choose the Woodbine for laid-back weekends and romantic dinners in the restaurant. Groups also book the Woodbine for meetings and banquets, and they find the grounds behind the hotel with its rose-covered gazebo a good spot for weddings.

Just two doors down from the hotel is the city's main attraction, the Madisonville County Museum, which was once the First State Bank building. The building houses rotating exhibits and displays photos of the Richardsonian Romanesque–style Madison County Courthouse, which burned to the ground in 1967 and was replaced with a modern building.

Madisonville is a pretty quiet burg except for each October, when the hotel becomes headquarters for the annual Texas Mushroom Festival in Madisonville—a day of dining, cooking demonstrations, wine tasting, live music, and family activities. Guest seeking lodging for the festival should book at least three months in advance.

Stagecoach Inn
Salado   circa 1860

This former stagecoach stop has become a beloved restaurant and is part of a peaceful compound that offers motel-style accommodations in the historic, art-loving village of Salado.

Overland stages traveling between Waco and Austin in the 1860s and 1870s once called at this historic inn, which sat so close to a feeder route of the Chisholm Trail that its owners erected a tall cedar fence to protect it from wandering cattle. Although overnight guests can no longer sleep in the original inn's wood-frame building, they can dine there, relax with a drink on its covered gallery, and stay in the motel-style rooms on the Stagecoach's expansive grounds.

The founding of Salado was synonymous with the founding of Salado College, which opened its doors in 1860 on land donated by Elijah Sterling C. Robertson. The college operated until 1885. Robertson also donated lots for Salado. Around 1860 Thomas Jefferson Eubanks purchased one of those lots across the street from the college for $100. While

Stagecoach Inn, Salado. Photo by Liz Carmack.

some sources state that in the early 1860s Eubanks built the building now known as the Stagecoach Inn, others cite W. B. Armstrong as the builder.

Salado was a growing educational, industrial, and agricultural center during this time, and eight flour and gristmills operated along Salado Creek, which is just a short walk from the inn and now bordered by a peaceful city park.

According to local lore, in 1861 Gen. Sam Houston, then governor of Texas, spoke against Texas' secession from the union from the balcony of the two-story inn, and Confederate Gen. Robert E. Lee and outlaws the Youngers and the James Brothers lodged here. Unfortunately, any records of these visits disappeared with the inn's early guest register, which was stolen decades ago. Over time, the inn changed hands, and owners operated the hotel under the names the Shady Villa Hotel, the Buckles Hotel, and the Salado Hotel.

ESSENTIALS

Contact: P.O. Box 97, 401 S. Stagecoach Road, Salado, TX 76571; 800-732-8994, 254-947-5111; fax: 254-947-0671; www.stagecoach-inn.com, lodging@ stagecoach-inn.com
Rooms: 82 rooms and suites, all with private bath; tub-shower combination; king, full beds.
Rates: $$–$$$
Room amenities: coffee maker, TV, hair dryer, iron and ironing board; deluxe rooms and suites have private furnished patio.
Facilities: Stagecoach Inn Restaurant, 11 A.M. to 4 P.M. and 5 P.M. to 9 P.M. daily; Stagecoach Inn Coffee Shop, 6:30 A.M. to 8 P.M. daily; Stagecoach Inn Club, 5 P.M. to 9 P.M. weekdays and extended hours on weekends; outdoor pool, group space for up to 200.
Smoking: designated rooms.
Credit cards: V, MC, AE, D.
Parking: free in hotel lots.
Accessibility: disabled access, many rooms are on ground floor.

Pets: yes, $50 fee.
Author's tips:—A short walk away, the 150-seat Salado Silver Spur Theater, 108 Royal Street, offers live vaudeville-style entertainment on weekends combined with silent movies in an old converted granary building. (254-947-3456, www.saladosilverspur.com)— Outlaws are said to have used a cave near a gnarled pecan tree on the inn's grounds as their hideout because of its constant supply of spring water. Visitors can see the entrance to the cave, which is now padlocked for safety.
National Register of Historic Places: yes
Texas historical marker: yes
Texas Heritage Trails Program: Texas Brazos Trail Region, www.texasbrazostrail.com
Visitor information: Village of Salado Tourism Office, 601 N. Main Street, P.O. Box 219, Salado, TX 76571; 254-947-8634; www.salado.com, saladotourism@vvm.com

A major turning point in the inn's history came when Dion and Ruth Van Bibber bought and remodeled the old building and reopened it in 1943 as a tearoom. The restaurant had a sophisticated atmosphere, and its southern-style dishes became so well known that the couple stopped taking lodgers and added dining rooms around a centuries-old bur oak tree. In 1959 the Van Bibbers retired. A nephew took over and added the motel and other facilities, which are conveniently positioned for motorists alongside the Interstate 35 access road.

The Stagecoach Inn complex now mixes modern conveniences with a historic legacy in a laid-back atmosphere. It has become popular with vacationing families and is often booked for group retreats. The western part of the Stagecoach Inn grounds includes the main lobby, motel buildings, coffee shop, pool, and conference center. These facilities sit amid manicured lawns and have easy on/off access to the interstate. The eastern side of the property fronts Salado's Main Street and includes a number of historic buildings, including the Stagecoach Inn Restaurant and Club. Diners today come from miles around to feast on catfish, southern fried chicken, and prime rib, finishing off with the restaurant's signature dessert, the Strawberry Kiss—a delicious combination of meringue, vanilla ice cream, and fresh strawberries. The restaurant has numerous dining rooms, but guests lucky enough to be seated in the original frontier vernacular–style inn can admire its original limestone fireplaces. The landscaping around these buildings is lush and dominated by the large bur oak, a large pecan tree, and other native vegetation.

All guest rooms in the four two-story motel buildings have sliding glass doors that open onto a patio or small balcony. They are comfortably fitted with modern pine tables and chairs and other furnishings. Deluxe rooms are 30 percent larger than standard rooms and include a writing desk. The roomy bathrooms have large vanities, and those in rooms around the pool were refurbished in 2007 with golden-colored granite. Suites include kitchenettes. I settled into a room with a balcony overlooking the pool. Children frolicked in the water while adults rocked and chatted underneath a large oak tree on the adjacent patio. If you prefer a bit more solitude, you could request accommodations in the "Jacuzzi building." It sits away from the patio and has easy access to an outdoor heated Jacuzzi filled with mineral water from the hotel well.

Across the street from the Stagecoach Inn are the Central Texas Area Museum and the ruins of Salado College. Lining Salado's Main Street are dozens of antique, gift, and clothing boutiques, cafés, and restaurants. Golfers can use the nearby Mill Creek golf course and its facilities, which is affiliated with the hotel.

Von Minden Hotel

Schulenburg ⚜ 1929

Cyclists and hunters of ghosts and game don't mind roughing it in this railroad hotel, the only combined hotel-movie theater still operating in Texas.

The Von Minden may be considerably less grand than the specter-filled hotel in Stephen King's *The Shining*, but it's every bit as creepy. The hotel's stuck-in-time ambience fuels the imagination of even the staunchest nonbeliever, especially after listening to enthusiastic ghost hunters describe their encounters with unregistered guests. Most days visitors can walk through the hotel's double, multipaned front doors to find a cluttered front desk left unattended and the lobby quiet and curiously empty. Behind the desk hangs a certificate commemorating the 2003 paranormal conference held here by the Spring (Texas) Spirit Seekers. After that event, word of the Von Minden's ghosts spread via the Internet. Now on many weekend nights, camera-wielding adventurers wander the hotel's dark hallways hunting spooks. The balls of light and smokelike images that appear in their photographs are supposedly restless spirits inhabiting the building, including that of a railroad worker who died here. Some say they've seen a lady wearing a wide-brimmed hat and a polka-dotted dress who vanishes into thin air.

Upon my arrival, a woman who visited regularly from Houston and claimed to be supernaturally sensitive

Von Minden Hotel, Schulenburg. Photo by Liz Carmack.

ESSENTIALS

Contact: Von Minden Hotel, 607 Lyons Ave., Schulenburg, TX 78956; 866-611-9818, 979-743-3716

Rooms: 9 rooms, all with private bath; tub/shower combination; two-bedroom Schultz House adjacent to hotel with sun porch.

Rates: $–$$

Room amenities: TVs in some rooms.

Facilities: Momma's Pizza Kitchen, 11 A.M. to 1:15 P.M. Tues.–Fri., 5 P.M. to 9 P.M. Sun.–Thurs., 5 P.M. to 10 P.M. Fri.–Sat.; coffeemaker in guest sitting area on third floor; no telephone available in hotel, but the Momma's Pizza Kitchen phone is available for brief calls.

Smoking: outdoors only.

Credit cards: cash or check only.

Parking: free in hotel lot.

Accessibility: all guest rooms reached by stairs.

Pets: not allowed.

Author's tips:—Stop by the Kountry Bakery, 110 Kessler Ave. (U.S. Hwy. 77), for *kolaches*, streusel, and other area favorites.

National Register of Historic Places: no

Texas historical marker: no

Texas Heritage Trails Program: Texas Independence Trail Region, www.texasindependencetrail.com

Visitor information: Schulenburg Chamber of Commerce, 618 N. Main St., Schulenburg, TX 78956; 866-504-5294, 979-743-4514; www.schulenburgchamber.org

used a "divining rod" made from coat hangers to help me select my room. The wires, which she balanced lightly on her index fingers, slowly swung toward one another and crossed when we entered some seemingly empty rooms, an indication, she said, of an otherworldly presence. I picked a room that was supposedly spirit-free and spent a restless night twitching at every drip of the faucet and creak of the stairs.

The Von Minden is also notable as the only hotel-movie theater combination still operating in the state. The Cozy Theater had already been open for a couple of years when Gerhardt Von Minden built his four-story, forty-room hotel. Some say the presence of Gerhardt's daughter Leonida and her husband, who ran the businesses for many decades, can be felt near the huge old gas boiler that still heats the 235-seat theater. For almost two years beginning in 1935 a radio show was broadcast live from the stage on Saturday mornings. The Gold Chain Bohemians played polkas and waltzes for audiences, and the broadcasts were transmitted via telephone line to a Fort Worth radio station. The old, faded scene backdrops used for such productions now hang behind its screen, which shows first-run movies six nights a week. In the projection room, decades of clutter and detritus make the cramped space feel like a time capsule. Dozens of 78 rpm records, mainly polkas and waltzes played for patrons before the movies began, sit dust covered in a cabinet. Stacks of large glass slides advertising area businesses fill a crumbling cigar box. Boxes now fill the seats in a small balcony that during segregation were occupied by black patrons who used a separate entrance from whites.

For Schulenburg area residents, the Cozy Theater is the only place in town to catch a movie. Admission is four dollars, and patrons can order a slice of pizza in addition to a bag of popcorn. The pizza comes from the adjacent Momma's Pizza Kitchen around the back of the hotel. Bill Petit bought the restaurant, hotel, and theater with his wife in 1979. An attorney, Petit has his office on the hotel's second floor. He opens the hotel only on weekends, but you'll find Petit in the theater's projection room most nights.

Couples who spent their wedding night at the Von Minden decades ago sometimes return for a nostalgic evening. A few might recognize the same chairs that were in the lobby back then and the same candy machine (now empty) in the guest sitting area on the third floor.

The hotel's basic accommodations are not for every traveler, but those who can appreciate its funkiness, dust bunnies, and cobwebs will enjoy the atmosphere. Nine guest rooms are available on the hotel's third floor, and a few permanent residents occupy the fourth. Public areas are not heated or air-conditioned, but the guest rooms have window air-conditioning units and space heaters. Rooms are wallpapered or painted and have simple appointments. Many have their original oak rockers and dressers, which show their age. All have private baths. Soap is provided, but guests should pack other toiletries. Bathroom fixtures are old enough to be original and include sinks with separate hot and cold taps. A more well-appointed home behind the hotel is also available to lodgers.

Aside from ghost hunters, the Von Minden also hosts cyclists touring the Fayette County countryside and hunters. The Schulenburg Chamber of Commerce has maps and tour information about the Painted Churches of Fayette County. The churches nearby in the Dubina, Ammannsville, High Hill, and Praha communities have elaborately painted interiors and date from as early as 1892.

Rogers Hotel
Waxahachie ⚜ 1913

Located across from one of Texas' most photographed county courthouses, this hotel during its early years was home to the Chicago White Sox and other professional baseball teams in Waxahachie for spring training.

One evening at the Rogers Hotel, I watched the sun dip behind the 1896 Romanesque revival Ellis County courthouse and its chiming clock tower. The sky slowly shifted from burnt red-orange to deep violet-blue. Then white Christmas lights lining the two- and three-story brick buildings along the turn-of-the-century square blinked on along with floodlights accentuating the courthouse's gargoyles and sculpted columns. A room at the Rogers Hotel is once again a front-row seat to this awe-inspiring show after a $1 million renovation and reopening in 2001.

The site of the Rogers has a long history. The hotel opened in 1913 and was named for the town's first homesteader and his wife, Emory W. and Nancy Rogers. They built their log cabin home, the community's first, here in 1847. In 1856 the couple built a two-story wooden hotel on this spot. Several major fires plagued the young town. That early hotel, and then another built at this location by the Waxahachie Real Estate and Building Association, were both burned. The last fire, in 1911 also destroyed a grocery, millinery, the Wells Fargo office, and several houses.

From 1890 through 1920, a strong cotton market and the town's criss-crossing railroad lines supported Ellis County cotton growers and

Rogers Hotel, Waxahachie. Photo by Liz Carmack.

ESSENTIALS

Contact: 100 N. College St., Waxahachie, TX 75165; 800-556-4192, 972-938-3688; fax: 972-938-3036; www.rogershotel.com, info@rogershotel.com

Rooms: 27 rooms and suites, all with private bath; tub/shower combination; king and queen beds; Bridal Suite has large living area and excellent view of Ellis County Courthouse and town square.

Rates: $–$$, includes continental breakfast.

Room amenities: phone, TV, coffee maker, hair dryer, iron and ironing board, free wi-fi.

Facilities: Fat Moe's Live, 5 P.M. to midnight Mon.–Fri.; 5 P.M. to 1 A.M. Sat.; group space accommodates up to 150.

Smoking: bar.

Credit cards: V, MC, AE, D, DC.

Parking: free on street or in hotel lot.

Accessibility: disabled access, elevator.

Pets: not allowed.

Author's tips:—Trains pass only two blocks away, so light sleepers should bring earplugs.—The menu at the College Street Restaurant and Pub, 210 College St., around the corner from the hotel, includes excellent burgers and daily specials seven days a week.

National Register of Historic Places: yes, part of Ellis County Courthouse Historic District.

Texas historical marker: no

Texas Heritage Trails Program: Texas Lakes Trail, www.texaslakestrail.com

Visitor information: Waxahachie Chamber of Commerce and Convention and Visitors Bureau, 102 YMCA Drive, Waxahachie, TX 75165; 927-937-2390; www.waxahachiechamber.com,

Waxahachie's cotton gins, warehouses, compresses, and textile mill. For a time Ellis County was the largest cotton-producing county in the nation. During King Cotton's reign, the Waxahachie Real Estate Building Association hired Dallas architect C. D. Hill to design a modern, "fireproof," four-story hotel. Gross Construction built the Rogers using reinforced concrete faced with dark, mottled brick and Bedford stone.

When the building opened it had sixty guest rooms outfitted with telephones and corner sinks. Outdoor dining and sunset watching were available on a rooftop garden covered with potted plants and a shade-providing arbor. On the eastern half of the roof, the hotel constructed a tented sleeping area for "the open air enthusiast," according to hotel literature from that time.

Cotton merchants and traveling salesmen favored the Rogers for its two large sample rooms, conveniently located near a freight elevator. Today groups can book the same rooms for functions and view the elevator mechanism. Hotel patrons also liked its convenient location on the Texas Electric Railway, an interurban passenger rail that connected Waxahachie with several cities including Dallas and Waco from 1912 to 1948. The tracks ran down College Street and the train stopped just outside the Rogers' west entrance, where the words "Rogers Hotel" remain set in the tiled foyer.

The floors in the hotel lobby and the former parlor and dining rooms also have their original tile. The square and octagonal one-inch tiles of grey, green, brick red, and yellow create different geometric patterns in each room. In fact, the layout of the hotel's first-floor public areas and most of the floor's original interior details have remained largely intact since the hotel's opening. They include a curving front desk and green-brown tile wainscoting in the airy lobby; a marble, wall-mounted artesian water fountain (which no longer works); and frosted-glass transoms set high over the lobby and parlor's many windows. The hotel's original black iron elevator cage, with its delicate ceiling scrollwork and lacy wall panels, make it the most attractive of Texas' hotel elevators.

Most spring seasons from 1916 to 1921, the Rogers lobby and dining room hummed with activity, and its guest rooms filled with members of major league baseball teams such as the Detroit Tigers, the Cincinnati Reds, and the Chicago White Sox. Players like Ty Cobb mingled with coaches and sportswriters at the hotel, and signed autographs for fans.

The Rogers turned its basement coal storage bin into a mineral water pool for team members to soak in after practices. I took a nighttime tour of the basement and found the former coal bin-turned-pool now filled with dirt and debris.

Daniel Newman purchased the hotel from its original owners in 1921, and he and then his son ran it until the early 1940s. The Depression and the subsequent slowdown in the town's economy eventually led to the hotel's shuttering. It sat largely unused from the 1950s until its recent rebirth. During its renovation by new owners Tony and Janice Cimino of Dallas, the upper floors were totally gutted and reconfigured to create nine spacious rooms and eighteen suites, all with private baths.

Large radiators with decorative moldings once provided steam heat throughout the hotel. Silver paint and the installation of central heating have transformed these into purely decorative sculptures that are the main conversation piece in the carpeted guest rooms and hallways. The accommodations are sparingly decorated and have relatively artless walls and few knickknacks on tables and dressers. They have modern furnishings and appointments, and some have their original push-button light switches and ceiling light fixtures. Large windows, and light-colored walls, blinds, and bed linens make the quarters bright. The bathrooms feature marble in muted tones, chrome fixtures, and pedestal sinks fashioned in an early twentieth century style.

A half block away are historical exhibits at the Ellis County Museum. Here visitors can pick up literature outlining driving and walking routes through Waxahachie's four national historic districts. The areas include parks, the city cemetery, and more than a hundred historic homes and public and commercial buildings.

South Texas Plains

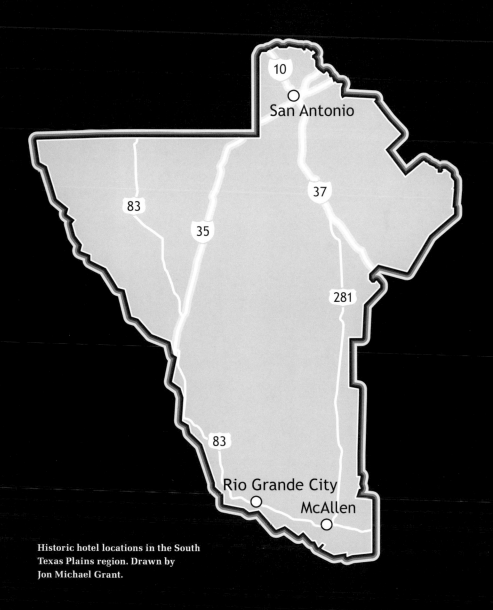

Historic hotel locations in the South Texas Plains region. Drawn by Jon Michael Grant.

Renaissance Casa de Palmas
McAllen ⚜ 1918

The flavor of the Lower Rio Grande Valley pervades the atmosphere of this mission/Spanish revival-style hotel and tropical courtyards.

As I sat in the Saltillo-tiled lobby of the Casa de Palmas late one afternoon, a trio wearing crisp white guayaberas and black slacks serenaded patrons with "Cielito Lindo." The Mexican folk music was a perfect fit to the atmosphere of this McAllen hotel, which provides plenty of reminders that you're in Texas' Lower Rio Grande Valley. Foremost among these is the hotel's mission/Spanish revival-style architecture (including red-tiled roof) and towering palm trees.

Designed by local architect M. L. Waller, the hotel was built by the Rio Grande Valley Hotel Company and opened in 1918. The project was launched by McAllen Mayor

O. P. Archer, bank president R. E. Horn, and other business leaders, who thought McAllen lacked a fine hotel. The land chosen along Main Street for the project had been a zoo, home to antelope, javelina, and deer. The hotel took its name from the dozens of multistory palms that line the street and remain a distinctive feature of the grounds and of McAllen's downtown.

After its opening in 1918, the hotel served traveling salesmen, people involved with the area's growing agriculture operations, winter Texans, and visitors on their way to Mexico. The hotel immediately became McAllen's social nexus and the scene

Renaissance Casa de Palmas, McAllen. Photo by Jeff Carmack.

ESSENTIALS

Contact: 101 N. Main Street, McAllen, TX 78501; 956-631-1101; fax: 956-631-7934; www.renaissance mcallen.com

Rooms: 165 rooms and suites, all with private bath; tub/shower combinations; king and full beds; Presidential Suite is 800 square feet and features one bedroom, Jacuzzi tub, and walk-in shower.

Rates: $$–$$$$

Amenities: phone, TV, coffee maker, hair dryer, iron and ironing board, free wi-fi, room service.

Facilities: Spanish Room, 6 A.M. to 10 P.M. daily; Lomax Cantina, 2 P.M. to 1 A.M. daily; gift shop, fitness center, outdoor pool; group space for up to 300.

Smoking: outdoors only.

Credit cards: V, MC, AE, D, DC, JCB.

Parking: free on street or in hotel garage.

Accessibility: disabled access, elevator.

Pets: not allowed.

Author's tips:—Alonsos Tres Rios Restaurant, 2101 N. 10th, is a short drive from the hotel and serves inexpensive, Mexican food in a cozy atmosphere.

National Register of Historic Places: yes

Texas historical marker: yes

Texas Heritage Trails Program: Texas Tropical Trail, www.texastropicaltrail.com

Visitor information: McAllen Chamber of Commerce, 1200 Ash Ave., McAllen, TX 78501; 956-682-2871; www.mcallen.org, nmillar@mc allencvb.com

of elaborate banquets attended by soldiers, many from the east, who had arrived in town in 1916 to quell disturbances along the Texas-Mexico border. Half of its sixty rooms offered private baths, and they all had hot and cold running water, steam heat, and private telephones, all of which were considered luxuries for a hotel at that time. A ladies salon, two private dining rooms, and well-lighted sample rooms where drummers could display their goods rounded out the top-notch facilities. Shortly after the hotel opened, most of McAllen sought refuge there during the "Corpus Christi Storm of 1919." The building emerged relatively unscathed from the hurricane.

As McAllen grew in the 1920s and '30s, the hotel changed hands, and when John Lomax and his wife became owners, they added a three-story wing to the south. The hotel bar is named for the Lomaxes, who were known across the valley for their hospitality and fine meals. In 1952 Marlon Brando, Anthony Quinn, and Jean Peters stayed here when Elia Kazan set up headquarters at the hotel during the filming of *Viva Zapata*. After a $2.5 million renovation and expansion in 1973 by a new set of owners, lightning struck the building, just two months before a grand reopening. The resulting fire almost destroyed its additions and damaged the older portions of the hotel. Repairs were made, and the hotel reopened in 1974. It underwent another renovation in 2001, this time to the tune of $8 million.

Guests enter through a large, stone-floored patio filled with lush ferns, large ficus and banana trees, and a gurgling fountain. The air smells wet and loamy. Vines from a towering African sausage tree hang dozens of feet below the tree's branches, sprouting blossoms and sausage-shaped fruit. Inside, the nicely appointed lobby looks out on a second courtyard and pool. The bilingual front desk staff switch easily between English and Spanish with guests, who are mostly business travelers, tourists, or individuals in town attending family functions.

Though it is tempting to nip inside to the hotel bar for a cool beverage while lounging poolside, guests are expected to cover up first. The hotel is serious about maintaining its relaxed but refined atmosphere in public spaces, and bathing suits are not welcome on elevators or in the hotel's lobby. The 165 guest rooms and suites all have private baths, handsome modern furnishings, and work desks. The rooms feature exposed ceiling beams, and their decor uses quality fabrics in greens, blues, crème, and gold. Bathrooms have black marble vanities. Many guest rooms have patios or balconies overlooking the interior courtyard and its pool.

Just south of the hotel along Main Street, shoppers from McAllen and Mexico fill shopping bags with imported T-shirts, tennis shoes, linens, and housewares. Locals sell cold drinks, *elotes* (roasted corn), and *raspas* (snow cones) from the backs of pickup trucks and sidewalk stands. Six wildlife refuges are within an hour's drive of McAllen, including the Santa Ana National Wildlife Refuge, recognized as one of the top ten birding sites in the nation. The Museum of South Texas History in nearby Edinburg offers the largest collection of exhibits and artifacts covering this area's heritage.

La Borde House
Rio Grande City ⚓ 1897

A French merchant established this hotel in his former home and mercantile. It has since become a celebrated example of successful historic preservation within the Rio Grande City Downtown Historic District.

In Rio Grande City, one of the oldest settlements in south Texas, the La Borde House is one of dozens of buildings more than a century old. Economic hardships and political turmoil have at times made their preservation a low priority, but city leaders proudly point to the La Borde House as an example of what determined individuals and hard-working nonprofits can accomplish when they invest in architectural resources.

Spanish colonization began here along the Rio Grande during the mid 1700s. By 1849 the first post office was established, and in the latter half of the nineteenth century, Rio Grande City had become a cattle ranching center. Flatboats brought passengers and cargo from New Orleans up the Rio Grande to this community and others, such as Roma. In 1897 French immigrant and merchant François La Borde constructed this building on land that at that time was one block from the Rio Grande. The meandering river has since moved several blocks away. The building served as a two-story family home and a one-story general store, office, and warehouse around a central courtyard. As the town's population and commerce

La Borde House, Rio Grande City. Photo by Jeff Carmack.

grew, La Borde decided to turn his home into a hotel. He modified the building's design and made it entirely two story in 1917 with the help of San Antonio architect Leo M. J. Dielmann.

The LaBorde family had to forfeit the Greek revival-style building during the Great Depression, and in the 1930s George Boyle and James Rodwell purchased it from a bank. Almost a half century later, the hotel had deteriorated, its wooden galleries collapsed and rotting—another among dozens of beautiful but vacant and neglected historic downtown buildings. Larry Sheerin, a San Antonio businessman with a Starr County

produce operation, bought the property and spent two years and $1 million restoring it in the early 1980s. The Texas Historical Commission and the U.S. Department of the Interior oversaw the project's details to ensure that La Borde kept its historical integrity. Local craftsmen rebuilt the double-hung, nine-over-six-pane windows. They carved wooden staircase balusters to match the originals, and they replaced and repaired the hotel's damaged wooden galleries, recreating their gingerbread detail when necessary. The tan brick on the hotel's exterior and in its courtyard, which is said to have come from a brickyard

ESSENTIALS

Contact: 601 E. Main, Rio Grande City, TX 78582; 956-487-5101; fax: 956-716-8560
Rooms: 7 rooms, all with private bath in original building; walk-in shower, claw-foot tub; queen and twin beds; 7 modern-style efficiency apartments.
Rates: $–$$
Room amenities: phone, TV; hair dryer, iron and ironing board available upon request; free wi-fi; small fridge and microwave; efficiency apartments have kitchenettes.
Facilities: Che Restaurant, 6 A.M. to 7 P.M. Mon.–Fri., 6 A.M. to 2 P.M. Sat.; 6 A.M. to 2 P.M. Sun., morning coffee served in lobby, business center services, group space for up to 75.
Smoking: outdoors only.
Credit cards: V, MC, AE, DC.

Parking: on street or in hotel lot.
Accessibility: one room is on ground floor, elevator.
Pets: not allowed.
Author's tips:—A short drive across downtown is Caro's, 205 N. Garcia, famous for its "puffy" fried tortilla chips and home-style Mexican food.
*National Register
    of Historic Places:* yes
Texas historical marker: no
Texas Heritage Trails Program: Texas Tropical Trail Region, www.texastropicaltrail.com
Visitor information: Rio Grande City Economic Development Corporation, 101 S. Washington St., Rio Grande City, TX 78582; 956-487-0672; www.riograndecity.net

across the Rio Grande in Camargo, Mexico, was patched with replacements ordered from the same manufacturer.

Shortly after the restoration, the Starr County Historical Foundation adopted the hotel. The organization's tight budget means the focus is now on keeping the plumbing working, the rooms clean, the roof leak-free, and the doors open to tour groups and guests. Travelers who choose the LaBorde over the chain motels on the developing eastern edge of town are rewarded with turn-of-the-century ambience made more comfortable by large guest rooms, private bathrooms, and free wi-fi.

The seven guest rooms in the oldest part of the building have high ceilings with tall windows whose sills reach the floor. Some rooms open onto the restored covered galleries. Many rooms have beautifully restored (but nonfunctioning) fireplaces featuring carved wooden mantels and hand-painted tile or marble surrounds. Victorian antiques installed in the 1980s, along with carefully restored original pieces from the hotel, fill the spacious environs. Furniture includes large mahogany beds with satin canopies, walnut armoires, and small, upholstered settees and chairs. The rooms are uncluttered aside from large mirrors, botanical prints, a pedestal sink, and the oc-

casional porcelain bowl and pitcher. Several rooms feature the same wallpaper used in the 1981 restoration of the Texas governor's mansion—a repeating Texas state seal of olive and live oak branches encircling a star. Oriental-style and English-made rugs, also from the hotel's 1980s renovation, cover hardwood floors of yellow pine and fir. Private baths in each room have Mexican tiles with simple designs in crème and rust, and each pull-chain toilet's tank is mounted high on the wall. The hotel also has seven efficiency apartments in the back of the building, all simply outfitted with modern furnishings.

The brick-paved interior courtyard features a few tropical plantings and a lion's head wall fountain. Around the corner is an old broken spiral staircase that leads belowground, to what some claim is an entrance to one of the many now-closed tunnels that crisscross subterranean Rio Grande City. These secret passageways supposedly ran from businesses and homes to the riverbank and were used to transport contraband, such as liquor during Prohibition.

The city's Main Street Program operates a bus tour of Rio Grande City's historic buildings twice daily. Stops include a number of buildings, the city cemetery, and Fort Ringgold. Hotel staff can provide information on the tour times and pickup location.

Crockett Hotel

San Antonio ⚜ 1909

This hotel, built by the International Order of Odd Fellows on an Alamo battlefield, features a pool with a leafy patio and is well situated between the famous mission and San Antonio's Rivercenter Mall.

Lounging poolside at the Crockett Hotel amid blooming hibiscus, palms, and a gurgling waterfall, it's hard to imagine that for thirteen days in 1836, this peaceful spot was part of the chaotic Alamo battlefield. Here Texians and Tejanos fought to their deaths against Mexican troops for Texas' independence. The Alamo mission is just west of the Crockett. So when the International Order of Odd Fellows built their combined IOOF lodge and hotel here in 1909, they named it for Davy Crockett, one of the mission's most notable defenders.

The Odd Fellows owned the Crockett until 1978, when they sold it to a British Columbian firm. In the early 1980s San Antonio native John Blocker bought the hotel and

Crockett Hotel, San Antonio. Photo by Liz Carmack.

ESSENTIALS

Contact: 320 Bonham, San Antonio, TX 78205; 800-292-1050, 210-225-6500; fax: 210-225-7418; www.crocketthotel.com
Rooms: 138 rooms and suites, all with private bath; tub/shower combinations; king, queen, and full beds.
Rates: $$–$$$$, includes continental breakfast.
Room amenities: phone, TV, hair dryer, iron and ironing board, coffee maker, free wired Internet.
Facilities: Ernie's Bar, 5 P.M. to midnight Mon.–Sat.; free wi-fi in lobby, group space for up to 50.
Smoking: in bar.
Credit cards: V, MC, AE, D, DC.
Parking: valet parking, $25.
Accessibility: disabled access, elevator.

Pets: not allowed.
Author's tips:—The hotel's spacious Driskill Suite offers the best view of the Alamo and its grounds.
National Register of Historic Places: yes, as part of Alamo Historic District.
Texas Historical Marker: no
Texas Heritage Trails Program: Texas Hill Country Trail Region, www.txhillcountrytrail.com
Visitor information: San Antonio Convention and Visitors Bureau, 203 S. St. Mary's, Suite 200, San Antonio, TX 78205; 800-447-3372, 210-207-6700; www.sanantoniovisit.com, SACVB@sanantoniovisit.com

pumped at least $10 million into a major makeover, restoring its exterior, modernizing its rooms, and adding a large atrium lobby. Today a banner bearing a portrait of the hotel's namesake hangs near the shiny brass-and-brick front desk in the lobby. The hotel's interior was thoroughly updated during the renovation, wiping out most original details, but the original coffered ceiling in the Crockett's former lobby was preserved and is now painted green, brick red, tan, and crème. The hotel serves a complimentary continental breakfast here each day.

Locals remember that the Odd Fellows' ballroom on the seventh floor (since turned into guest rooms) had a cork floor and that the hotel's original coffee shop once occupied space on the first floor, including part of what is now the hotel bar. A keen eye peering just inside the Crockett's original curved corner entrance at Bonham and Crockett streets can spot patched masonry. The patch covers the spot where, in 1909, the Odd Fellows placed a time capsule. The capsule was removed in 1984 and revealed an IOOF medal, a thimble, and April 29, 1909, issues of the *Daily Express* and the *San Antonio Gazette*.

The hotel has 138 newly renovated rooms and suites. All rooms have private baths and modern furnishings. Lodging in the seven-story building provides views of either the Alamo, downtown San Antonio, or the hotel's atrium. Guests have easy access to a small landscaped patio, pool, and hot tub.

The Crockett is popular with tour groups and people in San Antonio for meetings and special events. Tennessee Mounted Volunteers, including descendants of those who fought at the Alamo, make the hotel their headquarters when they gather in the city each year to remember the historic Alamo battle. The hotel is steps from the back gate of the Alamo's walled grounds, across the street from the Rivercenter Mall, and two blocks from the city's convention center.

The Fairmount

San Antonio ⚜ 1906

This San Antonio landmark, best known for its record-breaking move across town to escape demolition, now pampers with posh accommodations and personalized service across from HemisFair Park and La Villita.

The Fairmount has twice been reborn. When it was threatened with demolition in the 1980s, conservationists rallied and moved the 1,600-ton, three-story structure across town. Then, two decades later, a civic-minded San Antonio millionaire bought the landmark to save it from neglectful owners. He's since invested more than $1 million toward its rebirth as a luxury hotel.

The posh Fairmount Hotel had humble beginnings in 1906 at the corner of Bowie and Commerce streets. Veronica Felix hired local architect Leo M. J. Dielmann and contractor J. P. Haynes to design and construct the masonry, brick, and steel building. Rooms went for $1 a day to drummers and other railway passengers arriving at the nearby Southern Pacific Depot. During the Depression the hotel became home to many semi-permanent residents. Accounts of those times say some of them traded labor for rooms and meals. Like many early twentieth-century hotels, retail businesses, such as a grocery store and hardware store, operated on its first floor with guest rooms above. From 1934 to 1967, the Julius Kelfer family operated their furniture company here.

The hotel was closed during the 1970s and '80s, and in 1984 plans emerged to demolish the building to make way for construction of the Rivercenter Mall and San Antonio

The Fairmount, San Antonio. Photo by Doug Jacobson.

ESSENTIALS

Contact: 401 S. Alamo Street, San Antonio, TX 78205; 877-365-0500, 210-224-8800, fax: 210-224-2767; www.fairmountsa.com, info@thefairmounthotel-sanantonio.com
Rooms: 37 rooms and suites, all with private bath; shower/tub combinations, Jacuzzi tub, walk-in showers; king and queen beds; Monet Suite features onyx and hand-painted tiles, chandeliers; Gold Suite features golden-colored fabrics, furnishings, and 24-carat gold leaf bathroom tile.
Rates: $$$–$$$$
Room amenities: phone, TV, coffee maker, iron and ironing board, robes, free wi-fi and wired Internet, room service.
Facilities: Sage Restaurant and Bar, 7 A.M. to 10 A.M., 11 A.M. to 2:30 P.M., and 5 P.M. to 10:30 P.M. daily; business center; group space accommodates up to 150.
Smoking: designated rooms, in bar.
Credit cards: V, MC, AE, D, DC, JCB.
Parking: valet only, $19.
Accessibility: disabled access, elevator.

Pets: welcome, $75 fee; grooming and other pet services available.
Author's tips:—The Fairmount's second-story balcony provides great views of the New Year's Eve fireworks at HemisFair Park, which makes it a popular place to celebrate. It's best to call New Year's Day for reservations the following New Year's Eve.
—Azuca, 713 S. Alamo, is a lively locals' favorite that serves delicious Nuevo Latino cuisine and killer *mojitos* just a short walk from the hotel.
National Register of Historic Places: yes
Texas historical marker: no
Texas Heritage Trails Program: Hill Country Trail Region, www.txhillcountrytrail.com
Visitor information: San Antonio Convention and Visitors Bureau, 203 S. St. Mary's, Suite 200, San Antonio, TX 78205; 800-447-3372, 210-207-6700; www.sanantoniovisit.com, SACVB@sanantoniovisit.com

Marriott Rivercenter. But C. Thomas Wright, Virginia Van Steenberg, and Belton K. Johnson, the latter of the King Ranch family, would hear nothing of it. They enlisted the support of the San Antonio Conservation Society, and their efforts led to the Fairmount's relocation six blocks away on city-owned land at S. Alamo and Nueva streets. The move took six days, required thirty-six dollies with pneumatic tires, and landed the hotel in the *1986 Guinness Book of World Records.* After the move the Fairmount gained a three-story brick addition and an extensive renovation. It reopened its doors in 1986 to much fanfare.

By 1992 it no longer had a local owner. In 2001 San Antonio businessman Robert D. Tips attended a New Year's Eve party at the Fairmount and thought the landmark was showing signs of neglect. In 2004 he purchased the hotel with a plan to remake it into the city's first small, "European-style" luxury hotel. Guests today experience his initial investment toward that goal.

The small, tastefully outfitted lobby is filled with original art and looks out on a granite-floored courtyard. A case in the corner displays historic artifacts uncovered here during the hotel's relocation. They were left by one of Santa Anna's artillery batteries during their siege of the Alamo in 1836.

Each of the hotel's thirty-seven rooms and suites (eighteen are in the original hotel building) have been repainted and redecorated with quality fabrics adorning beds and windows. Each room has a singular feel thanks to handpicked antique armoires, marble-topped tables, and recently upholstered chairs mixed with pieces from its 1986 reopening. Walls display original art from local and regional artists. All rooms have private, wallpapered baths, and most feature gold-tone fixtures and chocolate brown marble-topped vanities.

The Gold Suite and the Monet Suite, the smaller of the two, are the hotel's standout accommodations. These rooms were completely gutted during the renovation, and workers and artisans used high-dollar materials in their transformation. Expensive touches include delicate crystal chandeliers with dimmer switches, hand-painted bathroom floor tiles, jewel-tone onyx tiles, elaborate crown molding, and cut glass wastebaskets and ice buckets. Each suite's bath has a walk-in shower with not one, but three brass showerheads set at different heights.

The hotel aims to provide personalized service. Its concierge will even help plan the excursion of your dreams. How about shopping on Los Angeles' Rodeo Drive or cruising the Gulf of Mexico while enjoying a pedicure? Just ask. The hotel's proprietor owns a fleet of limousines, a yacht, and private jets. Guests are limited only by their imaginations—and their means. Lodgers' pets also receive the royal treatment. The Fairmount arranges grooming services as well as guided tours of San Antonio's dog walks and pet-friendly markets for pets and their people.

The Fairmount is near San Antonio's River Walk and the shops, restaurants, and events held at La Villita, just across the street. To the east across S. Alamo lie HemisFair Park, the Institute of Texan Cultures, and the Tower of the Americas. The VIA Metropolitan Transit trolley stops outside the hotel and drops off visitors in the King William Historic District, which is filled with turn-of-the-century homes just south of downtown.

Havana Riverwalk Inn
San Antonio ⚜ 1914

Guests at this small hotel along a quiet portion of San Antonio's River Walk find modern amenities in an old-time, whimsical atmosphere.

The mood at the Havana Riverwalk Inn is part bygone era and part modern chic, seasoned with a dash of whimsy. An overnight stay feels like a visit to the comfortable, antique-filled home of a slightly eccentric great-aunt. Antique tables and light fixtures mix with artisan-crafted modern iron beds. Handmade white muslin bed linens and brown velvet pillows adorned with dozens of old buttons convey the hotel's earthy color scheme. Portraits of the 1927 San Antonio Indians baseball team, old plates (hung backward to reveal spiderweb-like cracks on their underside), and

thumbtacked snapshots from the 1930s appear in unexpected places—such as above a bathroom sink.

Edward Franz Melcher, a successful grocer, hired local architect Arthur J. Herman to design this Mediterranean revival–style building, which suits its semitropical environs along the San Antonio River. Melcher was one of the city's first German immigrants to move his trade to the north end of downtown. When it opened in 1914, the mercantile also lodged buyers who made overnight trips to San Antonio to purchase his goods.

In 1926 Melcher sold the property.

Havana Riverwalk Inn, San Antonio. Photo by Liz Carmack.

It changed hands several times until it was purchased in 1931 by the family of Morris D. Jaffe, a prominent San Antonio businessman. The Jaffe family operated the Havana as a rooming house and owned it until 1973. By 1988 the building was in the hands of the Resolution Trust Corporation. It had become a vandalized, boarded-up home to vagrants, its interior largely gutted by fires. See-ing the property's potential, current owner Theresa Greer bought the Havana and acted as general contractor during its extensive $2 million-plus reconstruction. It reopened in 1997, aiming for a clientele that travels child-free and enjoys the whimsical touches and period decor coupled with the hotel's special amenities, such as designer bathroom toiletries and free wi-fi.

ESSENTIALS

Contact: 1015 Navarro, San Antonio, TX 78205; 210-222-2008; fax: 210-222-2717; www.havanariverwalkinn.com, info@havanariverwalkinn.com
Rooms: 27 rooms and suites, all with private bath; modern tub/shower combinations and walk-in showers; king, queen beds.
Rates: $$–$$$$
Room amenities: phone, TV, hair dryer, iron and ironing board; free wi-fi; room service.
Facilities: Kayla's Cafe, 7 A.M. to 10 P.M. Tues.–Thurs.; 7 P.M. to 11 P.M. Fri. and Sat., 7 A.M. to noon Sun.; Club Cohiba, 4 P.M. to midnight Mon.–Thurs., 4 P.M. to 2 A.M. Fri. and Sat., 4 P.M. to 10:30 P.M. Sun.; morning coffee served in lobby, small rooftop patio, group space for up to 125.
Smoking: bar.
Credit cards: V, MC, AE, D, DC.

Parking: self-park in hotel lot, $10.
Accessibility: disabled access, elevator.
Pets: not allowed.
Author's tips:—Rooms at the front of the hotel tend to be noisier from traffic on Navarro.—The hotel considers itself a child-free zone, welcoming guests 15 and older.
National Register of Historic Places: yes
Texas historical marker: no
Texas Heritage Trails Program: Hill Country Trail Region, www.txhillcountrytrail.com
Visitor information: San Antonio Convention and Visitors Bureau, 203 S. St. Mary's, Suite 200, San Antonio, TX 78205; 800-447-3372, 210-207-6700; www.sanantoniovisit.com, SACVB@sanantoniovisit.com

Although much of the three-story hotel's interior had to be rebuilt from scratch, "The Havana," written in coffee-colored octagonal tiles against a white background on its front porch, greets guests as it did in 1914. The original, diagonally coffered plaster ceiling in the lobby has been artfully restored. In addition, carpenters rebuilding floors, doors, and millwork matched as closely as possible the building's longleaf pine, oak, and maple.

Two comely, lamp-holding bronze maidens adorn the newels at the base of the hotel's massive staircase. Greer had to retrieve and rehabilitate these ladies from a Jaffe family member who had converted them into table lamps. Sisal and Oriental-style carpets cover the hardwood floors throughout the hotel, including the wide-planked subfloors on the second and third stories that were refinished and left exposed. Woodwork throughout is stained almost black. Except for the large panes in the small, sunny lobby, the double-hung windows and their transoms are covered with shutters. The hotel's golden faux-finished walls contrast with these dark details.

Each of the twenty-seven rooms and suites has its own theme, and some are executed with tongue firmly in cheek. For instance, room 104's motif is based on threes. (That's right—threes not fours.) Three hats hang side by side on one wall; a trio of china serving platters decorates another. The hands on a vintage clock are frozen at three. In my room, old postcards in a rose motif lined the inside of the armoire, where the usual modern hotel conveniences—a TV, a hair dryer, an iron—were tucked away so as not to spoil the carefully crafted atmosphere. In my bathroom a cigar box dispensed tissues, and rustic wire baskets were stuffed with fluffy towels. A beveled glass mirror hung above the sink. All rooms have private baths.

Greer kept the building's original name and added the words "Riverwalk Inn" to play up the hotel's riverside location. Guests, who are usually corporate travelers or vacationing couples, can cross the street and step down to a quiet portion of the River Walk. A short walk or river taxi ride away are dozens of riverside restaurants, bars, and shops. The Havana has a riverside restaurant with glass-enclosed, climate-controlled dining. Club Cohiba is favored by locals for its friendly atmosphere, tapas, and mojitos. The San Antonio Municipal Auditorium, which hosts local and touring musical acts and special events, is next door.

Menger Hotel

San Antonio ⚜ 1859

This well-known Alamo neighbor is one of Texas' oldest hotels and has a guest list that includes famous authors, Civil War generals, and Texas legends.

The Menger must qualify as Texas' most well-known historic hotel. During my nearly two years of research on this book, dozens of people across the Lone Star state recounted in casual conversation fond memories of staying at the Menger. Many others cited some factual tidbit about the hotel, even if they had never visited. The hotel's celebrity is well deserved. For a start, it's one of Texas' oldest hotels. The Menger has sheltered travelers since 1859 (except for a short period during the Civil War when only its restaurant remained open). Many famous individuals have stayed within its walls, from Gen. Ulysses S. Grant and Oscar Wilde to Babe Ruth and Bill Clinton. And it's next door to the Alamo, considered the symbol of Texas liberty, having opened a little more than two decades after the decisive battle fought at the historic mission for Texas' independence.

The hotel's founder, William Menger, emigrated in 1847 from Germany to San Antonio, where he built kegs and barrels, and operated

Menger Hotel, San Antonio. Photo courtesy Menger Hotel.

ESSENTIALS

Contact: 204 Alamo Plaza, San Antonio, TX 78205; 800-345-9285, 210-223-4361; *fax:* 210-228-0022; historicmenger.com
Rooms: 316 rooms and suites, all with private bath; tub/shower combination, walk-in shower, Jacuzzi tub; king, queen, full, and twin beds; King Ranch Suite features one bedroom and a private balcony; Roy Rogers Suite is one large room that includes a game table and private balcony.
Rates: $$$–$$$$
Room amenities: phone, TV, iron and ironing board, hair dryer, free wired Internet.
Facilities: Colonial Garden Dining Room, 6:30 A.M. to 10 P.M. Sun.–Thurs., 6:30 A.M. to 11 P.M. Fri. and Sat.; Menger Bar, 11 A.M. to midnight Mon.–Sat., noon to midnight Sun.; fitness center, outdoor heated pool, spa, free wi-fi in lobby, group space for up to 750.
Smoking: designated rooms, in bar.

Credit cards: V, MC, AE, D, DC.
Parking: valet only, $25.
Accessibility: disabled access, elevator.
Pets: not allowed.
Author's tips:—Curious about the Menger's ghosts? Query the Menger's public relations director, Ernesto Malacara. Malacara, a thirty-year Menger employee, has given more than one hundred interviews on the topic and hosts the hotel's annual Ghost Disclosure Gathering conference.
National Register of Historic Places: yes
Texas historical marker: yes
Texas Heritage Trails Program: Hill Country Trail Region, www.txhillcountrytrail.com
Visitor information: San Antonio Convention and Visitors Bureau, 203 S. St. Mary's, Suite 200, San Antonio, TX 78205; 800-447-3372, 210-207-6700; www.sanantoniovisit.com, SACVB@sanantoniovisit.com

a small grocery. After he and his wife, Mary, wed, he purchased a plot of land immediately south of the Alamo mission and established a brewery. With Mary's help—she had experience running a boardinghouse—the Mengers added rooms to accommodate brewery patrons. Their lodging business must have done well. Menger next hired local architect John M. Fries to design a two-story, fifty-room hotel to replace his brew-

ery and boardinghouse. General contractor J. H. Kampmann built the hotel using limestone quarried from the Sunken Gardens area in what is now San Antonio's Brackenridge Park. (Menger's original hotel building is today the southwest corner of the much expanded Menger and includes the Victorian Lobby.) The hotel cost $15,712 and opened in 1859 to community praise and a glowing review in the *San Antonio Herald.* Business was brisk, and the Mengers quickly realized they needed more rooms. Within eight months, Menger added fifty more to the rear of the building.

The hotel became well-known for clean rooms, fine hospitality, and delicious meals at a time when the bed and board provided by many Texas inns left a lot to be desired. The Mengers did their best to create an elegant atmosphere for guests and ventured to New York and Europe to purchase furniture for the hotel. Following the Civil War and Reconstruction, well-traveled visitors made the Menger their choice for lodging when in San Antonio, and its reputation grew. Early registers, including a couple from 1871 and 1893 displayed in the lobby along with other hotel memorabilia, show signatures of guests from many Texas cities as well as New York City, Cincinnati, Mexico, India, and England.

After William died, Mary and her children continued to operate the hotel for ten years before selling it to the inn's builder, J. H. Kampmann, in 1881. The Kampmann family remodeled and expanded the hotel. Although the Menger had always had a saloon, the owners built a new hotel bar based on sketches of the House of Lords pub in London. This handsome room, which has a large mahogany bar, now sits in a different spot within the hotel, but it is filled with its original cherry wood paneling and beveled glass mirrors. It's here in the 1890s that Teddy Roosevelt recruited some of his Rough Riders, the United States' first volunteer cavalry. The

summer afternoon I visited, the bar provided a cool, dark respite from San Antonio's hot sidewalks. A local couple showing family from Mexico the sights stopped in for drinks before touring the Alamo.

In 1909 the Kampmann family hired architect Alfred Giles to remodel the hotel, in part to compete with the newly opened Gunter and St. Anthony hotels across downtown. Giles turned the Menger's original lobby, which early photos show had a wood floor and rather plain decor, into a grand space. Called the Victorian Lobby, the room has Corinthian marble columns, a floor of mini, six-sided white, blue, and green tiles, and a leaded glass skylight that arches over the room's two stories. The walls today display western art, including "Venting Cattle on the Frisco System," a large oil by Frank Lewis Van Ness from 1902, which was a prop in the 1956 film *Giant*. Across the room sits a square Steinway and Sons grand piano purchased by Mary Menger for the hotel in 1876. The lobby also has antique furnishings and several large planters of palms and bromeliads.

During the 1920s and '30s the hotel declined, and business dropped off so much that during the early 1940s, the hotel was in danger of being torn down to make way for a parking lot. The Mengers' savior was Galveston businessman William Lewis Moody Jr. His National Hotel Corporation, now called Gal-Tex, has owned the landmark since 1943. Moody constructed the larger of the hotel's two lobbies in 1948. Today, clothing, gift, and antique shops line the lobby's perimeter facing Alamo Plaza. Visitors can relax in the lobby or pull up a rocking chair in the adjacent Spanish Patio. The gardens now have formal plantings of manicured shrubs, palm trees, and a central fountain, but early photos show it was once jungle-like. Alligators even lived in a small pond in the patio for several decades.

The Menger has 316 rooms and suites. The decor, size, and atmosphere of each varies based on its age. Smaller rooms are furnished with more antiques and are generally found in the oldest part of the hotel. Larger rooms have more modern furnishings and are in the newer sections. All rooms are carpeted and have private baths. A few of the hotel's most popular suites, named for famous guests, are in the 1859 hotel building. One of those, the King Ranch Suite, is named for Capt. Richard King. This steamboat entrepreneur, livestock capitalist, and founder of the King Ranch in south Texas was a part-time resident at the Menger and died here in 1885. His bed remains in the suite, along with other original furnishings.

Additional notable guests include generals Robert E. Lee, Sam Houston, and William Tecumseh Sherman; entertainers Roy Rogers, Dale Evans, Buffalo Bill Cody, and Annie Oakley; and writers Sidney Lanier and Oscar Wilde. Spirits of past guests, famous or not, often make appearances in the hotel, according to staff and visitors. Manifestations range from ghostly figures appearing in photographs taken in its rooms or on its grounds, to hotel doors opening and closing on their own.

Writers have memorialized the Menger's ghosts, its celebrity guests, its dedicated owners, and the fascinating events that have occurred there in articles, poems, memoirs, and other writings. One of the best books on the hotel is by Docia Schultz Williams. In *The History and Mystery of the Menger Hotel,* Williams compiled many of the Menger's ghost stories and gives a comprehensive and entertaining account of this San Antonio icon.

The hotel is near the Alamo, which attracts more than 2.5 million visitors a year. The battle fought there in 1836 during Texas' struggle for independence from Mexico is considered the state's paramount patriotic event. Admission is free to the Alamo's eighteenth-century structures and landscaped grounds. The chapel is one of the most photographed buildings in the nation. The Alamo's long barracks holds a museum and library.

St. Anthony
San Antonio ⚜ 1909

When it opened, this hotel provided unheard-of luxuries such as in-room telephones, private baths, and guest room doorbells.

The painting of an eagle verging on flight perched on a cliff is unlabeled and probably goes unnoticed by many guests who rush past it to the St. Anthony's registration desk. Titled "Monarch of the West," this large oil by James Ferdinand McCann has a 22-carat gold-leaf frame, is supported by two pedestals, and is a remnant from the hotel's once large art collection. Ralph W. Morrison, a prominent rancher, businessman, and San Antonio civic leader, installed "Monarch," numerous other works of art, carpets, and French Empire furnishings in the St. Anthony after

he purchased it in 1935 for $475,000. His decision to invest in the deteriorating, foreclosed-upon hotel during the depths of the Depression was considered an incredible risk. More than twenty-five years earlier when it opened in 1909, the St. Anthony offered unheard of luxuries for a hotel of that time. Half of its 210 guest rooms had private baths. All had solid mahogany furnishings and telephones. Electric lights, powered by the hotel's private power plant, turned off automatically when guests exited and locked their doors. Brass number plates on guest room doors

St. Anthony, San Antonio. Photo courtesy St. Anthony.

ESSENTIALS

Contact: 300 E. Travis, San Antonio, TX 78205; 210-227-4392; fax: 210-271-1017; st-anthony.wyndham hotels.com

Rooms: 352 rooms and suites, all with private bath; tub/shower combination, bathtub, walk-in shower; king and queen beds.

Rates: $$–$$$$

Room amenities: phone, TV, coffee maker, hair dryer, iron and ironing board, room service, free wi-fi.

Facilities: Madrid Room, 6 A.M. to 2 P.M. and 5 P.M. to 10 P.M. daily; Pete's Pub, 2 P.M. to midnight daily; outdoor heated pool and hot tub, fitness center, business center, group space for up to 400.

Smoking: designated rooms, bar.

Credit cards: V, MC, AE, DC, D, JCB.

Parking: self-park, $15; valet, $20.

Accessibility: disabled access, elevator.

Pets: not allowed.

Author's tips:—For the best view ask for a room overlooking Travis Park or the hotel pool.—Lula's, 137 E. Travis, is a cheery little Mexican café a short walk from the hotel that serves tasty, inexpensive dishes.

National Register of Historic Places: yes

Texas historical marker: no

Texas Heritage Trails Program: Texas Hill Country Trail, www.txhill countrytrail.com

Visitor information: San Antonio Convention and Visitors Bureau, 203 S. St. Mary's, Suite 200, San Antonio, TX 78205; 800-447-3372, 210-207-6700; www.sanantoniovisit.com; SACVB@sanantoniovisit.com

included electric doorbells. These still work and are used by hotel staff when making deliveries.

A 1918 newspaper advertisement placed by the St. Anthony's original owners, A. H. Jones and B. L. Naylor, calls their hotel the "stockman's headquarters" and touts its artesian wells, ice and cold storage plant, and special facilities for "commercial men." Rates were $1.50 to $4 per day and included meals. In later years the hotel had five restaurants, including the Cascade Terrace, which featured a 20-foot waterfall. Each venue had its own set of china. Staff today say that fifty remaining place settings, a sample of which is displayed in the Jefferson Manor meeting room, are used for special occasions.

In 1946 a writer called the St. Anthony "the Waldorf on the Prairie" since it was the setting for countless high-society functions. Lately it has hosted the reception that follows the "crowning" of the Order of the Alamo "royalty" during San Antonio's annual Fiesta celebration. The hotel has been no stranger to national notables, either, as the photos hanging in its white marbled lobby attest. In one, Prince Rainier and Princess Grace of Monaco hobnob at a hotel reception. John Wayne appears in another shot. The actor stayed here during the filming of the 1960 movie *The Alamo.*

Over the years, the original eight-story buff brick hotel has been expanded to fill the entire block on Travis Street between Navarro and Jefferson. Facing Travis Park, it now stands ten stories. Little of Morrison's original collection remains in the hotel, but what is left is impressive. The pieces are displayed in Peacock Alley, a long, formally appointed room just east of the lobby. They include "Monarch," a few bronzes, and a handful of slightly worn French Empire chairs and marble-topped tables.

The hotel's 352 modern appointed guest rooms and suites all have private baths, and all are configured differently. The hotel's entire interior was slated for renovation in 2007. Large glass and brass doorknobs remain on all interior doors and are original to the hotel.

Business travelers and tourists frequent the hotel, which is in San Antonio's downtown and near the River Walk, the San Antonio Children's Museum, and the Buckhorn Saloon and Museum.

Sheraton Gunter Hotel
San Antonio ⚜ 1909

Settlers to the new Republic of Texas, U.S. Army troops, and Confederate soldiers all found shelter on this site long before the hotel celebrated its grand opening.

The site where the Gunter Hotel sits today has a long history of lodging travelers to Texas. In 1837, one year after the Alamo fell, the Frontier Inn opened here. The inn housed settlers hoping to find their fortunes in the newly formed Republic of Texas. When the Republic joined the Union in 1845 and the Mexican-American War began a year later, a two-story army barracks and quadrangle replaced the inn. Confederate soldiers later occupied the barracks during the Civil War. William Vance and his brothers, who owned the barracks, reclaimed them in 1872 and turned them into the Vance House hotel. In the late 1880s, Ludwig Mahncke and Lesher A. Trexler took over the Vance and renamed it the Mahncke Hotel.

At the turn of the century, investors L. J. Hart, Jot Gunter, and others formed the San Antonio Hotel Company, demolished the Mahncke, and sold stocks and bonds to finance the construction of the eight-story, 301-room Gunter. The project employed the latest building techniques using steel, concrete, and brick. At the time, Houston Street was a busy commercial corridor with a trolley line running in front of the hotel. At its grand opening dinner more than three hundred guests dined on "milk fed" chicken and broiled red snapper. Gentlemen enjoyed Caswell Club cigars with their after-dinner cordials as speakers

Sheraton Gunter Hotel, San Antonio. Photo courtesy Sheraton Gunter Hotel.

boasted that with the opening of the Gunter and the nearby St. Anthony Hotel, San Antonio would surely rival Los Angeles as a tourist destination.

Over the years the Gunter has been home to visiting entertainers, politicians, and other celebrities. Cowboy star Tom Mix frequented the hotel during the 1920s. The American Recording Corporation turned two of the hotel's rooms into a recording studio, and in 1936 it recorded songs performed by blues giant Robert Johnson. The hotel also lodged cattle-men, their families, and ranch hands. While in town for several days, the men conducted ranch business, while the ladies visited dressmakers and shopped for supplies.

I spent an hour studying the artifacts and black-and-white photographs that document the Gunter's colorful history throughout the hotel's public areas. In one photo from 1912, circus performers in full costume and greasepaint gather around a Christmas tree in the hotel's large, two-story lobby. The room's dark

ESSENTIALS

Contact: 205 E. Houston St., San Antonio, TX 78205; 800-325-3535, 210-227-3241; fax: 210-227-3299; www.gunterhotel.com

Rooms: 322 rooms and suites, all with private bath, tub/shower combinations; king, queen, and full beds. Rates: $$–$$$$

Room amenities: phone, TV, coffee maker, hair dryer, iron and ironing board, wired Internet and wi-fi for a fee, room service.

Facilities: Gunter's Bakery, 6 A.M. to 6 P.M. daily (open until 11 P.M. on theater performance nights); Barron's Restaurant, 6:30 A.M. to 2 P.M. and 5 P.M. to 9 P.M. daily; McLeod's Lounge, 2 P.M. to midnight daily; heated outdoor pool, whirlpool, fitness center, group space for up to 700.

Smoking: outdoors only.

Credit cards: V, MC, AE, D, DC.

Parking: valet only, $22.

Accessibility: disabled access, elevator.

Pets: dogs only, under 50 lbs.; no fee or deposit; welcomed with treats, dog bed, and water bowls.

Author's tips:—Visit the third floor near the hotel's executive offices for the best selection of Gunter historical photographs.—Yokonyu Sushi Bar and Restaurant, 301 E. Houston, offers Japanese food with a spicy Latin touch.

*National Register
    of Historic Places:* yes

Texas historical marker: no

Texas Heritage Trails Program: Texas Hill Country Trail Region, www.txhillcountrytrail.com

Visitor information: San Antonio Convention and Visitors Bureau, 203 S. St. Mary's, Suite 200, San Antonio, TX 78205; 800-447-3372, 210-207-6700; www.sanantoniovisit.com, SACVB@sanantoniovisit.com

walnut wainscoting and marble floors shown in the photo remain today. A wood-paneled Western Electric telephone switchboard, used from 1909 to 1979, sits in the elevator foyer. Labeled phone connections include the hotel's men's shop, the beauty shop, and the "coffee manager." The Gunter continues to operate a barbershop and shoe shine station in its basement. The basement was also once home to a cafeteria-style restaurant called the Caveteria—a favorite of servicemen and women stationed in San Antonio during WWII.

Hotel staff and guests have occasionally reported unexplained events at the hotel, hinting that it's haunted. Tales told include strange sounds that emerge from unoccupied rooms, lobby chandeliers that tremble, doors that open automatically, and lights that turn themselves on and off.

The hotel has 322 rooms and suites with modern furnishings and private baths. There are no fewer than twenty-six different sizes of rooms throughout the now twelve-story hotel. Some facing Houston Street have bay windows that overlook the 1929 Majestic Theatre. The historic Empire and Majestic theaters, still in operation, are a short walk from the hotel. Theater patrons for decades have called at the Gunter for a meal or a drink before taking in a movie or a live performance at one of these two landmarks.

About half the hotel's overnight guests are in San Antonio for conventions or business meetings. The other half are mostly leisure travelers who take advantage of the nearby River Walk and San Antonio's many other downtown tourist attractions.

Closed but Not Forgotten Hotels

In 1900 the American Hotel Association listed 380 Texas hotels in its *Official Hotel Red Book and Directory.* A mere three decades later, that list had grown to more than 600. Many of these hotels are gone today—victims of fire or the wrecking ball. Some stand empty, suffering the ravages of time. Fortunately, several hotel buildings have been transformed into museums, event facilities, housing, businesses, and chambers of commerce. This chapter touches on the stories of a handful of these hotels; information about many more can be found in the suggested reading at the back of this book.

VICTIMS OF FIRE

Fire took many of these early Texas hotels, particularly those built during the nineteenth century. Perhaps the most magnificent Texas hostelry to succumb to flames was Galveston's 200-room Beach Hotel. The three-story building, designed by prolific Galveston architect Nicolas Clayton, opened in 1883. In *The Galveston That Was,* Howard Barnstone describes the Beach: "Most rooms were corner rooms. Large windows ran from floor to ceiling, and an American Gothic two-story porch shaded the lower stories and provided terraces for rockers."

The hotel was built entirely of wood and was a colorful, imposing site on Galveston's beach. Its roof was painted in giant red and white stripes. Its delicate grillwork and numerous gables were mauve and its eaves a "golden green." The hotel was crowned by a multicolored octagonal dome that rose 125 feet above the sand. The Beach Hotel's interior featured cypress and curly pine wainscoting from Beaumont. Despite multiple precautions to avert disaster, including widely separated staircases and water hoses installed in hotel corridors, an early-morning fire that began in the Beach's boiler room destroyed the building in 1898.

The three-story brick and granite Algona Hotel opened in Llano in 1892, and it, too, succumbed to fire. The luxurious, sixty-room hotel was carpeted throughout. Its ballroom had an orchestra pit, and its parlors and music and dining rooms became the town's social center. On a cold night in February 1923, the hotel's many fireplaces were ablaze, warming overnight guests and local bridge players attending a dinner party. Within hours after the party ended, flames spread throughout the building. Lodgers escaped unhurt, but firefighters couldn't save the hotel. The Algona was completely destroyed

Beach Hotel, Galveston. Destroyed by fire in 1898. Photo courtesy Rosenberg Library, Galveston, Texas.

and never rebuilt. A lumberyard and general store are now where the Algona once stood at 602 Bessemer.

In 1882 a fire in Waxahachie destroyed a two-story wooden hotel constructed on the same spot where the brick and concrete Rogers Hotel now stands. That fire also spread to several homes, a grocery, a millinery, and the Wells Fargo office. In Kountze in 1925, the volunteer fire brigade was no match for the blaze that took down the two-story Commercial Hotel, which sat across from the railroad tracks. The wooden building with its covered galleries burned to the ground in less than forty-five minutes.

DEATH BY ECONOMICS

The law of supply and demand dealt many hotels their fatal blow. Declining business and the need for costly repairs and upkeep eventually caught up with them in the shape of a wrecking ball.

Hurricane Celia damaged Corpus Christi's Nueces Hotel building so extensively in 1970 that it was condemned and demolished a year later. At the time, it was employed as a retirement center, a common conversion for many old hotels. It had opened in 1913, and vacationers traveling by rail to the coast enjoyed the Nueces' banquet hall, two private dining rooms, sun parlor, and 205 guest rooms.

Marshall's Capitol Hotel opened in 1857 as the Adkins House, named for its original owner, Judge George B. Adkins. It served as a depot for stage lines, including the southern branch of the Butterfield mail line. It was famous for hosting Civil War conferences attended by the governors of Missouri, Arkansas, Louisiana, and Texas. According to local newspaper accounts, two of Adkins' slaves (who were both expert masons) constructed the large, three-story brick building. It was torn down in 1971. A garden dedicated to Lady Bird Johnson is planned in its place.

Fort Worth and other Texas cities have lost their share of aging hotels to downtown development. Such was the fate of the El Paso Hotel, which opened in 1877 in downtown Fort Worth. It was later called both the Pickwick and the Delaware hotels. The Delaware was razed to make way for construction of the Westbrook Hotel, which opened in 1911. The Westbrook fronted Main Street and also had entrances on Houston and Fourth streets. The Westbrook is perhaps best known as the favored hangout of wildcatters after oil was discovered in nearby Eastland County in 1917. Fortunes were made and lost at the hotel as speculators packed its expansive marble lobby to trade oil leases.

As time wore on, the aging hotel instituted improvements to keep its rooms filled. An article in the March 1942 issue of *Texas Hotel Review* boasts that the Westbrook had just completed a remodeling and redecorating program in which much of its equipment was "brought up-to-date." The hotel's manager explains in the article how older hotels may be made modern and comfortable without destroying their "old-fashioned" hospitality. By the mid 1970s, the deteriorating hotel was no longer favored by travelers. It closed its doors and was razed in 1978 to make way for a parking lot.

AN UNCERTAIN FATE

Today many deteriorating relics face an unknown fate on weed-filled lots near railroad tracks or on small-town squares. Some are large, architectural marvels languishing from vandalism, thievery, water damage, and the elements.

The Herring Hotel in Amarillo is one of these boarded-up behemoths. Preservation Texas, a statewide architectural preservation organization, named the hotel to its list of Most Endangered Places of 2006. Cornelius Taylor Herring built the fourteen-story brick building in 1926 during the area's oil boom. Herring was a pioneer cattleman, oilman, and banker. Only one of the hotel's western frescoes, painted by noted artist H. D. Bugbee, remains intact after a ruptured water main flooded the Herring's basement several years ago. The mural was one of many in the hotel's Tascosa Room, where cattle barons and oil tycoons once socialized. The 600-room hotel has been empty since the 1970s when for a short time, it was used as federal offices.

The art deco Hilton Hotel (also known as the Plaza Hotel) sits virtually empty at Mills and Oregon streets in El Paso. Conrad Hilton broke ground on this high-rise building shortly before the stock market crashed in 1929. As Hilton writes in his biography, *Be My Guest,* people eagerly awaited the opening of his hotel, which provided a glimmer of hope in 1930 during gloomy economic times. Five hundred invited guests danced at the opening ball. Hilton came close to bankruptcy shortly after the 300-room hotel opened, nearly losing the El Paso property and the fledging hotel empire he had begun to build in Texas.

The Hilton, which was designed by celebrated Southwest architects Trost and Trost, became the Plaza in the early 1960s. Now, except for a few retail businesses lining the sidewalks, its eighteen floors sit empty. The hotel's owners hope to restore the historic features of the building while redeveloping its guest rooms into condominiums.

Many hotels opened on the eve of the Great Depression, but the story of the 1929 Baker Hotel in Mineral Wells is perhaps the most unusual, and saddest, of Texas hotels that began in that era. This 14-story, 450-room landmark is the first thing travelers see today as they approach this community of about 17,000. It was the largest of numerous resort hotels and sanatoriums that sprang up in Mineral Wells, which was once nationally known for the supposed healing properties of its mineral springs.

Gene Fowler writes in *Crazy Water: The Story of Mineral Wells and Other Texas Health Resorts* that as many as 150,000 patrons a year visited the town during its heyday in the 1920s and 1930s. Some of these patrons were quite famous and included Judy Garland, Will Rogers, Jack Dempsey, and General John J. Pershing.

It took three years for Texas hotelier T. B. Baker to construct this massive, Spanish colonial revival building, whose facilities and design rivaled that of its urban contemporaries. The Baker's attractions included an outdoor swimming pool, bowling alley, veranda, gym, coffee shop, dining room, solarium, roof garden, and pavilion. Nationally touring entertainers and orchestras regularly performed in the Baker's ballroom. A young Lawrence Welk got his start there. Guests could play tennis, badminton, shuffleboard, keno, or bridge. Horseback riding, hiking, and golf were available nearby.

The hotel's main attractions were its mineral baths, steam cabinets, steam rooms, exercise equipment, and massage therapists. On my tour of the Baker, I found pink and blue paint chips peeled off weatherbeaten massage stall doors and piled on the floor, scattered by the wind whipping through broken windows. Exercise tables that once vibrated ladies' hips to "give resilience and tone to your muscles," according to a hotel brochure, sat rusting in the corner. The Baker claimed its mineral wells would relieve everything from rheumatism, fatigue, nervousness, and stress to poor posture.

The hotel's business declined in the 1950s and 1960s, and Baker closed the hotel in 1963. A group of local investors purchased and reopened the hotel briefly in 1965, but it closed for good in 1973.

Like many others, this hotel awaits a benefactor with big ideas and deep pockets to save it from the elements, vandals, and thieves. Over the years, the unscrupulous have stripped the Baker's interior of many of its original features. There are missing faucets, mirrors, and bathroom tile. Squares have been sliced from the stylish 1920s-era carpet in several guest rooms. The remaining carpet is now moldering. Most of the hotel's unusual "butler" style doors, which have an inset smaller door used to pass items between hotel staff and guests, have been hauled off, and many of the marble slabs in steam rooms are missing. Even the huge bell that once hung atop the hotel in its 40-foot tower has been stolen.

Baker Hotel, Mineral Wells. The 450-room Baker sits empty and decaying. Photo by Liz Carmack.

PRESERVED
FOR NEW PURPOSES

Fortunately, more than a dozen old hotel buildings in Texas have been preserved and remain open today as museums, chambers of commerce, businesses, and living quarters. Here are details on a few of these.

The National Museum of the Pacific War occupies the old Nimitz Hotel at 340 E. Main Street in Fredericksburg. The Nimitz, founded by Charles H. Nimitz, began as a stagecoach stop in the 1850s. Some of its more notable guests included Pres. Rutherford B. Hayes, Robert E. Lee, William Sydney Porter, and Ulysses S. Grant. The hotel offered patrons the entertainment of a combined theater-casino-dance hall and an on-site brewery. It's said to have provided the only hot baths between San Antonio and El Paso. The hotel's grounds included stables, barns, a smokehouse, orchard, vegetable garden, and rose arbors.

In Newton, the Powell Hotel on Rusk Street across from the Newton County Courthouse now houses the Newton County Chamber of Commerce Visitor Center and the Powell Hotel Museum. This 1889 building began as an educational center called the Ford Male and Female College. After the local public school district was established, the building was moved in 1914 to its present location and became the Powell Hotel. Its owners were Joseph Dallas Powell and Minnie Howard Powell, both former students of the college. In 2000 the Newton County Historical Commission raised $50,000 and restored the deteriorating structure. Exhibits include a re-created classroom, hotel parlor, and guest rooms that display personal items from some of its long-term residents.

Another hotel-turned-museum is in Van Horn. The Clark Hotel, constructed in stages between 1901 and 1911, is one of the town's oldest structures. The Clark began as a commercial building and housed everything from the county courthouse, professional offices, a community center, and newspaper printing office to a dance hall, pool hall, and saloon. Around 1919 Fred Clark purchased the building and converted it into a hotel. The Culberson County Historical Society has turned the building into a museum. The Clark Hotel Museum, 112 W. Broadway, displays exhibits on the history of Van Horn and Culberson County.

International hotelier Conrad Hilton began his dynasty with the purchase of the Mobley Hotel in Cisco in 1919. Hilton went to Cisco that year, during the oil boom that began in nearby Ranger, to purchase a Cisco bank. He balked when the bank's owner unexpectedly increased its sale price. Seeking accommodations, he saw the Mobley's owner was making money hand over fist by renting rooms in eight-hour shifts. He quickly bought the two-story brick hotel for $50,000.

Today the Mobley is known as the Conrad Hilton Center. The building contains the Cisco Historical

Museum; the Innkeeper Gallery, which details Hilton's life; the Cisco Chamber of Commerce offices; and a theater that features performances by Cisco Junior College students. The hotel's rehabilitation was funded by a $1.2 million grant from the Conrad N. Hilton Foundation of Los Angeles.

Hilton continued to buy and build hotels in Texas before expanding into California, other states, and abroad. The family of Hilton hotels now comprises more than two thousand properties worldwide, including the Waldorf-Astoria in New York City. One of the first hotels Hilton constructed in Texas was the 14-story, 200-room San Angelo Hilton. Today several floors

of San Angelo's tallest building, now called the Cactus Hotel, are home to apartments and offices of businesses and nonprofits.

Interior details in the Cactus' well-preserved two-story lobby and mezzanine include floors and wainscoting with original glazed tiles in blue-green, yellow, gold, and tan. The room also displays oak and mahogany woodwork and stenciled wooden ceiling beams. Four original ornate brass chandeliers hang above the elegant space. The ballroom features original crystal chandeliers, mirrors, and its restored, original hand-painted ceiling. The hotel hosts more than sixty weddings a year, and the Cactus

Mobley Hotel, Cisco. The first hotel owned by international hotelier Conrad Hilton is now a community center. Photo by Liz Carmack.

serves as a center for community social and civic gatherings.

Eastland residents are also fortunate to have a restored pre-Depression hotel to host such events. When the eight-story Connellee Hotel opened in 1928, the *Eastland Telegram* called it a "Hostelry Rivaling All in the Oil Belt." Each of its one hundred rooms had a private bath and ceiling fan. Floors displayed English Axminster carpets. The rooftop garden hosted balls on a maple dance floor and seated two hundred banquet guests.

The Connellee, which sits just west of Eastland's town square, closed its doors in 1972 and sat unused and empty for decades. In 1997 the city and local nonprofits acquired the building and began an effort to reopen it as a community arts center. The campaign faltered when the restoration work seemed overwhelming. In 2004 the Eastland Community Foundation adopted the project and, with the help of generous benefactors, reopened the Connellee's doors one year later. Its fully restored rooftop garden ballroom, lobby, and meeting rooms are once again serving the community of Eastland.

Sprinkled around the state are many old hotels that have been converted into public housing projects, senior citizen retirement centers, or apartments and condominiums.

The Hotel Beaumont is now a retirement facility with more than 130 apartments for elderly residents in downtown Beaumont. The $1 million, 250-room hotel opened in 1922 and quickly became the unofficial headquarters for the city's many civic clubs. During the 1990s, the National Development Council purchased the property and completed extensive pre-development work on the building. The City of Beaumont and Beaumont's Main Street Program joined forces on a restoration project that took eight years, raised $7.5 million, and succeeded because of close coordination between numerous national and local organizations.

The hotel's senior residents relax in the two-story lobby under ornate coffered ceilings, whose gold trim and detailed stenciling have been painstakingly restored. The lobby displays its original white marble floor and columns topped by gold capitals. The hotel's original front desk and mail slots are used today. The Texas Downtown Association named Hotel Beaumont Texas' Best Restoration in 2003. Hotel Beaumont's Rose Room and ballroom, the sites of many past galas, have yet to be refurbished. The Main Street program and the hotel are seeking donations for this effort.

Wichita Falls has recently completed a major campaign that raised $6.8 million toward the restoration and renovation of the Holt Hotel. The hotel opened in 1910 at Ohio and Eighth streets as the City National Bank, the city's tallest building. When it was sold in 1926, George Holt and H. S. Ford added two stories and converted the eight-story property into a hotel.

The building remained a hotel until the early 1970s. It then closed and was vacant for more than twenty years. A public-private partnership has redeveloped the Holt into loft-style apartments with ground-floor retail. Because of careful restoration, the hotel retains significant original features in the lobby and mezzanine, including elaborate plaster moldings and marble wainscots. Many of its original floors, of mosaic tile, hardwood, and terrazzo, were preserved and repaired.

One of Texas' best-known closed hostelries, the Rice Hotel, cost $2.5 million to construct and opened in 1913 on a site once occupied by the first capitol of the Republic of Texas. The hotel's owner, Jesse Jones, expanded the hotel in 1925–26. After it closed in the 1970s, the Rice sat empty at Main Street and Texas Avenue for decades. In the late 1990s a private company restored and redeveloped the downtown landmark into retail, restaurants, and loft apartments. The Rice's restored Crystal Ballroom, which was Houston's first ballroom to be air-conditioned, is leased for events. The hotel's two-story lobby is topped by a restored skylight.

One of the more colorful happenings at the Rice occurred in 1936 when hundreds of rowdy cattlemen arrived for a meeting of the Texas Cattlemen's Association. The conventioneers, some of whom were toting guns, roped downtown pedestrians from the hotel's balcony and staged a square dance in its lobby.

Old hotel buildings in many communities now house business offices, restaurants, or retail stores. In El Paso the eleven-story Hotel Cortez today is filled with offices and retail at 310 N. Mesa across from San Jacinto Plaza. Designed by Trost and Trost, the $1.2 million Spanish colonial revival building makes a significant contribution to the flavor of El Paso's downtown.

When the hotel first opened in 1926 as the Hotel Orndorff, it was promoted as "A Castle of Old Spain on the Plaza of El Paso." Today tourists stop on the sidewalk outside the hotel to admire the elaborate exterior, which features three-dimensional busts of Spanish conquistadores and the Spanish coat of arms.

Steps from the main entrance lead to the beautiful lobby, which has its original Spanish tile floor and wainscoting, a heavy beamed ceiling, and arched elevator entrances. A restaurant and retail businesses occupy the Cortez's ground floor. The remainder of the building is filled with offices. The building's owners lease the original ballroom and tearoom for special events.

The two-story Southwestern Hotel in Henderson opened in 1913 as a grocery store and was converted into a hotel in 1922 to serve travelers arriving by train. Today several business offices occupy its ground floor at 114–122 Marshall St.

The Van Horn State Bank purchased the closed El Capitan Hotel in Van Horn in the early 1970s and now uses the building for its offices.

The hotel, designed by Trost and Trost, opened in 1930 and had sixty rooms. Its architectural design and layout is very similar to the mission-Spanish revival style of the Hotel Paisano in Marfa, another Trost-designed hotel.

A Mexican restaurant occupies part of the first floor of the former Texan Hotel at the corner of Cage and Kelly in Pharr's Historic Main Street District. Brothers Lloyd M. and Elmer Bentsen opened the two-story building in 1951 with 54 guest rooms and a 75-seat restaurant. The Texan's top floor is still empty, but Pharr's Main Street/Downtown Office helped the Habanero Café locate in space that had been empty for more than a decade. A chaps-wearing cowboy on the hotel's original neon "Texan" sign tops the building.

The ground floor of the two-story Nelson Hotel in Celina is now home to business offices. The building, at 222 W. Walnut on the town square, was built in 1914 by early Celina settler Richard Tinsley Peterman and was a grocery store and home to other businesses before becoming a hotel in 1922.

HOTELS ARE EVERY-WHERE AND EVER-CHANGING

Texas' historic hotels are in a constant state of flux. Businesses close and move, and the ownership of buildings changes. At any time a closed hotel may find a benefactor willing to invest in it and reopen its doors. Of the operating hotels in this book, half a dozen were for sale and some were undergoing renovation while I was writing.

As you travel around Texas, remember that many closed or repurposed hotels have no historical markers, fading signs, or other clues to alert you to their past lives. But if you have a keen eye, take the time to visit with residents or stop in the local library or history museum, you'll be surprised how many you'll find.

Individuals interested in historic hotels in their corners of Texas provided me with many leads during my research. I welcome further news about Texas' historic hotels and comments about this book through my Web site dedicated to this subject, www.historictexashotels.com.

Sources and Suggested Reading

In addition to interviewing more than eighty individuals around the state, I gleaned information from more than 230 documents, including books, monographs, unpublished manuscripts, newspaper and magazine articles, meeting minutes, historical photographs, and original hotel materials including menus, brochures, and advertisements. In addition, I collected data from more than fifteen Web sites.

My research included information from dozens of historical accounts about particular hotels and the cities, counties, and Texas regions where they're located. I found this information mostly in historical archives, public libraries, and museums across Texas, as well as in the Texas Historical Commission's library in Austin. The *Handbook of Texas Online,* www.tsha.utexas.edu/handbook/ online/, sponsored by the Texas State Historical Association, was another excellent resource for historical information about particular Texas communities and individuals. Many of the hotel properties I featured are on the National Register of Historic Places and/or have a Texas historical marker (either a subject marker or a marker noting it as a Recorded Texas Historic Landmark). I relied upon the narratives describing these buildings in the THC's Atlas Database, atlas.thc

.state.tx.us. They were invaluable for architectural and historical details.

For readers whose curiosity has been piqued, here is a list of the *essential* texts and Web sites I used while researching this book. It is not a complete bibliography.

Printed Resources

Barnstone, Howard. *The Galveston That Was*. Houston: Rice University Press and Museum of Fine Arts, 1993.

Bauer, Linda, and Steve Bauer. *Recipes from Historic Texas: A Restaurant Guide and Cookbook*. Lanham, TX: Taylor Trade Publishing, 2003.

Beasley, Ellen, and Stephen Fox. *Galveston Architecture Guidebook*. Houston: Rice University Press and the Galveston Historical Foundation, 1996.

Berkman, 'Cele. *Treasures of the Adolphus*. Dallas: The Adolphus Hotel, n.d.

Bull, David, and Turk Pipkin. *The Driskill Hotel: Stories of Austin's Legendary Hotel/A Cookbook for Special Occasions*. Austin: The Driskill Hotel, 2005.

Carson County Historical Survey Committee. *A Time to Purpose: A Chronicle of Carson County, Vol. I.* Hereford, TX: Pioneer Book Publishers, 1966.

Carter, Kathryn Turner. *Stagecoach Inns of Texas*. Waco: Texian Press, 1972.

Casey, Clifford B. *Mirages, Mysteries, and Reality: Brewster County Texas, The Big Bend of the Rio Grande*. Hereford, TX: Pioneer Book Publishers, 1972.

Cohen, Judith Singer. *Cowtown Moderne, Art Deco Architecture of Fort Worth, Texas*. College Station: Texas A&M University Press, 1988.

Cutler, Morene Parten. *Stagecoach Inn: Iron Skillet & Velvet Potholder*. Salado: Village Press Inc., 1981.

Dannelly, Elizabeth. *The History of the Jessie Allen Wise Garden Club, Jefferson, 1939–1989*. Unpublished manuscript, n.d.

Eagle Lake Historical Committee. *A History of Eagle Lake*. Austin: Nortex Press, 1987.

Engelbrecht, Lloyd C., and June-Marie F. Engelbrecht. *Henry C. Trost: Architect of the Southwest*. El Paso: El Paso Public Library Association, 1981.

Farwell, Lisa. *Haunted Texas Vacations: The Complete Ghostly Guide*. Englewood, CO: Westcliffe Publishers, 2000.

Fowler, Gene. *Crazy Water: The Story of Mineral Wells and Other Texas Health Resorts*. Fort Worth: Texas Christian University Press, 1991.

Greene, Shirley Brooks. *When Rio Grande City Was Young*. Edinburg, TX: Pan American University, 1987.

Groth, Paul. *Living Downtown: The History of Residential Hotels in the United States*. Berkeley: University of California Press, 1994.

Gruver, Cynthia. *Country Inns of Texas*. San Ramon, CA: 101 Productions, 1989.

Haywood, John. *A History of the Queen Isabel Inn of Port Isabel, Texas*. Unpublished manuscript, 1990.

Hilton, Conrad. *Be My Guest*. New York: Simon and Schuster, 1957.

The Hotel Limpia Cookbook, A Collection of Favorite Recipes. Highland Village, TX: The Hotel Limpia, L. C. Cookbook Resources, 1998.

Jakle, John A., et al. *The Motel in America*. Baltimore: Johns Hopkins University Press, 1996.

Jasper County Historical Commission. *Swann Hotel*. Jasper County Archives. Unpublished manuscript, n.d.

Johnson, Linda, and Sally Ross. *Historic Texas Hotels and Country Inns*. Austin: Eakin Press, 1982.

Kulhavy, Pamela Aronson. *A Survey of Nacogdoches Hotels 1830–1910*. Unpublished manuscript, 1980.

Landry, Wanda A. *Boardin' in the Big Thicket*. Denton: University of North Texas Press, 1990.

McComb, David. *Galveston: A History*. Austin: University of Texas Press, 1986.

McDonald, Archie P. *Hotel Fredonia: For the Convenience of Travelers and Guests*. Nacogdoches: Hotel Fredonia, 2005.

Metz, Leon C. *El Paso Chronicles: A Record of Historical Events in El Paso, Texas*. El Paso: Mangan Books, 1993.

Oatman, Wilburn. *Llano, Gem of the Hill Country: A History of Llano,*

Texas. Hereford, TX: Pioneer Book Publishers, 1970.

Official Hotel Red Book and Directory. New York: The American Hotel Association Directory Corporation, 1900, 1920, 1930, 1940, 1950.

Olmsted, Frederick Law. *A Journey through Texas: Or a Saddle-Trip on the Southwestern Frontier*. Lincoln: University of Nebraska Press, 1857.

Ruff, Ann. *A Guide to Historic Texas Inns and Hotels*. Houston: Gulf Publishing Company, 1982.

Smith, Joanne. *The Adolphus Cookbook*. Dallas: Taylor Publishing, 1984.

Stott, Kelly McMichael. *Waxahachie: Where Cotton Reigned King*. Charleston, SC: Arcadia Publishing, 2002.

Texas Hotel Review. Issues from the 1930s, 1940s, and 1950s.

Thompson, Cecelia. *History of Marfa and Presidio County*. Austin: Nortex Press, 1985.

Van Orman, Richard A. *A Room for the Night: Hotels of the Old West*. Bloomington: Indiana University Press, 1966.

Why Build a Community Hotel? Harrisburg: The Hockenbury System Inc., brochure, circa 1950.

Williams, Docia Schultz. *The History and Mystery of the Menger Hotel*. Dallas: Republic of Texas Press, 2000.

Wills, Rosetta. *The King of Western Swing: Bob Wills Remembered*. New York: Billboard Books, 1998.

Wlokarski, Robert, and Anne Powell Wlokarski. *Texas Guide to Haunted Restaurants, Taverns, & Inns*. Dallas: Republic of Texas Press, 2001.

Web Sites

Hospitality Accommodations of Texas, www.hat.org

Hotel Online, www.hotel-online.com

National Trust for Historic Preservation, Historic Hotels of America, www.historichotels.org

Preservation Texas, www.preservationtexas.org

Texas Escapes, www.texasescapes.com

Texas Historical Commission, www.thc.state.tx.us

Texas Historical Commission Historical Sites Atlas, atlas.thc.state.tx.us

Texas Parks and Wildlife Department, www.tpwd.state.tx.us

Texas State Historical Association, The Handbook of Texas Online, www.tsha.utexas.edu

🦋 Index